Dear Pitman Publishing Customer

IMPORTANT – Please Rea

We are delighted to announce a special free servic

Simply complete this form and return it to the FREEPOST

A Free Customer Newsletter

B Free Information Service

C Exclusive Customer Offers – which have included free software, videos and relevant products

D Opportunity to take part in product development sessions

E The chance for you to write about your own business experience and become one of our respected authors

Fill this in now and return it to us (no stamp needed in the UK) to join our customer information service.

Name: Position:

Company/Organisation:

Address (including postcode):

Country:

Telephone: Fax:

Nature of business:

Title of book purchased:

ISBN (printed on back cover): 0 2 7 3 ☐☐☐☐☐ ☐

Comments:

Fold Here Then Staple Once

We would be very grateful if you could answer these questions to help us with market research.

1 Where/How did you hear of this book?

- ☐ in a bookshop
- ☐ in a magazine/newspaper (please state which):
- ☐ information through the post
- ☐ recommendation from a colleague
- ☐ other (please state which):

2 Where did you buy this book

- ☐ Direct from Pitman Publishing
- ☐ From a bookclub
- ☐ From a bookshop (state which)

3 Which newspaper(s)/magazine(s) do you read regularly?:

4 When buying a business book which factors influence you most?

(Please rank in order)

- ☐ recommendation from a colleague
- ☐ price
- ☐ content
- ☐ recommendation in a bookshop
- ☐ author
- ☐ publisher
- ☐ title
- ☐ other(s):

5 Is this book a

- ☐ personal purchase?
- ☐ company purchase?

6 Would you be prepared to spend a few minutes talking to our customer services staff to help with product development? YES/NO

We occasionally make our customer lists available to companies whose products or services we feel may be of interest. If you do not want this service write 'exclude from other mailings' on this card. The Customer Information Service is liable to change without notice.

Written for managers competing in today's tough business world, our books will give you a competitive edge by showing you how to:

- increase quality, efficiency and productivity throughout your organisation
- use both proven and innovative management techniques
- improve your management skills and those of your staff
- implement winning customer strategies

In short they provide concise, practical information that you can use every day to increase the success of your business.

Using Questionnaires and Surveys to Boost Your Business

■

To Stephanie, my wife

PITMAN PUBLISHING
128 Long Acre, London WC2E 9AN

A Division of Pearson Professional Limited

First published in Great Britain 1995

British Library Cataloguing in Publication Data
A CIP catalogue record for this book can be obtained
from the British Library

ISBN 0 273 61181 X

1 3 5 7 9 10 8 6 4 2

Typeset by Northern Phototypesetting Co. Ltd, Bolton
Printed and bound in Great Britain by
Bell and Bain Ltd, Glasgow

The Publishers' policy is to use paper manufactured from sustainable forests.

Using Questionnaires and Surveys to Boost Your Business

■

NICK EVANS

The Institute of Management (IM) is at the forefront of management development and best management practice. The Institute embraces all levels of management from students to chief executives. It provides a unique portfolio of services for all managers, enabling them to develop skills and achieve management excellence. If you would like to hear more about the benefits of membership, please write to Department P, Institute of Management, Cottingham Road, Corby NN17 1TT. This series is commissioned by the Institute of Management Foundation.

Contents

Acknowledgements

■

I would like to thank Sally Wellman of *Search Consultancy*, Bristol, for advice, help and sample materials; David Schofield of *David Schofield Consulting Ltd*, Bradford, for advice on quality assurance matters and for quality management forms; the *Market Research Society* for permission to use abstracts from their published works; and Mike Ormian for permission to use the college questionnaire.

Thanks are also due to Corporate Communication Associates for the use of the persona personnel profiling questionnaire, *West Sussex County Council* for permission to reproduce the Cycling survey; *Longman Group* for the Skills Audit Questionnaire; Inspector Brian Jenkinson of *Cambridgeshire Constabulary* for permission to use the victim questionnaire; and, especially Pete Cole, author of *PinPoint for Windows*, for permission to use sample materials from the product, and for writing the software in the first place.

What is this book about?

- What is a questionnaire?
- Not all questionnaires actually ask questions (forms)
- Reasons for undertaking a questionnaire
- How the desired outcomes from the survey predetermine the questionnaire's format

From large corporations to sole trader companies, from hospital managers to personnel directors, from quality managers to customer service departments, this book is designed for use by anyone who wishes to use a questionnaire or survey to enhance their understanding of their business or profession, its clients and customers, and the forces which govern its success. This is not a learned thesis on statistics nor is it a professional's market research manual. It has been written by someone who has had to get to grips with the entire process of surveys from their initial design and implementation, through data collection, to analysis and presentation of results. If you know little about data structures, less about statistics and nothing at all about the process of formulating a questionnaire which will work, then you share the same attributes as those with which the author began his current work.

The information here assumes that you will use some electronic means for creating your questionnaire, collecting and analysing its results. For the purpose of consistency the work draws on the facilities of *PinPoint for Windows* with which the author has been closely involved both in terms of development and marketing. The software is published by Longman Logotron. Although it is not necessary to have the software in order to use this book, much of the exemplar material may be found in the *Working Model* disk which is available free of charge from Longman Logotron. In order to run the Working Model and see the examples which are used in the text you will need a computer which runs Microsoft Windows 3.1 or later. To obtain the software, simply call Longman Logotron on Cambridge (UK) (0)1223 425558.

WHAT IS A QUESTIONNAIRE?

This may sound like a silly question so early in this book, yet a questionnaire can be many things and take many forms, as will be seen as you dig deeper into the subject. The questionnaire form itself is only part of the story, although an important part, it is only one factor which contributes to the overall usefulness of the exercise. In addition, the data entry, analysis and presentation of information allow the person conducting the survey to extract and infer much more information than is available when every element is taken singly. By combining, comparing and contrasting sets of data the user is able to uncover trends, relationships and influences which could not otherwise be seen. For that reason, the questionnaire is more than the sum of its processes or parts.

The most familiar questionnaire to many people is the one such as that propped up in the hotel room, asking for your comments on their facilities and services. It is a means by which you can make your feelings known, whether good or ill, and it encourages you to approach the subject in a structured way, looking at all the areas of the hotel you might have used.

This type of questionnaire on customer satisfaction has, until recently, been the most prevalent use of the technique where the respondents are left to themselves to answer the questionnaire. A growing trend nowadays has people with clipboards stopping you in the street to ask about your preferences in soap powder, your opinions about advertising or to collect your views on a particular public service. These interviews use questionnaires to structure and guide the conversation, but are led much more by the interviewer who guides and encourages you to answer with prompting and with suggestions.

Similarly, on telephone interviews, a survey of your opinions about the current state of government or your needs or otherwise for double-glazing, are directed by a questionnaire form in front of the interviewer. In this case it is quite likely that the form is actually on a computer screen and the questions are being 'routed' automatically so that your trail of responses follows a path predetermined by a structure in the questionnaire itself.

Collecting information by any of the available means gives different benefits according to the method. Paper questionnaires filled in at home by the respondent are less likely to be influenced by the 'pleasing the company' syndrome, particularly if they are anonymous. On the other hand, the chances that the respondent is giving the questionnaire their full attention is minimal. Telephone interviews can be more focused in some respects. The interviewer can listen to the responses, clarify the questions that have been poorly framed, but conversely may influence the outcome by 'interpreting' the questionnaire to give a particular result.

Face-to-face interviews are the most effective but are also the most expensive! The interviewer may read the expression, mood and body language of the respondent and thereby guide the questioning appropriately. This sort of work is really best tackled in a much more free-form type of questionnaire than is discussed in these pages.

It is often the case that companies wish to collect sensitive information from their clients. Who is likely to give the best picture of the way things *really* are? If you want the truth perhaps you don't always ask your friends. It may be more informative to survey the people to whom it is difficult to talk: the malcontents, those with a grievance, those whom the system has failed. For that reason, in large businesses there is a central market research office which undertakes client surveys. The individual regional offices would probably only talk to the 'nice' people!

WHEN IS A QUESTIONNAIRE NOT A QUESTIONNAIRE?

Questionnaires are not the end of the story. Never believe that questionnaires are simply carried out by market research agencies; a questionnaire might be designed to discover your level of entitlement to aid, your eligibility for a mortgage or simply be a form which you fill in to apply for a driving licence. The principle is still the same: collect the information in a sensible fashion so that, afterwards, you can do what you want to with it!

Practically any form which you complete, be it for a mortgage or insurance application, as a method of providing an audit trail for processes in your work or simply as an order form for goods or services, can be seen as a questionnaire. It is, after all, the same process – collecting information in a structured way, ensuring that nothing of importance is missed. Increasingly there is a convergence between questionnaires and other data collection systems which use forms, particularly in those areas where quality management is an integral part of the process. Questionnaire forms are ideal for this type of work, particularly when used in conjunction with appropriate software (see Chapter 10 *Technology Tools*). This book attempts to demonstrate how best to collect that information through simple techniques of design and planning.

REASONS FOR NEEDING A QUESTIONNAIRE

If you believe that you need to undertake a survey of your customers or pass round a questionnaire among your colleagues then it will be a result of having identified a need to collect information in a structured way. It is likely that as you work through this book there will be ideas of how you could use questionnaires more frequently in your work, both inside and outside your organisation. Questionnaire fatigue can be a very real problem if they are used too enthusiastically. The key is variety and clarity of purpose. The respondent must feel that completing the questionnaire will be of benefit either personally or to the organisation. Where questionnaires actually form a part of the day-to-day process as forms or data collection systems, then familiarity must not breed contempt. The importance of information tracking and record-keeping is central to the success and responsiveness of any organisation. The following sections tackle questionnaires from a variety of standpoints. Perhaps you will say, 'I'm not involved in Quality Management so I shall skip this bit', however, you may find that there are ideas which can transfer from other disciplines to your area of expertise. Some of the main reasons for needing questionnaires are considered below.

Performance of your organisation

Internal and external factors affect the way in which any organisation (company, institution, public service, etc.) operates and the effectiveness of its services. Measuring those factors allows you to examine them without prejudice, based upon facts rather than anecdotal evidence. Once the evidence is measured it is possible to frame a plan of action to compensate for the problems that have been found or the issues that have been raised.

QUALITY ASSURANCE AND TOTAL QUALITY MANAGEMENT (TQM)

BS5750, ISO9000

The drive to promote quality throughout businesses and institutions is now international. The British Standard BS5750 and ISO9000 of the International Standards Organization, both lay down criteria for managing and tracking processes and services; these criteria must be met in order that an organisation may be accredited. Having gained certification the organisation must then consistently maintain these processes in order to retain accreditation. The objectives are to improve customer satisfaction with the product or service being generated; to improve efficiency and thereby cut costs and raise profitability; and to improve the workplace and its practices so that employees are content and therefore are more productive. This may be achieved by defining the effectiveness of internal procedures or staff efficiency, both of which are examined later this chapter, or by testing and monitoring the relationship between procedures which have an impact upon the overall process. Equally it may be to do with the quality of materials and services being purchased by the organisation from external suppliers or the appropriateness of processes and procedures which lead to the end-product.

The system is the same whether you produce goods or provide a service. At any stage in the process it should be possible to examine the factors which have led to a given state of affairs so that the quality of the system at any point may not only be measured but tracked back through its constituent processes.

Towards accreditation

The route to accreditation for these standards is complex and demanding and is not the subject of this book. However, one of the major tools involved is questionnaire and survey work. Surveys will help gain an overview of the way in which your organisation impacts on the external community. Questionnaires will enable you to monitor the processes by which it operates and its impact on its staff and suppliers. The key is maintenance of records, allowing an auditor to backtrack any given process from a particular point to its origin. This type of record-keeping is not unlike accountancy! The audit trail must be complete and consistent if the system is to work. The sensible structuring of questionnaires and forms which enable any of these processes to be tackled, is a key to success.

Once you have achieved your objective of accreditation, and set in place processes and procedures by which quality may be controlled, it is then necessary to ensure that those systems are maintained and continue to provide the control you require. Constant audit of processes and personnel are vital to ensure that there is no slippage and once again regular, simple questionnaires may be used for this purpose. Examples of questionnaires which are used in this context appear later in the book.

Forms and quality tracking

Having your finger on the pulse is the key to successful management in both the public and private sectors. The structured collection, storage and retrieval of information will enable that process to be more successful, although it will not in itself make you into a perfect manager! Rather, it will give you a base from which to make informed decisions and, more importantly for others' perception of your role, allow you to produce the information required at the press of a button. The ability to report on processes, performance, systems management and all other factors which govern your organisation's operation is central to success at management and board meetings. All of the factors in the following sections can be controlled and tracked using questionnaires, whether they be of the 'What is your opinion . . .' type or simply forms on which processes are recorded.

Frequently reiterated throughout this book is the fact that you will need to determine what you want out of this system before you put it in. Consider the reports, the output, which will help you to manage better. Consider the way in which you need to have access to information and the ways in which it will need to be presented. Then read the sections hereafter which will help you to achieve that objective.

Tenders

Tendering nowadays has become an exact science. Information about the company, its services, its ability to deliver, the quality of its goods and its services all play a part before the magic brown envelope is taken into consideration. For many organisations the bottom line is no longer simply which quotation is the lowest, but which organisation will provide the best service in terms of product quality and reliability, value for money, and whether the organisation can be trusted to deliver on time.

Measuring all of those factors is not only time-consuming, it also is a headache when it comes to analysing and comparing the merits of a variety of organisations. For example, if out of ten tenders received there appear to be six which fit your needs, how can you determine which company should take the order. Guesswork, hunch and a lucky streak will no longer do! You need to be able to measure all of the factors which contribute to a company's appropriateness, score them and come out with a result which tells you who, on balance, should be considered most likely to take the order. The system is not foolproof and it does not deny the need for management judgement to override the 'decision' which a computer has made. It does, however, provide you with a tool (a yardstick) which will dispassionately measure all of the contenders and present the results in a form from which you can make an informed decision.

Approved suppliers

In a similar fashion to that which applies to tendering, suppliers change, grow, merge and are generally in a constant state of flux. As you adopt new suppliers and monitor the status of existing ones, so you will need to have a systematic method for evaluating their services and for recording their commitment to fulfilling your needs. Moreover, records of your interaction with the suppliers, particularly in terms of their record for quality in goods and the service they provide should be maintained along with the supplier record. Continually updating, amending and extending those records is a task which is best undertaken by questionnaire, whether administered on paper or by telephone dialogue.

Client records

Tracking your clients is not simply a question of stacking their orders and invoices in a folder and scanning the information on paper. Their performance (the amount of business they do with you, its regularity and its volume) is a key indicator of the strength of your organisation. By recording your interaction in a structured way you can not only look at their business over a year but you can also compare it with other similar companies and their patterns of buying and examine moving trends to see whether your line is going up or down with any individual or group.

Although these records are probably not questionnaires (it would be a poor company which had to ask its clients how much business they did with them!) the form in which and, for that matter, on which you collect that information has as its basis the design principles and structures which also apply to questionnaires.

Inspection reports

Simply logging materials in as they arrive is a form-based occupation. It is not satisfactory for someone to say 'Yes, they look OK' and place the goods into stock. The criteria by which you measure how 'OK' those goods are quite often change and certainly are not the same for a stack of timber as they are for a high performance computer system. Consequently, the right form, phrased in the right way, with the correct content and structure will not only make the process easier for those performing it and provide predefined control over it, it will also mean that records can be tracked back easily using simple computer technology.

Non-conformance reports

These reports monitor where your quality system fails. A supplier sends the wrong goods; despatch send to the wrong customer; the goods or services are ineffective or inappropriate or any other situation which calls for remedial action. A non-conformance report is simply a form which logs the problem, establishes a process for correction and monitors whether the action was actually carried out. Forms such as simple questionnaires, held in an efficient data structure can assist the quality manager in tracking such information and proving that work has been carried out.

Moreover, if the data are structured appropriately they will also allow the manager to build a profile of where non-conformance occurs and represent it in a graphical or statistical format. This then allows analysis and highlights problem areas in the organisation.

EVALUATION OF INTERNAL SERVICES

'Internal services' covers a multitude of operations which vary from company to company. Internal effectiveness is an aim of quality management in which the company's services, performing in concert, provide an efficient end-product with a minimum of duplication, waste or conflict. Although individual services within the organisation may be effective they may not marry perfectly with related departments, causing ripples in the calm of an otherwise efficient system.

The evaluation of services is undertaken in a number of ways:

- Employee attitude surveys.
- Systems audits.
- Departmental customer satisfaction reports.
- Supplier questionnaires.

It is possible to measure the relative importance of services as perceived by the people who use them. Questions which ask employees to rank the importance of tasks within their department, the importance of their operations in the whole process and the value of the work which they undertake can highlight problems of perception which lead to discontinuity in the process.

Each department of a company (production, development, marketing, finance, sales, personnel, purchasing) has its own quality requirements. The processes in any one department may not be directly linked or similar to those in another – indeed there may well be competition between them which can create a blockage in the system. The key for the quality manager is to identify where the blockages occur and to provide a continuity so that the process overall is smooth. A number of factors can affect these processes and their continuity:

- methodology
- equipment
- personnel

and these can be further subdivided into:

- methodology – processes, materials
- equipment – information, 'hardware', software, services
- personnel – skills, training, attitude.

The interaction of all these factors is the subject of the quality manager's scrutiny. With appropriate systems a continuous loop of establishment of procedures, implementation, recording, evaluation and modification can be undertaken. The key process for your skills with questionnaires and forms is recording. Those records provide the audit trail and the means whereby any part of the loop may be assessed.

INTERNAL AUDIT

The internal audit department of a company is central to the effectiveness of any drive towards quality. Its processes and operations monitor in 'helicopter view' every activity to ensure harmonisation within the company. Reporting is a key to controlling the business. By tracking and mapping reports, one can detect patterns of behaviour or of incidence of events which can help to pinpoint factors such as inefficient work practices, lapses in security and fraud. Such work is part of an overall structure of *key controls* which enable the auditor to track the operation of every aspect of the business. This begins with statements of policy made known to all employees and continues through documents for reporting all aspects of the operation (in the form of questionnaires or simple forms) into structures for analysing those processes on a constant basis, monitoring change and non-conformance, and then taking appropriate action.

Not only will these structures benefit the company directly when correctly implemented, they will also have knock-on effects with other organisations. Insurers, for example, will be more willing to cover risks that are backed by sensible control processes. In addition, security of data, for example, will minimise the risk that fraud can take place, particularly where that fraud might involve breaches of the Data Protection Act (individuals masquerading as others or even as companies can leave your organisation open to litigation if you have not adequately protected your data – monitoring that situation by sensible audit procedures is a fundamental task).

Your staff and yourself

PERFORMANCING APPRAISAL AND MONITORING

Your staff's and your performance govern the productivity of the company. Keeping a handle on where things are going well and where things could do with adjustment is central to effective management. The process of optimising your workforce to gain the greatest productivity per person at the most economical cost and with the greatest quality is a fine equation to try to balance. As is the case with all these situations, the collection and interpretation of information is key relating to all the variables which contribute to good performance.

Performance appraisal is likely to be a yearly or half-yearly activity within your company, probably with intermediate reviews from time to time to monitor progress and for the two-way communication which characterises good appraisal practice to take place. Performance can be defined not just in terms of the productivity of an individual but also in terms of their attitude, satisfaction and their ambition.

All of these elements need to be measured in a way which enables you not only to chart their progress in fulfilling their own desires and your objectives, but also allows you to map the skills and desires in your company. Such mapping or profiling will give you a picture of what comprises your organisation. Nor is this a static thing. Once an initial appraisal has taken place, the next appraisal is seen, not in isolation but in the context of the comments and objectives which were defined in the previous appraisal. The intention is to provide a curve of development which will benefit both the employee and the company.

The performance appraisal document is essentially a questionnaire, although it is also a basis for a structured discussion between manager and the managed. As such it falls neatly into the definition of a questionnaire and the processes which underpin questionnaire design in good practice should also obtain when structuring performance appraisal. A further development of this area is examined in the following section where the employees, skills and attitudes are matched with their needs in order to develop a training or development plan.

TRAINING NEEDS ANALYSIS

How do you assess whether your staff have the skills they need for their work? How do you test whether the skills that they are using are appropriate or whether, with training, they might become more effective and productive? How, in fact, do you audit the pool of skills that is available to you in the company so that you might better select the right person to tackle specific projects?

The only people who really know what your staff can or cannot do are the staff themselves. They know their previous history, the skills they learned in past employment, the hobbies and interests which may, indirectly, prepare them for a different role in your organisation. The untapped resources which lie in your staff may be a significant factor in improving your organisation's performance – or not! Tapping into that information can only take place by analysing people's skills, partly through performance appraisal (see above) or through the analysis of skills and needs where the skills that they have already are mapped against the role that they fulfil now or are destined to fill. The end result is a map of deficiencies (needs) and surpluses (additional skills) which allows managers to plan more appropriately how they dispose their staff and the type of training that they need.

Training needs analysis is about getting information on existing skills and identifying where related skills are in short supply. The example later in the book which analyses an individual's IT literacy (their computer skills) emphasises 'What can you do now?', and then 'What could you do/what do you want to do with additional training?'

PROFILING

Much of what has been said in the previous section can apply to profiling the people in the outside world. Where you have a need to understand the people and organisations with whom you interact, there is a need for a framework within which you can collect information and then analyse it. Mention has already been made of profiling suppliers, both existing and potential, but here we concentrate on customers.

Your customers or clients

Customers or clients are the people with whom you do business, whether they are purchasing a service or goods from you, whether you supply a service to them in the public arena such as health, water supply, policing or any local government activity – they are still called customers. Rail networks no longer talk of passengers, prisons no longer talk of prisoners and job centres do not refer to the unemployed – they are all customers. The use of the word implies something about the viewpoint from which these people are seen. If you call people 'customer' then the theory is that they will be treated as such. (Is the customer always right?)

Understanding your customers is a process which falls into a number of areas:

- Their satisfaction with your service or product.
- Their needs and how you fulfil them or otherwise.
- Their behaviour and opinions.
- How those factors influence their perception of your organisation and the services/products which it supplies.

CUSTOMER SATISFACTION SURVEYS

How pleased are your customers with you? Do you 'delight' them with your products and services? Is dealing with your organisation hard work for your customers? After the event (the sale, the service, the advice) do your staff continue to support the product or service in the way the customer wants? How could the interaction between your customer and your facility be improved?

Such questions are the motivating force behind customer satisfaction surveys. In such a questionnaire the service provider offers an opportunity to customers to have their say. This is often an uncomfortable experience but one which is ignored at your organisation's peril. If *you* are not doing the job properly someone else probably will.

As ever, the motivation for undertaking such a survey must be based upon what you will do about it when you find out that your customers have a poor opinion of aspects of your service. What exactly do you want to discover? Are you simply looking for a pat on the back (in which case you may have a nasty surprise) or do you have a genuine desire to see the situation from your customer's viewpoint? Begin with your expectations, move on to the consequences if those expectations are or are not fulfilled. You may already have an inkling that your customer service in the area of invoicing or technical support is less than satisfactory. Your questionnaire will probe your customers' experience of that service and will give you evidence, on the basis of which you will do . . . what? That very much depends upon the circumstances and is, of course, not the province of this book.

Feedback

Use the questionnaire to gain feedback (reactive information) upon all aspects of your organisation's activities which directly impinge on the consumer or customer.

- *Your product/service:* How does your product appear to the customer? Is it of sufficient quality? Does it fulfil their needs? Is it delivered in an appropriate way? Does it meet their needs in every respect? If not, in what ways could it be modified in order to improve its relevance to the customer?
- *Your support:* After the sale or the initial tranche of service has been provided, what quality of support is provided to the customer? Are their queries answered in a satisfactory way? Is additional help, material or support provided appropriately and at a satisfactory cost? Does the customer have confidence that, upon returning to you for advice and further support, they will get what they require?
- *Your sales and ordering process:* Is purchasing goods or services from your organisation easy and pleasant or is it like getting the proverbial blood from a stone? Do procedures help or hinder the purchasing process? Are the services which support the sale (delivery, invoicing and all general fulfilment services) performed satisfactorily? If things go wrong (goods out of stock or unavailable, staff off work) are the procedures for informing the customer satisfactory?
- *Pricing or cost effectiveness:* Do the goods or services which you supply represent good value for money? Is the price too low – no-one will tell you this and yet it is something which can be discovered by careful questioning. Are there more cost-effective solutions available and are people considering these in preference to your product?

All these and more are questions which can be answered easily by strategic use of questionnaires. Their outcome is crucial to your organisation's success and it is therefore worth your while investing time and money and, if necessary, also staff in the integration of survey work into your operation.

UNDERSTANDING YOUR CUSTOMERS' NEEDS

So who are your customers? Do you actually know? This may sound facile and yet profiling your customers, identifying who they are, where they come from, what characterises them means that you can target more people who are just like them by seeking them out and telling them about your organisation. Your customers have needs, otherwise they would not be your customers. To what extent you fulfil those needs will be determined in a customer satisfaction questionnaire. There is more, however, than merely saying 'We gave you the product – what did you think of it?' You are also likely to say, 'We have a new product in design or development. What do you think it should do?' Or, 'We are considering changing our procedures to tackle X, Y and Z. If we do this, will you be pleased? What facilities will you expect from such an extended service? And (in a slightly more subtle way) how much will you pay?'

Researching the market, establishing whether your customers have a need for what you will produce in the future is very much central to a good development plan. There is little point in coming out with an all-singing all-dancing widget complete with every bell and whistle imaginable if no-one is going to buy it. There are plenty of examples of products which have failed because of lack of research: Clive Sinclair's C5 car is the one most often quoted. Consider also institutions such as the UK Poll Tax which may never have seen the light of day had proper research been conducted.

On the other hand, successes such as Death™ cigarettes, 'green' toilet cleaners and detergents, or Hedgehog crisps are all the result of good research and lateral thinking. Market research reveals whether people are interested and, more importantly, whether they will pay and how much.

Evaluating

This type of research allows you to assess a variety of aspects which impact upon the product and on the market.

- *Opportunities for new products:* Is there really an opportunity now for this new product or service? Do people really want that or are they just saying so? Will they pay for it? These questions are all answered once one identifies the potential customers. This is probably the most difficult task – who exactly will make use of what you have to offer and, having discovered that, how will you talk to them? The important factors here are to profile the size of the market which is available to you if it is not big enough then it is not going to support the product adequately to make it viable. Secondly, how best can you attract those people for whom your product is the answer to their prayers (if only they knew it)?

- *Enhancements to existing range:* When you intend to extend, or in some way modify, your existing product, you need to be sure how your existing customer base will react. They are, after all, your core market. Your questionnaire will undoubtedly tell them of your intentions and then seek their reactions and opinions about the things you have omitted.
- *Problems in order to find a solution:* You know you have a problem, your customers also know that there is a problem. The best way of finding a solution is often to ask those who are closest to the problem itself – the customers. How does this problem affect them? What do *they* feel could be done about it? How would they react if you attacked the problem in this way or that way?
- *Predicting customers' behaviour in the face of change:* One of the greatest difficulties in a world of constant flux is keeping your customer when you change the way you do things. Some readers who left *The Guardian* when it changed style have never returned – a calculated gamble on the publisher's part. A survey will indicate to you the likely effect of implementing any change in your product, service or procedures. The question to answer here is likely to be 'If we lose X customers, will we gain Y more as a result of the change?'
- *The impact of your services on the community:* Many organisations actually have a statutory duty to survey their customers. Not only must they know their opinions and their needs, but they must also be able to measure how much impact their services have upon the community. A good example of this is the health service where health authorities must monitor the general health of their population and hope to show a gentle increase in improvement over the years as their preventative medicine policies impact on the patient sector. The *only* way to do this type of monitoring and evaluation is by collecting information in the form of surveys.

UNDERSTANDING YOUR CUSTOMERS' BEHAVIOUR

Categorising your customers into types is often essential to understanding their needs and providing them with the goods or services they require. Although this is simply another facet of an overall customer profile, it is something which is identifiable as a separate aspect of any customer's personality – what do they do, how do they behave, how do they react? By answering all these questions you begin to understand what makes a typical customer and how best you can serve them.

Evaluating

The process involves assessing a variety of factors including:

- *Regional preferences: 'Diff'rent strokes for diff'rent folks'* as the Americans have it. What regional or environmental factors affect the sale or promotion of your goods or services in areas other than your traditional market? This is, of course, marked in venturing into overseas markets and you would expect to have to try to understand French, German, Australian or Chinese markets if those were appropriate to your goods. So equally, why not when you venture into Wales, Scotland, Ireland, Yorkshire, Dorset or wherever else your work takes you? Each different territory has a different way of reacting to particular aspects of products, marketing techniques and advertising. You need to know these, understand them and compensate for them before you begin an expensive marketing campaign. What are the right words? What are the differences in legislation which may affect your product – for example, in tackling the education market in Scotland, there is a completely different curriculum which bears little resemblance to England's National Curriculum. Say the wrong words, trot out the wrong jargon and the customer is left with the distinct (and correct) impression that you do not understand the people to whom you are talking.
- *Price sensitivity:* The price that the market will stand in the City of London is unlikely to be the same as that which holds good in deepest Lincolnshire. Your survey must uncover how sensitive the market is to price, not just in terms of competitors and their product, but also in terms of how much value regional purchasers of your goods and services are likely to place on what you provide. Assessing this is more subtle than a 'How much do you want to pay, John?' approach. Gauging price sensitivity can be done by comparing products or services which you consider to be in a similar bracket to your own so that, without mentioning your own area, you have a yardstick by which to measure it.
- *Seasonal variations:* Although most seasonal variations will be familiar to you in your work, venturing into new markets may reveal unforeseen variants – the Lancashire Mills' Holiday, for example, or the fact that schools in Scotland have a summer holiday a month in advance of those in the rest of the country. These factors can seriously affect the impact of a campaign and ruin an expensive media push.
- *Responsiveness to advertising/promotion including in public service:* Monitoring the effectiveness of advertising is a constant operation which must have high priority in any business. There is little point in persisting with an expensive media campaign unless you have evidence that it is working. The only way to check that evidence apart from monitoring a sales line, which does not apply in every organisation's case, is to poll people's perceptions about the campaign.

For example, an advertising campaign to raise awareness about the perils of drug abuse or drink driving can only really be measured by asking people whether:

- they noticed the campaign
- they took heed of and understood its message
- they retained the facts (names, injunctions, products) associated with it.

It is only later that one can measure the effectiveness of such work through a decrease in convictions or hospital cases and a general raising of awareness. That is too late for most organisations which generally need to have some immediate feedback about how the money spent is going to produce a pay-off. Therefore, a survey targeted at those most likely to be the focus of the campaign must be undertaken.

There have been many fine television advertisements which have stuck in the memory over the years (clever catchphrases, sensational images and great humour which exceeds that provided by scheduled broadcasting) but can you remember the product which was being promoted? Marketing magazines usually keep a running survey of the effectiveness of campaigns, polling individuals about those which they remember seeing (unprompted) and those they recall in detail (prompted). The two are quite revealing and show the effectiveness or otherwise of advertising spend.

In a smaller scale business, where your advertising may consist of local newspaper advertisements, or in a public service where you wish to promote the local volunteer service, the talking book service or some other aspect of facilities available to the community, it is necessary to find those people at whom the campaign is aimed and discover whether they have heard about it and secondly, whether they have taken any notice.

- *What are the messages that turn them on?* At the same time it is worth assessing which images stay with them; what is it that makes them sit up and take notice; what buttons do you need to press on people in a similar situation in order to effect the right reaction?
- *What is the most effective medium for that message?* It is also worth checking that the medium through which the message is being delivered is the most appropriate. Is there more than one local free newspaper? Which one do people read? Where best should one display posters to target this audience? Which national dailies do your target read? Have you classified the target groups correctly in order to define the mailshot which you are undertaking? If any of these are wrong then you may well be wasting a good deal of money. The only way to find out for certain is to undertake a survey with a sample group who represent the larger population.

SELLING TO YOUR RESPONDENTS

You can easily be lulled into thinking that as you survey your respondents you could sell a product, your product, to them as a consequence of their answers. This practice is actually frowned on by reputable market researchers who call the practice 'sugging'. The 'I am doing a survey on driveway finishes and would be pleased if you could answer a few questions' practice which ultimately always leads to 'From your answers I can see that what you need is StikkyStuf Driveway . . .' is an underhand way of getting your respondent to tell you their needs before you hit them with the sell.

However, there are ways in which the practice of raising awareness (for such it should be) can be undertaken reputably and with respect for the respondent. The key factor is that the respondent's answers are not immediately matched with a sales pitch. A questionnaire which genuinely seeks to gather information in order to profile your potential customer community could easily finish with a small tickbox with the question: 'Would you like more information about StikkyStuf Driveway finishes?' The respondent is not cornered and does have the option to follow up your initiative if they have been moved to think about the driveway in a positive way.

Focusing thoughts

Essentially your aim is to collect information, but in so doing you may also focus the respondent's thoughts on the issues that make your product indispensable – otherwise, why would you be asking them if they were interested? Your discretion and respect for the respondent must be paramount above any desire to sell to them through the medium of the questionnaire. Having discovered that 50 per cent of your respondents really would benefit from StikkyStuf, *then* send them a carefully worded mailer after the survey. You have detached yourself from the accusation of sugging and have rightly followed up on the information you have gathered – the very purpose of the questionnaire in the first place.

Raising awareness

Questionnaires do raise awareness of products although the rather tacky approach from a catalogue company (Fig. 1.1) makes you wonder what mental age they consider their agents to have.

Buyers

Market Research Department

fashion questionnaire

spring/summer 1995

Please fill in your details below:-

Name ____________________

Agent Ref No. ____________

Please read each of the following questions and answer as you see fit. Your answers are of course in confidence

Do you feel that the Buyers Spring/Summer '95 catalogue gives an excellent variety of choice for everyone young and old?

☐ Yes ☐ No

Who do you buy for, mainly?

Yourself ☐ Family ☐ Friends ☐ Other ☐

Would you like us to make more superb special offers such as those featured on page 408?

☐ Yes ☐ No

Do you consider the range of children's wear on pages 667 to 678 meets the needs of all your children?

☐ Yes ☐ No

Do you believe that the we have the latest in up to date sportswear such as the Super AirLite Nuke Mega-Trainers from SportsStars? (See pages 345-346)

☐ Yes ☐ No

Finally, how can we improve our excellent service?

____

____

____

____

Thank you

Fig. 1.1 Questionnaire from catalogue company to its agents

The competition

Who are the competition? Do you have any? What edge do they have over you? How do your customers perceive them? What is it about them that makes customers buy their product and not yours? What is it about their *customers* which makes them different from yours? Surveying for competition analysis is an activity which enables you to draw a profile of your competitors by asking their customers about them. Assuming that you are able to address these customers in some way, through a mailing or by interviews, then you may be able to highlight their strengths and weaknesses.

The first key is to find a way to address those customers. As they are not your customers you are unlikely to have a mail-list for them. In which case, assuming that you are surveying a product or service which is fairly widely used in your area, and assuming for the sake of argument that you reckon the competitor to have 30 per cent of the market, then a mailing to a sample group from the population should reveal around 30 per cent of people who use that product. In order to isolate those as a group at the analysis stage you will need to ensure that at least one question in your survey highlights which product they use.

If you have written this survey as being clearly from you, the manufacturer of a competing product, it is less likely that people will confess to using the competition! People will often answer in the way that they think you want them to. Therefore it is a good idea to remain anonymous in the survey process. There is little advantage in performing the survey with your company name emblazoned at the top if the consequent answers you get are invalid. Although you may raise your profile a little to those who shop with the competition, it is better to mail them afterwards, having collected valid information.

FINDING OUT

Your task in the survey is to *find out*, not to inform. Irrelevant detail will clutter the questionnaire and the data set. Keep the questions brief and to the point. There may need to be only three or four questions which can be answered quickly, stuck in the (reply paid) envelope and sent off for your analysis. Your questions need to focus on a number of factors from which you gain an insight into the competing firm's products or services, selling and advertising techniques, support and the characteristics of their customers.

What makes them effective?

Why exactly are they effective? If this is at your expense then it is a question of differentiation. Your questions must probe firstly which product

Which pain relief product do you most usually purchase?

❍ PainGo
❍ Adanin
❍ Aspiril
❍ Parashootemal
❍ Nuro
❍ Other (please specify)

What are your reasons for choosing the product you use?

❍ Its effectiveness in relieving pain?
❍ Its price?
❍ Its packaging?
❍ The brand name?
❍ The manufacturer's name?
❍ The advertising you have seen?
❍ Something else – please say what it is

Fig. 1.2 Finding out about the competition

they buy and then search for the detail about their reasons (Fig. 1.2). This probing may be done either by multiple choice questions or, if an interviewer is used, by suggesting possibilities to the respondent in a varied order. It is likely that if any of these answers is chosen that you will then want to know more about that particular factor. For instance:

In what way do you find this product more effective at pain relief? ____________

The question now is, do you give them the answers that you have at your finger tips (the stuff works quickly; it has no side-effects; it's more pleasant) or do you let them tell you in their own words? Remember that if you let them tell you, then you have not forced them into the answer. The data are more accurate and you may still record them using the codings that you have already thought of (see the section on coding free text answers, p. 83). You need to have thought out carefully beforehand what the reasons for any of these choices might be. Do this by testing your survey on an informed sample group (see the section on '*Dry running the Questionnaire*', Chapter 2).

The data you collect in this section needs to be cross-referenced with other factors in order that you might have an overall impression of who purchases the product (age group, social factor, etc.), who prefers what (price, pack, product, etc.) and derive from that the characteristics needed in your product to convince them to buy yours in preference to the other. Sounds easy on paper, doesn't it?

What they are missing?

You may also wish to probe your respondent about the shortcomings of the opposition, whether or not they are the manufacturer of the chosen product, e.g.

What features do you feel are missing, if any, from your chosen make of lawnmower?

You have asked the question since you know perfectly well that there is some dissatisfaction with Lawnotron's electric mower because it does not have a safety cut-out on the power plug, CloseCut's petrol mower lacks a reliable grass collection system and people have remarked on the inconsistency of cut in SnipSnap's LawnRazor product. By asking the question you are focusing people's minds on features which you know are missing and, more importantly they will then think of other problems that have occurred to them. This is not the time to hit them with 'Well our product does this much better!' Do it later with a mailshot which highlights the benefits of your product against the shortcomings of others on the basis of your accumulated data – after all, that's why you are doing the survey in the first place.

Where you can beat them?

There are areas where your product will win. You may like to ask people to compare your product and its price and features with the opposition's. Don't expect to gather any sense however. They will say all the nice things you wish to hear, particularly if you put the words in their mouths with multiple choice options.

Who are their customers?

This, more than the product specification itself, will tell you a good deal about the characteristics of a typical sale. Accumulating information on the make-up of your opponent's customers gives you the power to target your product more closely at them either by direct mailing, advertising in appropriate magazines or journals, or simply by making the product appeal more to that group in any way that seems practical. Can it be, for example, that you have been missing a major market for your product which your opponent is tapping? Did you know that your product can be used for this particular task in waste reclamation/hang-gliding/social services? Could you, with a little tweaking, make your product applicable or more appealing to a wider audience?

Discover the characteristics of the population using the product. Who are they, where are they? What do they do? Why are they choosing X instead of Y?

- *Region:* Regional variations can make a big difference to perception about a product. Consider the differences in preference for beers between north and south, or the language used to describe bread rolls in any part of the country, or the price of products in the affluent south-east against the price in the north-west. Find where the groups lie and look for clustering of buyers in those areas. Map those clusters against factors such as advertising campaigns, regional preferences, price sensitivity until an identifying pattern emerges.
- *Lifestyle/social group:* The same principles apply to the social groupings. Although we are told that we live in a classless society, sociologists still continue to classify us into the groups that seem to characterise us. Groups' preferences for different things may be well known, but the evidence is often anecdotal. Check it against your findings.
- *Differentiating characteristics:* Language can be a barrier to sales – part of your questionnaire can test reaction to slogans, sales lines and the language and images of your promotions.

What is important to them

In your survey, use features and benefits lists so that the respondent can classify or rank features in order of importance (Fig. 1.3). Discovering where emphases lie is central to configuring your product and/or your campaign to hit the target centrally.

Please rank the following features of an effective office cleaning service in order of importance (1 is Most Important and 5 is Least Important)

❍ Cost
❍ Flexibility of hours
❍ Effectiveness
❍ Trustworthiness of staff
❍ Previous references
❍ Size of company

Fig. 1.3 Ranking features of importance

And by analysis

You will be able to try '*What if . . . ?*' tests until you discover the patterns that you are seeking. Chapter 7 '*Getting Out More Than You Put In*' will help you decide exactly how to do that. It is important to realise that this is not just a once-for-all operation. When you survey you take a snapshot in time of **now**. That **now** is past within a short time and things have moved on. Questionnaires, regularly applied, will help you to track how things are moving. To do that you must ensure that:

- your questions suit the need
- your questions remain constant
- your sample remains constant in characteristics
- your surveys occur at regular intervals.

The sample type and the questionnaire must stay constant so that anything else which moves will show up clearly. Following that structure will enable you to:

- follow movements in the market
- track changes in opinion
- observe how fashion alters.

A simple example would be a questionnaire which tracked preferences in buying canned beer (Fig. 1.4). It would look at the characteristics which influenced the purchase of any particular brand, enabling you to identify the brand leaders and the reasons they are there. A fragment is shown in Fig. 1.4.

Which of these canned beers have you bought MOST of in the last 14 days?
Tick one box only

❍ Treble X
❍ CastleBrew Main
❍ Hop-u-like
❍ Pintasuds
❍ Fasters
❍ Budwester

On average, how many cans of ANY beer do you think you buy per week?

❍ None
❍ 1 to 3 cans
❍ 4 to 6 cans
❍ 7 to 12 cans
❍ More than 12 cans

What is it that makes you choose the beer you buy? Rank the following features in order of importance, putting 1 against the MOST important down to 8 for the LEAST important

⎵ Taste
⎵ Alcoholic Strength
⎵ The Brewer
⎵ The Brand Name
⎵ The Advertising
⎵ The Cost
⎵ Special Offers (free cans, competitions etc)
⎵ Anything else (please say what it is here)

Fig. 1.4 Preferences in canned beer

DISCOVERING RELATIONSHIPS

It was mentioned earlier that by cross-referencing data (plotting one set of factors against another often using a technique called cross-tabulation) one can see trends emerge that might not immediately be apparent. A common primary question against which others are plotted is age. Another is sex. Either of these can be a determining factor in identifying behaviour, purchasing patterns or opinions. Take, for example, a survey of people visiting an hotel. They all come there for a purpose which your questionnaire has identified. Each respondent has said which age band they fall into. Plotting one against another reveals the not too startling fact that men between the ages of 35 and 55 are generally visiting the hotel on business. Further investigation can identify the fact that women are more likely to be there for conferences and pleasure than are men, but that men are quite likely to visit for the indeterminate 'Other' option whereas women never do. No surprises here, yet you are able to confirm a trend which was previously only suspected. Your marketing of your product or service can now match the pattern of behaviour of the age and sex groups.

CONFIRMING UNDERSTOOD OR ANECDOTAL KNOWLEDGE

Ultimately, if you have any sort of handle on your business or profession you will know what you feel is true about the state of the world as it affects you. Although your survey may ultimately confirm your opinion you must not design it to set out to do so.

Is what you think is true, actually true?

As has been mentioned before in this book, if you put the idea into people's heads they will feed you back your own thoughts. The power of a company to invoke a self-fulfilling prophecy was never so vividly shown as when Gerald Ratner, of the jewellery chain *Ratners,* stated that most of his products were 'crap'. The public believed him and his empire crumbled. So, too, your respondents will believe what is put in front of them. Your task is to build objectivity into the survey and shun bias (see the section on bias, p. 66, for further details).

Although your thoughts need to be confirmed this can only be done so indirectly by gathering evidence dispassionately and keeping the issues at arms' length. Your analysis may show trends which are not comfortable for you. Do not reject them as being unreliable, on the contrary, worry at them. Manipulate the data to see whether you can prove any more about them by comparing and contrasting with other groups, other products or, other surveys from the past. If what you fear still persists then devise further research which will tackle that issue head on and highlight the problem, its causes and perhaps, in the process, the remedy.

Forming hypotheses based on the information collected

As will be discussed further '*Getting out more than you put in*' (Chapter 7), the information you have collected can be juggled and massaged in order to make it work for you. Asking 'What if . . . ?' questions is central to forming hypotheses and then testing them. Since the whole purpose of your survey is to test the thing which is being investigated, you should aim to perform on the data as many relevant variants of analyses as possible in order to uncover trends.

REFINING AND ADDING FURTHER RESEARCH

You will find that the information you have gathered may be limited in some areas – the best laid plans for research will often fall down because an unexpected variable has crept into the analysis. Once that variable is identified it is then a question of setting up follow-up research which will build on the information received to date. It is worth bearing in mind that, since the information will be complementary, there is no reason to collect the original data a second time (unless you feel that your current data are invalid in some way) and therefore your questions should be framed in a way which enable the new information to be mapped onto the existing information in a logical and practical way. Therefore:

- Keep answer ranges the same to enable comparison of like with like.
- Keep question types the same – don't collect one set of answers as numeric when a similar set in the previous survey were undertaken as a range.
- Survey a similar or the same subset of people to ensure that the style and weighting of answers is maintained.

Setting objectives based on new or confirmed knowledge

And when your data has been collected, the analyses performed, the follow-up research undertaken and the final report has been prepared – what then? At the beginning of your survey specification you will have stated your objectives and the consequences which will befall in any given situation. Now is the time for consequences, based on clear evidence which may or may not be backing up your own gut-feeling about the state of the world.

The process of creating a questionnaire

- **The whole process of creating a good questionnaire**
- **How the type of respondent influences the questions asked**
- **The different means for administering questionnaires**
- **The need for clear objectives before writing a questionnaire**

Having decided on your approach you come actually to sit down and write your questionnaire. It is at this point that theory goes out of the window and you create the questionnaire according to your instincts. Some basic precepts are important, however, and they can all be summed up in one phrase: collecting information by design.

COLLECTING INFORMATION BY DESIGN

The implication that you are about to *design* the questionnaire rather than just jot down a few questions indicates that you are following some ground rules and that there is a level of skill involved. It has been said earlier that skill in this respect comes only from experience: the more you do it the better you will become at it. As ever, it cannot be overemphasised that trialling your work before you unleash it on your target sample will pay dividends.

The questionnaire provides a skeleton upon which the flesh of the facts may be hung. The skeleton not only supports the questions which elicit the facts, it provides an orderliness which makes the process of gathering and arranging those facts and opinions much more easy, logical and straightforward than it otherwise might be.

The structure of your questionnaire provides a number of benefits:

1. It guides the interview so that all the necessary information is gathered (research structure)

Without a formal structure, an interview (because that is the only way it could happen) would be directionless. A paper questionnaire would be impossible, or at best, random. The questionnaire allows you to control the flow of the questions, relating topics together and providing a structure for a stream of thought which results in your respondent's answers.

Your set objectives for the questionnaire are realised in the questions you ask. There is no redundancy in the questions, no irrelevance, the respondent will keep to the topic, all necessary facts and opinions will be gathered and all will be for the best in this best of all possible worlds! Perhaps a little idealistic, but that is your objective.

2. It ensures that everyone answers each question exactly as you intended and in a similar fashion (interview structure)

A vital part of any research system is the need to keep outside variables constant. When testing animals or humans under laboratory conditions, the environment, the diet and all other outside factors must be maintained in exactly the same way for all concerned. If not, how do you know that they have not influenced the outcome in some way? So with your questionnaire, it is important that each respondent encounters the same questions, asked in the same way, with the same set of possible responses made available to them, unless of course that can be seen as biasing the outcome.

Paper questionnaires do not suffer from variance nearly so much as interviews, either face to face or over the telephone. Provided that you only have one version of the paper questionnaire then all people who use it will have the same questions and answers, good or bad, useful or useless, and will therefore answer consistently – bear in mind, however, that if your questionnaire is poorly structured and your questions are poorly framed, they will answer consistently badly! Interviews are the area where variance creeps in. Simply the tone of voice in which a question is asked, the emphasis put on different words in the same sentence changing the shade of the question can bias the respondent who picks up on the interviewer's thoughts. The friendly interviewer who 'helps' the respondent when no help is required, prompting and probing when you, the designer, would have wanted them to keep quiet in order to see what the respondent said unprompted, can wreck the validity of your questionnaire.

For this reason, questionnaires administered by interview have very strict instructions and guidelines to which the interviewer must adhere. It is impossible completely to eradicate variance in this situation, but much can be done to minimise its effect (see '*Framing a question*', Chapter 3 for more detail on this topic).

3. It ensures that the respondent gives an accurate (not 'right') answer

What is the right answer? There is no such thing in a questionnaire. The concept of the 'right' answer must always be outside the compiler's mind since it is the answer which is relevant to the respondent which is the key to unravelling the complexity of any survey. The compiler's focus is on extracting the information in a structured and logical way.

Your objective is to discover what people feel and think, not to tell them. Therefore you must pay attention to:

- making your intentions clear in your instructions
- asking the question clearly and concisely
- giving the correct options or opportunities for an appropriate answer.

The only way in which you might consider the concept of 'correctness' for an answer is when the respondent gives you the type and content of answer you need.

4. It organises the answers, ready for analysis (data structure)

The order of the questions is important. Their content and style are both vital. However, the method by which you capture the information, the data structure, will determine whether you get out what you put in, or better still, whether you get out even more than you put in. Answer types will be dealt with at length later. Ensure that you have the correct type of answer structure to receive the data from your immaculately designed questions.

Pay attention not only to the answer type but also to the interrelationships of data. If you need to cross-correlate information, ensure that it is in a form which will allow that to happen easily and will make your presentation readable. For example, if you intend to cross-tabulate the age of your respondents with their preference for flavour of ice-cream, the choice of numeric answer style will prove fatal at the analysis and presentation stage. The reason? Simply because, if you have 50 respondents, all with different ages there will be 50 lines across, each one with one cross-reference to a flavour of ice-cream. Group your respondents into age ranges, say five of them, and then look for trends across the five rows of the cross-tabulation.

The pitfall with such a system is ensuring that the ranges give you all the information you need. What, for example, if all the vanilla lovers were in your first age range because you had specified it too broadly? The information being returned to the ice-cream manufacturer would be distorted.

How will the respondent answer?

For the purposes of this book there are three methods by which respondents will respond to your survey. The type of questionnaire needed for each is different. The first two are very much open to the skills of the interviewer to interpret the responses of the interviewee. They can encourage, cajole and assist the interviewee by interpreting the intention of the question if it was not quite clear. Whereas in the paper questionnaire, the respondent relies entirely on your skill as a compiler.

IN A PERSONAL INTERVIEW

The interview is controlled by the questionnaire. It provides the tracks along which the interview rolls but the interviewer, as an engine driver, can slow down, speed up or stop at will. The instructions in such a questionnaire have to be accurate and specific (see the section on '*Providing Instructions*', p. 55, for more details).

As the interviewee chats, the interviewer notes down the responses in the predetermined format that you, the compiler, have set out. However, they will filter out the noise, the irrelevant ramblings, the blustering and general nonsense that may have been exactly what you were looking for all along. Care must be taken that interviewers do not 'protect' you from the very data you need. Again this is achieved by sensible instructions, clear statement of objectives and a thorough briefing of experienced interviewing staff. A good interviewer will help you get to the meat of the issue, using your questions as the compass by which they will steer the interview. An amateur interviewer will only be as effective as your skill in compiling the questions

IN A TELEPHONE INTERVIEW

Similar rules apply to telephone interviews as to those conducted face-to-face. However, your interviewer is not able to pick up on body language, facial expressions and other indicators of mood, opinion and behaviour.

BY THEMSELVES

Your respondent may be on their own, in their office or house, possibly surrounded by children, washing up, with the television on, interrupted by the telephone, a meeting, a colleague or the coffee break. Under these conditions they are filling in your questionnaire without really paying attention to the loving detail which you have crafted into it, ignoring the skilful way you have asked that tricky question on access rights to the playing fields, glancing over the concise nature of the question on street lighting provision, in fact – not paying attention at all. It's just the way that we all answer questionnaires when we really don't care one way or the other. Most of the respondents to your questionnaire will be in that frame of mind and getting the best out of them will be a test of your skill and resolve.

Getting people simply to consider filling it in needs a motivating force of some kind. Keeping their attention over ten pages of tricky questions will be beyond the powers of most people. Postal questionnaires must be short, pithy, to the point and easy to complete. If that works you can always send another one – 'Thank you so much for the valuable help you gave us in a recent survey. Your remarks were so interesting that we would like to follow them up with a few more questions if you could spare us a little more of your time. As a gesture of thanks please accept . . .'.

These ground rules apply whether you are mailing thousands of questionnaires to households to discover preferences for soap powder or polling the opinions in your company of 120 employees. Only those with an axe to grind will pay attention and their dedication to their cause can sometimes swing the balance of your data.

ASKING QUESTIONS BEFORE YOU START

One of the main problems encountered by people who tackle questionnaire specification for the first time is that they tend to be directionless. Scratching their heads and sucking the end of a pencil they rough out a few questions that seem perhaps to be the right sort of thing if you were doing this type of questionnaire . . . maybe! Unfortunately, this approach is rarely productive and can end with:

- baffled respondents who do not understand what you are getting at
- irrelevant, inaccurate or illogical data
- unreliable results and therefore unsound conclusions.

A range of factors influence your questionnaire's reliability and effectiveness:

- Your objectives and the outcomes you propose
- The make-up of the 'population' which you will survey
- The degree to which your questions target the issue
- The style in which the data are collected and (as a consequence)
- The manner in which the data may be analysed.

All of these topics are tackled in this book. As the title of this chapter suggests, a whole range of questions needs to be answered before you can put pen to paper and design your questionnaire. The time taken in this process will pay dividends later on.

DEFINING A QUESTIONNAIRE

The process of specifying a questionnaire, entering data, analysing and presenting the information you have collected must begin with a definition of your aims. It must also be modified by an understanding of the influences which may skew the outcome.

Setting your objectives before you start

Not only will you need to have a clear idea of the aims and of the intended outcomes, you will also wish to have a plan of campaign which can be implemented when the results have been analysed. A fine questionnaire, excellent analysis and then no consequences is a waste of time, effort and money.

KNOWING YOUR SUBJECT

Strangely, it is necessary to know all about your subject before you research it. Without that foreknowledge both the questions you ask and your interpretation of the results are likely to be flawed. This will be because the questions are not asked from an informed base and may therefore fail to address the subject adequately, and your analyses will equally possibly miss the point entirely. Without prejudging the issue, you need to have some idea of what you are looking for and also of what you are likely to find.

Preliminary research to establish a working model for the question

Before you begin, preliminary research (or experience) will be necessary. You need to establish:

- Who are the people in your 'population' – the people who can answer on an informed basis?
- What proportion of those will make a valid 'sample'?
- What are the major issues and influences you need to address?
- What language is appropriate? Do you need to avoid or include jargon?
- What are the scales and units by which variables are measured in this situation?
- What sensitivities may people have to the issues you are raising?

Each of these can affect the validity of the outcome, either because your respondent does not understand the question, is not willing to answer the question, is insulted by the question, or because the variables are not representative of the situation they understand or the wrong issue is being addressed.

What are the issues?

Any questionnaire is tackled because an issue or a number of issues have been raised – Should we have a bypass around the village? Is the current work practice/shift system/incentive structure appropriate? Does the provision of facilities in the department meet customer needs? Can we continue advertising in these journals or should we look at new areas? All these questions are specific issues which are to be addressed by our questionnaire. There is no question here of prejudice; we know what we want to find out and the questionnaire is designed to tackle that. However, even these must be written from an informed viewpoint and must accommodate all shades of opinion. The issue of the bypass around the village may be easily argued by those who will lose the traffic rumbling past their front door, but the people whose land will be affected by the development must have an equal opportunity to weigh in with their argument. Prejudging or bias can take place if the wrong person writes the questionnaire! How would you feel as the landowner most affected by the bypass if the question below appeared on a questionnaire?

3. Do you feel that it is unreasonable of the local landowners to deny purchase of land for a bypass which will protect the safety of our children?

Biased? Emotive? I think so! The wrong person has been charged with writing the questionnaire in this instance. Bear in mind that the same polarisation relating to issues can happen whether you are from a parish council or a multinational, whether the survey is directed at the population of a village or the staff of a company.

It is when the issues are *not* clear that we are in danger of prejudging: Why is there little use of the new shopping area by residents of the Markham Estate? Why do patients from Eastchester prefer to go to Westchester Hospital, even though it is further away? What is it that has caused a fall-off in use of the 97 bus service? We may think we know the answer but is it *really* because there is dissatisfaction with the timetabling or might it be as a result of the local supermarket's shopper bus service or perhaps even some other factor, unknown? If we make the assumption that it is because of poor timetabling and create our questionnaire to prove that point then we shall not uncover the real truth at all except, perhaps, by accident. These questions have no definitive answers and we are asking the questions because the issues are not clear. The questionnaire in this case is a groping in the dark in the hope that we may grasp something which tells us the answer. This type of questionnaire needs a good deal more thought and planning than one where your objective is simple.

What needs to be uncovered?

If one takes it as read that simple issues can be addressed with simple questions then the corollary might be that the more complex issues require more complex questions. This is not necessarily true. They probably require *more* questions in order to provide a chance of hitting an answer that makes sense. Uncovering the issues will not be achieved by asking complex questions. Build up a picture of where the problems lie by asking a series of direct questions relating to a number of pertinent topics. If necessary, take the questionnaire in two or more stages. You will uncover more of the information you need by a systematic and steady approach than by charging in headlong with questions which baffle and confuse.

If you have determined what are the issues, then you will have some idea of the nature of the information which needs to be uncovered. Returning to our bypass situation for a moment: we know that there is a traffic congestion problem in the area of the village. It has already been the cause of a number of accidents, there is damage to local buildings due to heavy traffic and there is a feeling that the air quality in the area has deteriorated, particularly during the summer. Equally, the proposed (and only logical) route around the village passes through a nature conservancy area, a market garden which employs 20 per cent of the village's population and the land adjacent to a private mansion.

The issues and opinions are many, varied and heated! There needs to be a compromise which, although it might not please all, does the least damage and provides the greatest benefit. What is it? *That* is what needs to be uncovered. The same situation might occur, in different terms, in a company, in a hospital, in a public service – anywhere where self-interest, public interest, availability of cash and a will to change opinion all clash on the battlefield! Therefore it is essential that an independent, unbiased person who can look objectively at the situation should compile the survey. In a company or institutional situation this is not always easy. The questionnaire will come from 'The Management' and will be almost certain to interpret their viewpoint.

Where objectivity may be an issue, a small group of fair-minded people drawn from all parties can thrash out the basis for an investigation. However, beware of the 'committee effect'. The chance of a survey being lean and mean when emanating from a committee is small. Nonetheless, God almost certainly used a committee to design the camel – it may not be beautiful but it works well in the situation!

KNOWING YOUR RESPONDENT

The person who answers your questions is critical to the success of your survey. Regardless of the area in which the survey is carried out and regardless of the number of people involved, your respondent should be:

- Representative of like-minded people in the *population.*
- Capable of answering the questions.
- Willing to answer the questions.

Alienated, disaffected or downright contrary individuals may skew the data with their unrepresentative answers. For this reason your sample size should be sufficient to allow those people's answers to be absorbed into the whole without wrecking the analysis. Unless, of course, it is the case that the extreme view is the common view!

In smaller surveys, within a company for example, the question of finding a representative *sample* is less likely to occur since you will probably survey all or most employees during that project. In this case your *sample* is in fact the whole *population*.

Anonymity

Every respondent to a questionnaire always wants to know what the consequences are of responding. Your intentions may be the most benevolent and you may have no desire to use the data collected in any other way than for the purposes of your analyses. The paranoid public, employees or customers all see a conspiracy or entrapment behind the questions. There are ways of overcoming these fears and it is important that you do so since, if you have failed to put them at their ease, you may only get the answers that the respondent believes you *want* rather than those which are the truth.

Anonymity allows the respondent to answer questions without ever being traced. This is the ideal situation from their point of view, as they have complete freedom to spill out their feelings onto the paper and the answers you receive may contain much which is unexpected and possibly undesirable. Anonymity is only achieved by paper-based questionnaires. Interviews, either face to face or by telephone always carry the risk of identification.

Most reputable market research agencies subscribe to a confidentiality code. Accordingly the agency pledges that the outcome of the interview is for research purposes only and that at no time will the names of individuals be linked to their responses. This code is enforced by professional bodies such as the Market Research Society to whom people with grievances may take their case.

. . . but still keeping track

There is a major problem with anonymity as far as you the compiler is concerned. It may well be that you need to know some details about your respondent: where they live, in which department they work, or the area of the establishment which they visit regularly. You may need to capture them by time (all the out-patients who visited the hospital during specific hours of the day over a period of a month, for example) and for that reason you will need to have some means of identifying the source of the responses. A few of the simpler methods which might be employed follow:

- *Colour coding:* In order to identify particular groups (respondents from an area of a town, county or the country; or perhaps identifying respondents from design, manufacturing, fulfilment and so on within a large business) a system of colour coding will enable you to group questionnaires together. Print the forms on different coloured paper for each area to be represented and ensure that they are delivered appropriately. By adding a code according to colour at the analysis stage the data may then be segmented by type.
- *Sequential numbering:* Forms may be numbered sequentially by the printer or by the addition of an automatic stamp. However, if respondents see an identifying number they are then aware that that number might trace the form back to them. For that reason it is advisable to ensure that there is no link between the delivery system, i.e. the address label on the envelope – and the form inside. If the form contains no personal data the respondent is likely to feel more secure than if their address is printed on it! It may be that forms can be numbered when they are received back for analysis since their point of origin might be known (postmark, departmental mail and so on) but this system is unlikely to be totally reliable.
- *Identity marking:* Any marking at all can be used to identify forms. The only criterion is that you should know the code. The positioning of a logo, for example, might be changed in order to identify the target group although this is no more effective than printing on different coloured paper. A further method is the use of systems such as barcodes which bear a unique serial number.

Whichever method is used, it is still most important to reassure the respondent that the number, code or barcode is not linked directly to their name, rank and number in the personnel or data file.

Getting a sample

The sample is the group of people which has been chosen to represent the views of the whole population. The population is the entire set of people about whom the survey is being conducted. In terms of a national shopping survey, the population is literally that – the population of the country. In terms of a survey of the clients of a supermarket the population is all those people who shop there. For a job centre, the population is all those people who visit the centre looking for work or advice. For a business the population may be all its customers (and potential customers?) if the survey is outward looking, or all its staff if it is inward looking.

The sample which is chosen from the population must represent the population fairly. That is to say, it should take a good cross-section of all shades of opinion from all the different strata of the group being surveyed – the different classes (much as we may hope that there is not such a thing), the different levels of employment in the company or the different types of visitor to an institution such as a hospital (out-patients, emergency patients, long-term patients, visitors, patients from different sectors of the hospital's service) everyone whose views may make an impact on the outcome of the survey.

When the complexity of any population is examined it becomes clear that it is very important to understand that population before trying to collect information from it. For this reason it is a good idea to create a profile of your target population by informally identifying all the different groups or layers which comprise the whole. The sample is then drawn from all those layers in representative proportions so that the sample reflects the type of distribution that is present in the whole population. In a company setting this might just mean selecting at random a number of people from each of the departments or divisions of the company. In a supermarket it might mean giving a questionnaire to every tenth customer who comes into the store for a period of ten minutes every hour, every day for a week.

Missing persons bureau

It is important to look for the missing person, the person or group which has been omitted from your cross-section because they fall outside the normal parameters. These are the night-workers, those people who work off-site, the customers who only shop on a Sunday, the match supporters who only go to away games, the readers of the magazine or journal who read it because it has been passed on to them and are not the named subscriber, indeed anyone who for some reason does not conform to the normal pattern and yet is part of the representative population. Their views may not only be equally important as others, they may also throw a different light on the situation simply *because* they are different.

Importance of sample size

Your sample will need to be of sufficient size to make the exercise valid. To a certain extent, that process is common sense. If the entire population being represented is only 50 people or companies, then surveying only five of them may be 10 per cent of the whole, but it is likely to omit important views unless all are of roughly the same mind. Equally, in a population of 58 million, a sample of 10 per cent is going to be enormous and unwieldy. Apart from being impractical, the increase in accuracy for this size of sample is so small as to make it unworthwhile. A sample of 10,000 carefully chosen subjects would be likely to provide similar reliability. The following points should be borne in mind:

- The larger the sample, the more likely it is that it will represent the views of the whole group
- A small sample from a small population may miss major contributors to the significance of the data
- The larger the sample, the more expensive it is to administer
- The larger the sample, the more the extremes of behaviour/attitude/opinion will cancel each other out
- Practical considerations will limit the size of samples drawn from large populations
- For a sample to be random the population from which it is chosen must be sufficiently large to represent all shades of opinion

Standard error calculation

Standard error is a measure which enables you to predict, broadly, how reliable information may be which is gathered from a sample. That reliability (or otherwise) is expressed as $\pm X$ per cent (plus or minus X per cent) where X shows the level of uncertainty about the reliability of the answers you receive. The formula for calculating standard error has two variables; the number of people in the sample and the percentage of those people who answered a question in a specific way. The formula may be calculated mathematically, but for most purposes the process is better shown using the table below (Fig. 2.1). By drawing a line between the two variables you may see the measure of standard error automatically indicated on the middle bar. But what does it mean?

If we take an example of a sample of 100 people who have been asked their opinion of the effectiveness of the government's policy on county planning then we could expect them to respond in fairly predictable ways.

What does it all mean?

Your sample of respondents represents, you hope, the opinions of the whole population which you are polling. There will always be variance in the accuracy of their opinions against those of the whole population; a measure of that likely variance allows you to judge how much store to put on the results. For instance, if your calculation shows that there was a standard error of ±1 per cent then the true result of asking the question of the whole population is likely to be 1 per cent on either side of the result

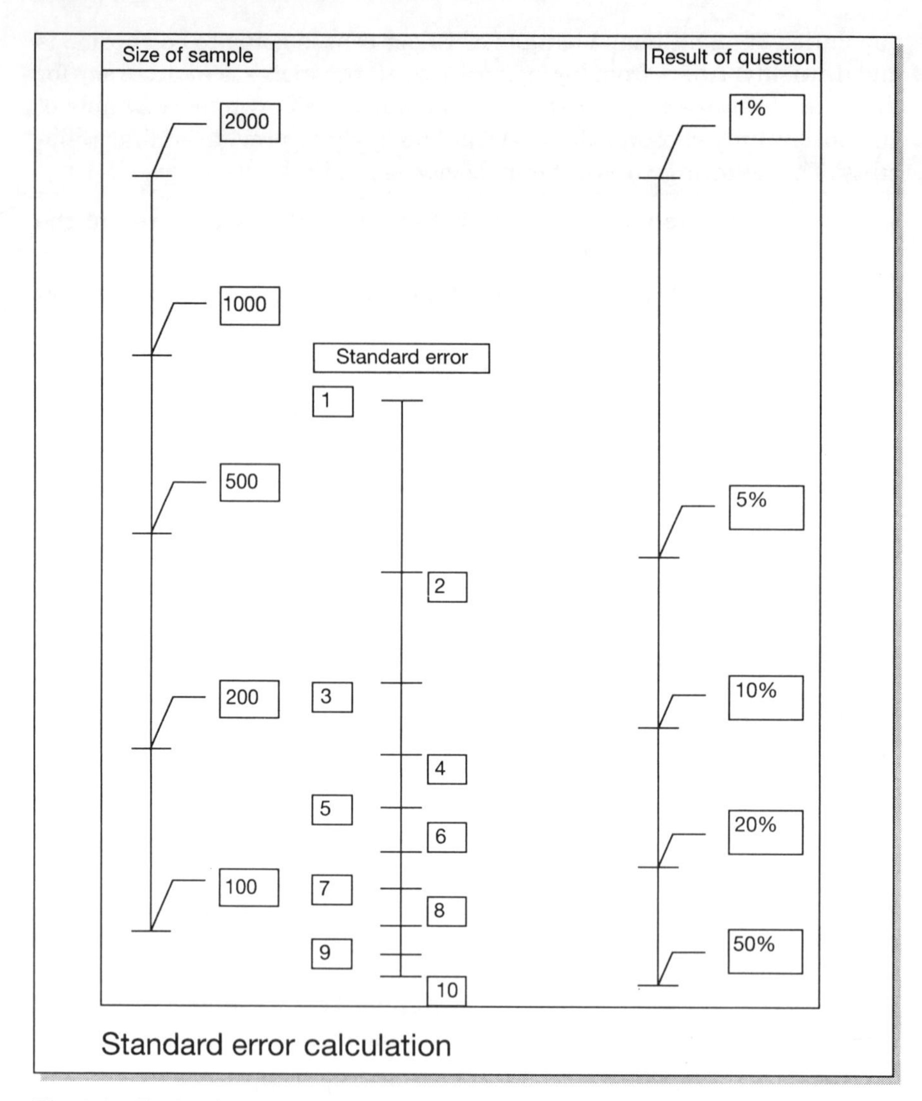

Fig. 2.1 Evaluating standard error

you have collected. So, in your survey of satisfaction with the hotel's reception procedure, if 5 per cent of respondents thought that it was 'Excellent' from a sample of 200 people, then by drawing the line between the 5 per cent mark on the right-hand scale (Sample result) and 200 on the left-hand scale (Sample size) it is possible to see that standard error is ±3 per cent. In other words, in the population as a whole satisfaction with the hotel reception could be 8 per cent, but it could equally be 2 per cent!

Having an acceptable range of error is fundamental to any survey. You know that the group of people who are responding to your questions may not have identical opinions to everyone else. Your efforts must go into minimising the problem this can be done mainly by increasing the sample size: the larger the sample, the more it will reflect the opinions of everyone else. However, there comes a point at which the benefit of increasing the sample size is outweighed by the costs of undertaking the survey.

It is also important to notice that there may be other factors which can cause an imbalance in the opinion being expressed. A faulty questionnaire which frames the questions poorly, bias, misunderstanding and errors in any aspect of the process – all these might affect the results.

Taking the error into account

When specifying your questionnaire and attempting to describe the set of respondents who you wish to complete it, you should take into account standard error. It can be a tool which will help you feel more comfortable about the results you receive. Therefore, build in the margin of error that you would find acceptable into your survey. If you can cope with a 5 per cent error either way (this is perfectly possible) then you will be able to fix the parameters for your sample before you begin.

GETTING THE BEST FROM YOUR RESPONDENT

Even with the best prepared questionnaire, if you have not taken into account those factors which will encourage your respondent to answer your questions, there will be little point in administering it. Superficial factors are:

- Your respondent may need an incentive to begin filling in the questionnaire. This is particularly true in surveys which 'cold call' – that is, turn up unexpectedly in the mail or by telephone. Why *should* the respondent fill in all this nonsense when they may never even have heard of you? A simple incentive is to give them coupons, money-off vouchers, entry to a free prize draw, a free gift with the questionnaire and so on. Simple and basic marketing techniques will tell you what is best for the sort of people to whom you talk regularly.
- Having encouraged them to fill in the questionnaire, make sure they return it. A prepaid addressed envelope is essential otherwise you will have little response.
- Try to ensure that you get their name and address correct – nothing irks people more than having their name spelt incorrectly.
- Then, more importantly, ensure that they know why they are replying (see '*Providing instructions and information*', Chapter 3, which explains about introductions). Ensure that they know the benefits that may ensue for them personally or in the products or services which you offer to them.

Ability

However, beyond all the above factors, it is important to know the ability of your respondent to answer the questions. In a large scale postal survey which has a random sample of the population this is a difficult task. In this case one must assume the lowest common denominator. Questions therefore should be:

- short and simple
- few in number
- jargon-free
- easy to understand.

In a more specialised environment (a business surveying its suppliers or its employees for example) there is an assumption which one can make about the level of understanding that the respondents have. None the less, the four points above, which may be summarised by the key points of *clarity* and *conciseness*, should still apply.

Understanding of the subject and context

The respondent must have an understanding of the subject or the setting in which the subject exists before they can answer either with any credibility or with any authority. For this reason it is always a good idea to avoid hypothetical questions which start as '*If you were given the opportunity . . .*' or '*If the company did so and so . . .*' or '*Imagine if the college moved to a new site . . .*'. Most of these types of question assume that the respondent can hypothesise and will give an accurate picture of what life will be like under the hypothetical situation. This is a dangerous assumption since hypotheses can only be made upon the facts that are available to you at the time.

Understanding of the language used

Your respondent must also understand your language. Jargon will baffle those who are not in the club which understands it. Asking a computer-illiterate person whether their ideal machine would have a CD-ROM drive is not advisable. The level of jargon must suit the sample and, if there is any doubt, all jargon should be omitted, or at the very least explained clearly whenever it is used.

The reading level of the text should also be carefully considered. It is important to keep language simple without patronising the reader, avoiding flowery and pretentious words and phrases. They will simply mislead because not only may your understanding of the words and that of your respondent differ, but the respondent may also be unwilling to show their ignorance and will pretend to understand, making up their own interpretation and therefore their answer.

Understanding of timescales

Be careful with time. Asking people to remember a long way back in the past with any accuracy is dubious. Asking them to separate events one from another, particularly where they have occurred in the same place is also tricky. For instance, in a hospital survey it may be necessary to ask people to remember conditions during a number of visits to out-patients. Keeping the events from separate visits compartmentalised is nearly impossible.

Similarly, where people are used to dealing in certain timeframes (ordering a product on a monthly basis, visiting a store weekly or performing a routine task daily) it is impractical to ask them to cast their minds back a year or six months. For the same reason, avoid asking people to predict the future unless they are qualified to do so. Asking a shopper in a supermarket whether they feel the price of tomatoes will rise in the next two weeks is asking them to guess.

Dealing with difficult topics

Naturally, the topic of the questionnaire should be relevant to and understood by the respondent. However, there are circumstances in which the relevance may be acute to the point of embarrassment. In the same way that one would not pose a direct question about marital infidelity to a member of the Royal family, one must tread carefully around topics which are sensitive in nature either because they are taboo for some reason or because they have a direct relationship to the respondent's state.

Researchers who wish to collect information about HIV-positive people, those who have recently been bereaved, or those who indulge in extra-marital affairs or have peculiar sexual preferences, must phrase their questions carefully in order to avoid giving offence and also to encourage the respondent to be frank in difficult circumstances.

The same ground rules apply when requesting sensitive information from company directors, institution managers, politicians or anyone else who, in the normal course of events, would not answer your question directly. There are many more ways than one to skin a cat!

Ask difficult questions towards the end of the interview

It is important that a rapport is established between interviewer and interviewee, even if this is through the medium of a paper questionnaire. Therefore, keep the tricky questions until the end. At worst, if they refuse to reply to them, you will have the earlier information intact. Asking the questions towards the end of the questionnaire will assist the process because they will have become used to answering what you ask to a certain extent. Your questions should lead naturally to the sensitive subject – don't hit them with the heavy stuff with no preamble!

Distance the respondent from answering personally

It is possible also to aid the process of responding by putting the respondent at arms' length from the question. Under normal circumstances they might be unwilling to answer the question directly but may be willing to generalise via the *'buying it for a friend'* analogy.

In this situation, put the respondent in a position where they are able to pretend to be answering on behalf of others. Questions which begin as:

'People in your situation . . .'
'Companies such as yours . . .'

keep the respondent detached from the situation. They are able to be comfortable that the question does not relate directly to them, although they are not fools. They may well realise your intentions but can recognise that they are not implicating themselves. However, once the facts about the 'other people' have been established, it may be possible to try a question which brings the matter nearer to home. Bring the issue back to their own situation by asking questions such as:

'And does this tie in with your own feelings/opinions/experience?'
'In what ways does this vary from your opinion . . .?'

Avoid direct facts by using ranges

A further technique is to use the ballpark estimate. Although you may not be able to get explicit figures for a particular issue, you may well be able to encourage the respondent to commit to a range in which the true figure lies. By asking this type of question the lady does not have to tell her true age (Is this really still a problem?), the managing director does not have to reveal the true sales figures and the heavy drinker can feel that they have not let the cat out of the bag about the extremes of their habit. When using ranges, please note that there are conventions for creating this type of question. For further information please see Chapter 3 on *asking questions* and refer to the Market Research Society *Standardised Questions* booklet.

CHOOSING APPROPRIATE COLLECTION METHODS

It may seem obvious to say that an effective questionnaire depends upon asking effective questions. It also depends upon ensuring that the right method is used and the right people are surveyed. Although all these are dealt with in more depth later, it is worth noting the following points at the planning stage.

The right questions

Asking the right questions involves a number of factors. Naturally, the questions should focus on your objectives. The questions should avoid bringing irrelevant data into the process – in other words, don't collect what you don't need. Conversely and confusingly, the questions should give the opportunity for issues that may be lurking under the surface to rear their heads. This is usually found in the 'Other Comments' style of open question where, having been interrogated the interviewee unleashes those points which have been burning them up – 'So why haven't you asked me about the ten-deep queues at the checkouts on a Saturday morning?' or 'I notice you have avoided the subject of telephone calls into this office and the fact that there are too few people to field them properly.'

The right survey technique

The right technique is essentially making sure that the way in which you collect your data is appropriate to the people who are being surveyed. For instance, it is unlikely you will get much joy from a face-to-face interview on the shop floor of a machine room. Equally, a telephone interview will probably be inappropriate for your Managing Director – he is, after all, in the same building as you! Paper-based questionnaires tend to be the standard, although the data then needs to be entered back at base. This process is therefore duplicated: once by hand, once by keyboard or scanner. Looking at an overview of techniques they fall into the following groups, although a complete survey may contain any combination of appropriate methods:

- Paper-based questionnaire by post or internal mail.
- Paper-based questionnaire administered by interview.
- Paper-based questionnaire administered by telephone.
- Computer-based questionnaire administered via disk or network.
- Computer-based questionnaire administered by interview.
- Computer-based questionnaire administered by telephone.

The benefits of any direct computer-based method is that the data are entered only once – directly by the interviewer or even by the interviewee. This assumes a level of knowledge of both the subject and of the computer system on the part of either of these people.

It should be borne in mind that remote interviewing does not allow the presentation of pictures, samples or interpretation of people's expression and attitude while being interviewed.

The right interviewees

Your sample of interviewees must reflect a broad sweep of the opinion groups you aim to question. There is little point in asking directors of businesses their opinions about the capabilities of school-leavers with any particular skill – the answer will always be that they are inadequate and 'What do they teach them nowadays?' This is because managers and teachers are working to different agendas. The manager has specialised requirements: trainees are needed who have experience of CNC lathes, the ability to use Microsoft Word, skills in answering the telephone, and the ability to make a decent cup of tea. The schools on the other hand are concentrating on providing a broad education, training minds to be trained, and not providing robots for the industrial machine (although there is an argument for drawing the two camps much closer together!).

Consequently, the right groups will fall into the following categories:

- A broad base of opinion – the larger the sample the more representative will be the data.
- Having relevant experience – in other words, qualified to comment on the topic.
- Having the ability to respond – are they free to do so, and do they have the skills to do so?
- Lack of bias – little point in interviewing your competitor about the quality of your products!

KNOWING WHAT YOU WANT OUT BEFORE YOU PUT IT IN

Just as with computer technology, the GIGO principle (Garbage In Garbage Out) holds true for questionnaires. An understanding of what information particular formats of report and analysis may offer will help you to decide how to collect your information appropriately. Unfortunately, even with modern technology it is not possible to construct sensible charts, graphs, cross-tabulations and other reports from inappropriate data.

Analyses

What analyses do you need to perform? There is a tendency for people simply to request streams of raw data (how many people responded 'Yes' to question 1, 'No' to question 2 and so on) whereas the correlation of data and its analysis using simple statistical techniques can highlight hidden information. For example, if you know in advance that you are going to need to look at the relationship between people's ages and their preferences for specific flavours of your patent ice-cream product then it will be important to gather information about their age in a sensible format.

Should it be as years and months, as years only or as a range – between 21 and 30, for example? The choice of your ice-cream flavours should also be given. Should you allow them more than one choice? How will they know whether they like it if they have not tried it, and therefore how reliable might their opinion be?

For your analyses to be worthwhile you will need to have a measure of confidence in their reliability. There are simple analytical techniques that can help you measure how reliable your data are and the conclusions that you may draw from them.

Reports

A report is the medium by which you communicate your findings to other people in your organisation. It is important that it is clear, concise and above all can be understood even by the most obtuse of your colleagues! Show them reams of paper full of columns of figures and their eyes will glaze – you've lost them. Show them some attractive pie charts, a quick cross-tabulation or two and a three-dimensional bar graph illustrating the improvement in opinion from last year's survey to this year's (as a direct result of your efforts of course!) and you may stand a better chance of success.

A report might contain not only the graphs, charts, cross-tabulations and tables needed to deliver the meat of your findings, but it will also probably contain a narrative – your commentary on the findings and some initial conclusions, perhaps drawn from derived data that has been compiled using some simple statistical functions. The report is the showcase of the project. Get this wrong and you will be unable to prove that the effort, money and time that you expended were worthwhile.

So what do you want that report to contain? You must know before you begin the project. What are the salient points which will be drawn out by your investigation? Do you have a specific objective – to prove that the market for fresh fruit in the winter months is diminished by advertising from canned fruit producers? To illustrate that, despite what your Managing Director believes, there is a correlation between the advertising push in the local papers and performance in the supermarkets? To show that the provision of wheelchairs in the out-patients' department is inadequate during weekdays or that the quality of service provided by the department is severely impacted by lack of planning of holidays in the summer months? All of these can be demonstrated very simply by an effective report with a couple of simple graphs.

When you have decided what it is that you wish to illustrate in the report you can begin to examine the specifics more closely. What do you need in order to generate that type of report? What type of data lends itself readily to cross-tabulation or scattergram distribution? Do you need to look at the reliability statistics associated with the data? How may this information be expressed in a number of ways the better to illustrate the point?

Charts and graphs

In the context of the report, the graphs and charts are the pictures in the child's storybook. Very few people enjoy raw data and, if like the author, you find spreadsheet tables of data very hard work indeed then you will be aware how important it is that your story should have pictures. Graphs and charts in all their different formats enable you to express numeric data (frequencies, percentages) in a form that immediately shows trends very clearly. The climbing (or falling) sales line illustrated by a red line on a grid is an instant indicator, not only of present performance but of the history of a product's sales and can also be an indicator of its predicted future. Choosing the appropriate type of graph is not difficult, and knowing in advance what you wish to illustrate graphically will help you choose the right type of data to collect.

- *Line graphs* illustrate the state of a particular variable against another (often time or another similarly predictable flow). You would use a line graph in order to show the changing state of sales, response to mailshots, frequency of visitors to your theme park or hospital, all against a time line divided into suitable intervals (days, months, years). Line graphs illustrate the ebb and flow of demand.
- *Bar graphs* illustrate the status of a number of variables in a snapshot in time. In our survey today (this week, this month) the opinion about the cleanliness of the streets in the borough of Kirkby was as follows: *X* per cent thought it was excellent, *Y* per cent thought it satisfactory and *Z* per cent believed it was poor. The bars of the graph illustrate the relative levels. Bar graphs may also have the attribute of area which enables two-dimensional data to be plotted.
- *Pie Charts* show how the pie is divided among the different opinion groups in your sample. Although a bar chart may be able to provide the same information, a pie chart allows you to show the relationship between the different groups more clearly – we have all tried to divide a portion of favourite cherry pie equitably among a hungry group of people! The relationship between the slices is easily shown and when one can separate the prime slice from the rest it is possible to highlight the area which is most affected in the survey.
- *Scattergrams* show the relationship between two sets of data. Is there a correlation between the weight of a baby at birth and the weight of

the child at 12 years old? Is there any relationship between the incidence of a particular crime and the area in which it is committed? How far could you say that people's opinions about the service you provide and their age make a difference? A scattergram will allow you to plot each of the data points and then show a line of best fit correlation – a measure of whether you are illustrating a trend or whether your data are totally random!

THE CONSEQUENCES OF ANY RESULT YOU MAY FIND

So there are your results. Now what? Data are useless without interpretation. Although graphs and charts may help, it is quite likely that the real result is in your ability to extrapolate or infer from that data the fact that yes, although your sales in barbecues are declining, this is probably due to external forces – not least of which is the fact that a 'drive-thru McDonalds' has just opened down the road! That will not come out in the data, unless you have been clever enough to predict that as a factor, but is an informed judgement made on the basis of the information provided by the data.

The actions you will take on the basis of that information

So what do you do about it? When you are planning your questionnaire you need constantly to have in your mind 'If I find that X is the case then I shall be able to do Y'. Outcomes which are not contingent on the findings are generally ill-advised or rely totally on 'hunch' rather than information. How will you react if any given scenario is found in your data – you must know before you start otherwise Murphy's law will intervene once more. (Murphy's law states that 'if a thing can go wrong, it will'. There is also O'Toole's Amendment to Murphy's law which states 'Murphy was an Optimist!')

. . . IN SUMMARY, YOUR OBJECTIVES

Yes, in summary you have defined your objectives by knowing what the outcomes will be in any given situation. Your data are correctly structured to provide the analyses you require; you have considered the type of report you will make and the essential elements – and Murphy has been bound and gagged and put into the coal cellar.

Your objectives are everything and without them, the whole exercise will be a waste.

In summary:

- What do you need to know?
- How will you collect that information?
- How will you present that information once it is collected?
- How will you react to the findings of your survey?

Caveat

One of the most common faults in survey and questionnaire design is where the person specifying the survey predetermines the outcome. This is not wilful distortion of the facts nor is it an attempt to deceive. It is quite simply that they have a fixed idea of what it is that they are looking for before they begin. That in itself is not a bad thing – planning and a sense of direction are essential when setting out on a journey. However, in this situation the compass has been locked in one quadrant and you have no choice but to go north, even though the problem is to the east. As one commentator has said: 'Some people view everything as a nail, because they have a hammer. Others view everything as a screw, because they have a screwdriver.'

Pre-determining the result means that:

- If you are looking for an issue or a problem you will probably find it because you will have put the idea into people's heads, whether it is really there or not.
- You may miss the real issue because your questions have not been sufficiently flexible to allow any other issue to rise to the surface.

For example, you may believe that the problem to tackle is the ineffectiveness of your promotion against a rival company and therefore concentrate your research efforts on that factor. In reality the problem lies in your own inability to provide successfully a reliable supply of goods to the retailers who are therefore refusing to stock them.

DRY-RUNNING THE QUESTIONNAIRE (PILOTING)

And so you have created a questionnaire. It is a gem. Perfect in every way. Are you going to spend all the money that is involved in administering it without trying it out first to see whether it works? Probably not a good idea. A dry run of your masterwork will highlight inadequacies, inconsistencies and simple nonsense that will almost certainly have crept into this, the first pass.

Piloting is undertaken with a small and reliable group drawn from your sample. Reliable because you know that they will be able to comment critically upon what you have written. They need to know about:

- The situation being tackled.
- The people answering the questions.
- The likely issues that will be raised.

Ask them all the questions as if it were the proper questionnaire. Ask them to comment on:

- Problems with the way in which you have phrased questions.
- Difficulties with ranges and option choices.
- Misunderstanding about instructions.
- Missing elements in the scope of the questionnaire.

Check whether anything made your respondents feel uncomfortable or intimidated. Were some of the questions difficult to answer because of the nature of the information required? Did you give enough opportunity for all the responses that your respondent would like to make?

Trying a variety of versions of the same questions on informed respondents

It may be that you have had a problem deciding which is the best approach to tackling your problem through a questionnaire and therefore you have created a number of questionnaires which come at the problem from different angles. Test these out on the same set of test respondents and discover which set of questions they felt most comfortable with and seemed to them to address the issues that were important.

Discovering that some questions may need modification before they are capable of response

Inevitably you will make changes and will then be thankful that you took the trouble to test the questionnaire. *Changes should not detract significantly from the original shape of your questionnaire.* If they do then it is likely that the original is fundamentally flawed and you should begin again. The detail changes you make to the questions will affect more the way in which they are addressed by the respondent or the scope of the topic which they address.

If this is not done then the consequence is: simply that your questionnaire will be unreliable. It must be based in some sort of understanding of the subject before you begin. The signs are easy to spot.

QUESTIONS WITH INADEQUATE RESPONSE OPTIONS

You have asked about the range of times at which the respondents have had access to the hospital shop, as follows:

At what times do you have access to the hospital shop?

- ○ 9.00 am to 12.00 noon
- ○ 1.00 pm to 3.00 pm
- ○ 4.00 pm to 7.00 pm
- ○ After 7.00 pm

Unfortunately, not only is there a missing hour in every series but the actual opening times of the shop have been ignored. Similarly, the following question poses problems:

Please give your opinion of the leisure facilities and the bar.

- ○ Excellent
- ○ Good
- ○ Poor

Apart from the fact that the respondent has been given only three options, two of which may be interpreted as 'satisfactory', they may not wish to apply them to both facilities simultaneously.

Please enter your hair colour ________________

Suppose you have brown hair – Is that what you call it? Brown, auburn, chestnut, mousy all describe the same thing. Moreover, you are asking for trouble with this style of response when it comes to data analysis if the type of answer is not consistent throughout the set of information. Similarly, when asking for someone's age, has the appropriate answer type been chosen?

How old are you? 24.3 years

How do you measure age in decimals? Choosing to use years and months, however, has its own special problems, both for capturing the data and for analysing it. Do you need to ask for months as well? A better option is usually to group people into ranges or to use a system which will calculate their age from their date of birth.

INAPPROPRIATE OPTIONS (RANGE)

Just as bad is the ill-informed set of options given in:

Which bus service do you use from Littlehampton to Bigtown?

- ○ East Coast Bus Co.
- ○ Central Line Buses
- ○ Great National

A pity that Central Line do not run that route because it is uneconomic and most people go from Littlehampton to shop in Westchester in any case. A bit of preliminary research would have shown those facts.

A situation where too few or too many options are given is a problem for the respondent. For example:

Is the standard of service in the hotel generally . . .

- ○ Excellent?
- ○ Poor?

It's more likely to be rather in the middle! Some aspects are good whereas others . . . Your position on the scale of Fig. 2.2 will depend upon your interpretation of it. Too many variables will give too much leeway for inaccuracy, built in because of personal interpretation. (Yes it was a silly example taken to an extreme!) When using any semantic scale (one which involves words rather than numbers) it is important that you and your respondent share the same understanding about what you mean.

How well would you rate our service overall?

○ Superb	○ Poorish
○ Reasonably superb	○ Poor
○ Excellent	○ Quite poor
○ Reasonably excellent	○ Very poor
○ Good	○ Extremely poor
○ Quite good	○ Quite dreadful
○ Fair	○ Dreadful
○ Quite fair	○ Appalling

Fig. 2.2 Too many options

Multiple choice questions providing no appropriate choice can create havoc with your data accuracy. This problem is easily avoided, however, with an 'other' option (Fig. 2.3). 'Other (please specify)' is the universal catch-all and should be built into practically every multiple choice question by default! Coding these answers is important because they will otherwise be left out of the main analysis.

Please select your favourite colour

- ☐ Red
- ☐ Blue
- ☐ Green
- ☐ Other (Please specify)__________________

Fig. 2.3 Adequate choice

'Don't know/won't answer' is also useful. If this option is not available where appropriate then people who do not wish to or cannot answer will simply leave a blank. You get more information from knowing that they did not answer because they could not or would not than you do from an empty data space! Indeed, it may be important to the accuracy of your data that you know that they had no idea of the answer.

3

The questions and how to ask them

- **In this section the entire process of asking questions is examined in detail**
- **The importance of clear instructions is discussed**
- **The grouping of questions by type is illustrated**
- **Common problems with question design are shown and rectified**
- **The relevance of asking specific questions is investigated and strategies for keeping questionnaires concise are examined**
- **Types of questions and the answers that they produce are discussed, in the light of the need to generate particular types of data for specific analyses**

The key to the success of your questionnaire lies in the questions – this is not a world-shattering discovery! The type of question, the way it is framed, the type of response that you expect from it and the way that it interacts with other questions all affect the outcome. This section looks at why you ask particular types of question and what answer types will yield appropriate data for analysis.

Asking questions involves skill, experience and common sense in fairly equal measures. The first is really a product of the last two and they are simply a product of getting out there and doing it. Perhaps the best reason for dry-running a survey is to see whether your ideas and experience are actually based on anything other than fantasy! Common sense will tell you when you have made a mistake – or so you would think. Some of the crazy questions illustrated in this text are drawn from actual questionnaires (although the details have been changed to protect the embarrassed) and the compilers of those forms thought they had got it right. A second, third or fourth opinion can highlight inaccuracies which your eye will have skipped over. It does mean, however, that you need to be open to criticism.

Chapter 2 showed that you should know what you want out before you put it in. The type of analyses you can expect to get from your data are dependent not so much on the way in which you ask the question (that is more likely to be an influence on the respondent) but more on the way in which you capture their answer. The following section looks at the question and answer types and summarises the reasons for asking questions.

FRAMING A QUESTION WHICH WILL WORK

Having decided what you will or will not ask, whether it is relevant or not, whether it will be biased or not, whether it will upset or intimidate your respondents, you then need to compose or find questions which will work. This need not be as laborious as it sounds. The volume of questionnaires commonly in use has risen rapidly over the past few years. It seems that every institution and organisation sends out a survey after each contact with you. These questionnaires are a rich seam of expertise for you to mine. Although the questionnaire itself may well be copyright, the individual questions, their style, structure and direction are all available for you to emulate and even replicate.

Someone's already done it! (libraries of questions)

Questionnaires that have been distributed by major institutions and corporates will have been composed by highly paid professional researchers. The intelligent dissection of this material will help you to create your own questionnaire. Similarly, in the world of local government, health, education and professional associations, questionnaires are now a standard requisite of the marketing manager, quality manager or public relations officer. Associations and professional bodies have already compiled standard questionnaires which may be tailored to your needs. Seek out the experts in the field (the guru for your profession) and get information about publications and materials which will help you. Also seek out the leading practitioners in your line of business – someone will be at the cutting edge and, with a few telephone calls, it is easy to begin a relationship in order to share resources.

There exist also libraries of questions which you may use. The Market Research Society for example publishes the booklet *Standardised Questions* for a small charge. The information and examples in there will save you a good deal of time and effort. Training packs produced by professional associations and groupings of institutions will also be a source of material.

CREATING YOUR OWN ARCHIVE

Once you begin to create questionnaires, build your own archive. Collect every questionnaire you can lay your hands on, whether or not it is relevant to your subject. As you build your own questionnaires, keep track of those which are most effective and, drawing from your archive, re-use the question sets which have worked well in subsequent surveys.

Software for questionnaire design usually comes complete with example materials. These may be useful, but in any case, as you create your questionnaires you will be able to copy and paste from one form to another one, meaning that you will only have to create your question sets once (see Chapter 10 '*Technology Tools*' for further details).

Providing instructions and information

Instructions are the link which gives relevance for the responder to all that you are doing. Without instructions and some background information they will have little or no idea of the purpose of the questionnaire and will therefore not be in the most advantageous position to answer questions constructively. Your instructions and the way you frame your questions should:

- Inform.
- Guide.
- Illuminate.

INFORM – LETTING THE RESPONDENT KNOW WHAT IS GOING ON

If you have no clue what is going on then your answers will emerge from the fog of your ignorance. A serious respondent will want to know why they are being asked questions and therefore you should use:

- *the opening statement* in which you declare who you are (if necessary) and the intentions of the questionnaire. This will include a number of factors all of which will make the respondent feel more comfortable and at ease, and therefore more likely to respond to your questions.
- *the declaration of objectives* where you set out what it is you intend to achieve. This may be a simple statement such as:

> *Thank you for agreeing to be interviewed in the staff satisfaction survey. As you may know there has been some discontent about the incentive and bonus scheme among staff of Cracker Inc. This questionnaire is part of an investigation which aims to uncover the reasons for this dissatisfaction in order that something constructive may be done.*

- *the privacy of their opinions:* All questionnaires are a private consultation. As such the value of the respondent's views and also their confidentiality must be implicit in the questionnaire. Expressing that privacy must be given a high priority, particularly where it is obvious that the responses given may be traced back to an individual. A statement which sums up all the issues might be:

> The views you express in this questionnaire will go no further than the analysis of the data. In that analysis your opinions will blend with those of your colleagues. A reference number is on the front of this form in order to categorise where the information came from. This enables the researchers to group opinions in a sensible way. It is important that you understand that no responses will be traced back to you as an individual.

Or, in the case of a more public customer satisfaction survey:

> In agreeing to answer our questions you are not in any way making your views public. All your answers will be treated with the strictest confidentiality and will only be used as part of the final analysis.

- *the results that are hoped for:* If you tell people what your ultimate aims are they are more likely to co-operate with you, particularly if those aims are to their benefit. Therefore, express clearly and simply what it is that will happen as a result of the analysis of the questionnaires. Tell them:
  - What the problem/issue is.
  - How the answers to their questions may help you to resolve that issue.
  - Possible outcomes that may occur because of the survey.

Be careful of promising the earth in order to collect significant data. You can do it only once!

GUIDE – HOW DOES YOUR RESPONDENT KNOW WHAT YOU MEAN?

Guiding the respondent is a process which begins with the entire structure of the questionnaire, which should be logical and should have a natural flow (see Chapter 5 on questionnaire structure). Thereafter it is important that you interpret the technical aspects, and make clear your intentions behind every question. You should be sure, in creating questions, to differentiate between the question itself and the instructions which are tied to it. If the respondent cannot separate the two then there may be confusion, particularly if instructions and question are both lengthy. The example of Fig. 3.1 shows how they may be separated clearly – such a style might be used throughout the questionnaire.

In the following questions, please choose ONE option only in each set of answers. If you have no clear opinion about the topic then choose the last option – Don't know.

Q4. I believe that a bypass will benefit our community

○ Agree
○ Neither agree nor Disagree
○ Disagree
○ Don't Know/Won't Say

Fig. 3.1 Separate instructions from questions

In professional market research questionnaires, administered by an interviewer, instructions for the interviewer are usually written in capitals. By differentiating instructions from question by a change of typeface, capitalisation or some other highlight, your intentions are made clear. In the example of Fig. 3.1 the important factor in the instruction (that only one choice should be made) is highlighted with capitals. The instructions have also been printed in a different style from the question.

Instructions which are separate from the question enable the respondent firstly to have a grip on what your intention is and *then* to focus on the core of the question. Blending the two into one lumbering sentence will only serve to confuse.

If you find that your instructions are becoming long and rambling it is probably because the question itself is too complex and should perhaps be split into a number of separate smaller issues. The reliability of the answers you receive will be in inverse proportion to the complexity of your instructions and questions!

Being economical with instructions

When questions are sensibly grouped, only one set of instructions will be needed per set. Not only does this type of conciseness help the respondent to understand the questionnaire and complete it more easily, it is also much easier to compile in the first place.

Keeping instructions consistent

Consistency in the way in which you present your instructions will also link with the way in which the question itself is asked. Although variety may be the spice of life, moving the goalposts around in the style of the questions will only serve to confuse. One school of thought has it that by swapping options you will keep the respondent on their toes. This may be the case, but it defies the *keep it simple* rule. The instructions for similar sets of questions should preferably be framed in a similar style *unless* you need to make a specific point by changing the style – highlighting the need to select *more* than one choice in a set, for example (Fig. 3.2).

The amount of tutorial time is . . .	❑ Too much	❑ About right	❑ Too little
The length of the college day is . . .	❑ Too long	❑ About right	❑ Too short
The number of breaks throughout the day is . . .	❑ Too many	❑ About right	❑ Too few
The duration of breaks is . . .	❑ Too long	❑ About right	❑ Too short
The information you were given initially about the course proved to be . . .	❑ Very useful	❑ Adequate	❑ Inadequate

Fig. 3.2 Consistency in instructions

In summary so far:

- Keep instructions separate from questions
- Mark out instructions with a clear difference in text style
- Keep instructions consistent and simple

ILLUMINATE – GIVE BACKGROUND INFORMATION TO SPECIFIC QUESTIONS

Never assume that your respondent knows what you are talking about. At the risk of stating the obvious, always give an opportunity for background information to be displayed, either on the form or as a separate card or sheet of text and/or pictures. Keeping these elements separate from the main questionnaire makes the survey look less daunting to the respondent and also means that there is no need to skim and skip if they already understand the topic.

However, if the information is brief, include it as part of the instructions for the question. Be sure to separate the instructions from the question itself so that there is a quite clear definition to what the respondent is being asked to do.

Using questions together

Questions may be grouped together in order to facilitate understanding of the objectives on the respondent's part; in order to make a more logical progression through the questionnaire – for example, keeping all personal details gathered under one group heading; and also to make the analysis of the data more logical. Questions which are grouped might be identified with colour backgrounds, borders, separate pages or any other typesetting device which seems appropriate.

GROUPING QUESTIONS IN SENSIBLE WAYS

Grouping should allow you to do the following:

- enable clarity
- enable flow
- emphasise appropriate links.

The way in which linking or grouping takes place should not strain the natural flow of the questionnaire. In fact, quite the contrary, it should make the questionnaire easier to use, more logical and should aid the respondent in filling in their responses.

Questions may be grouped, for example, as:

- Personal information.
- Questions about preferences.
- Questions about opinions.
- More difficult and probing questions (keep these until near the end).

Question grouping using appropriate questionnaire software will also allow you to move entire sets of questions around, examine related data by group and to extract information from the group of questions independently from the rest of the set.

CREATING DATA WHICH IS INTERDEPENDENT

Part of the reason for grouping may be in order to cross-correlate information more easily. For example, if it is important for you to find a relationship between your customers' ages and their preferences for X then you may wish to cast your eye over response forms in order to establish easily a trend before you perform your analyses. Keeping the questions close to each other will help this 'by eye' analysis.

The concept of interdependent data is not one which necessarily affects the design of the questionnaire but certainly is important in the analysis area where you wish to ask 'What if . . .?' about the relationship between different elements which affect your market, people's opinions or the decisions of purchasers or managers.

The presentation of the data is not the only important factor. Remember that in order for data to be cross-correlated it must be collected in a form which will allow that process to take place. For example, in an hotel questionnaire you may wish to draw out the relationship between your clients' age and their reason for visiting the hotel. This could be in order more effectively to target mailshots to them or in order to identify subgroups which have particular needs and preferences in order further to analyse them.

REPEATING THE SAME FORMAT IN MULTIPLE QUESTIONS

It is quite likely that you will ask series of questions which carry the same set of predetermined (multiple choice) responses. In this case it is advisable to group them together so that there is a consistency of response pattern in each set. Varying the response pattern during a series of questions will affect the reliability of the data due to the confusion of the respondent. So, for instance, a customer satisfaction questionnaire benefits from this consistency of approach in Fig. 3.3.

OUR PEOPLE

How would you rate staff in terms of:	Excellent	Good	Fair	Poor
Friendliness	1 ☐	2 ☐	3 ☐	4 ☐
Efficiency	1 ☐	2 ☐	3 ☐	4 ☐
Reliability	1 ☐	2 ☐	3 ☐	4 ☐
Anticipating your needs	1 ☐	2 ☐	3 ☐	4 ☐
Attending to your needs	1 ☐	2 ☐	3 ☐	4 ☐
Ability to resolve problems	1 ☐	2 ☐	3 ☐	4 ☐

Fig. 3.3 Grouping multiple choice questions

Providing variety of types of question while avoiding confusion

In a subsequent question group you may decide to ask for similar responses but change the order or the types of response in order to add variety. This is perfectly acceptable and gives a means for keeping the respondent's mind alive, particularly during large sets of repetitive questions. The secret is to avoid confusion.

- Don't mix types of responses within groups unless necessary.
- Don't mix the order of responses within groups.
- Provide variety of responses from group to group.

Pitching the question correctly for your audience

The final detail that you need to consider when assembling your questionnaire is the level at which it is pitched (see the section on the respondent, p. 39). Clarity, from the responder's viewpoint, is deeply affected by the assumptions which you make about their ability to understand the question or instructions and then to answer appropriately. Getting this wrong will invalidate all of the questionnaire, not because your respondent will not answer, on the contrary, they will. However, they will be making it up!

WHAT EXACTLY DO YOU MEAN BY . . .

Mistakes, misunderstandings and downright deceit!

The way in which a question is asked will determine its response. So many factors can influence a respondent, not only in the content of the question, but also in possible answers offered as choices, the order in which options are presented, the time, place and conditions under which the information is collected. Consequently, it is true to say that there is no such thing as a perfect questionnaire. A useful exercise will point up this situation very easily.

Select a couple of groups of people from your organisation who would be able to comment critically about language used in such things as advertising, press releases, publicity materials and so on. Ask them to write a series of questions which are designed to discover staff's opinions about a mildly contentious issue: allocation of company cars, use of the staff of kitchen or the need for an in-house bulletin. Then ask them to comment critically upon the other group's efforts using the following criteria:

- Is the question unambiguous?
- Is the question leading the respondent?
- Will the question elicit the type of responses which are being looked for?

The end result will be anarchy! It is always possible to pick holes in any questionnaire. The desired objective is to minimise the extent to which the questionnaire might misfire, mislead or be misinterpreted. The following factors should be taken into account.

Clarity

The clarity with which you ask your question and express the intention about the type of answer you expect will govern what you get out of the interaction. You may *think* that your question is clear but to your respondent it may not be so, for a number of very simple reasons.

JARGON

Never assume that the respondent will understand technical or specialised language. Abbreviations and acronyms which are common parlance in the circles in which you move may be gibberish to someone unfamiliar with the language. The 'granny test' is always worth a try – if your granny can understand what you are getting at then so will most other people. It isn't always necessary to avoid technical terminology totally provided that it is explained in the context of the question – unlike the example of Fig. 3.4. Acronyms might well be used once you have established what they stand for – or at least ensured that the respondent knows what is going on.

LIST DOS MEMORY RESIDENT PROGRAMS (eg QEMM, 386MAX, etc) AND CONTENTS OF CONFIG.SYS AND AUTOEXEC.BAT:

____

____

____

Fig. 3.4 Is jargon understood by respondent?

CONTRADICTION

Questions which contradict, or appear to do so, are often asked in order to test whether the respondent is paying attention. If they *are* paying attention, they will probably be insulted!

DOUBLE-EDGED QUESTIONS

The double-edged question attempts to tackle more than one thing at the same time and ends up confusing the issue. For instance,

Do you believe that the windows or doors should be painted blue or white?
○ Blue
○ White

could be solved by asking two multiple choice questions (Fig. 3.5).

Do you believe that the windows should be painted blue or white?
○ Blue
○ White

Do you believe that the doors should be painted blue or white?
○ Blue
○ White

Fig. 3.5 Splitting double-edged questions into two

Similarly,

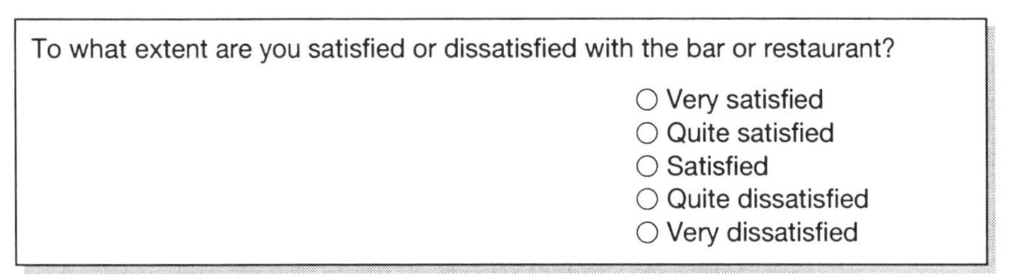
To what extent are you satisfied or dissatisfied with the bar or restaurant?

- ○ Very satisfied
- ○ Quite satisfied
- ○ Satisfied
- ○ Quite dissatisfied
- ○ Very dissatisfied

Fig. 3.6 Too many questions in one

What is the answer to the question in Fig. 3.6 – YES? Such questions are disentangled by subdividing them into two or more simple questions as in the previous example.

UNCLEAR QUESTIONS

An unclear question (one which does not make apparent its intention) is likely to gain little worthwhile data for you. At best, response will be mixed because the respondents have sometimes misinterpreted the question or have not been sure of the form of answer which you require. You may have been unclear for any of the reasons above or simply through carelessness and lack of forethought. Lack of clarity is often a function of the compiler's understanding of the topic. If you are not familiar with the parameters being assessed then inconsistencies which would jump out at an expert will pass you by. Another good reason for dry-running your survey!

Impractical ranges

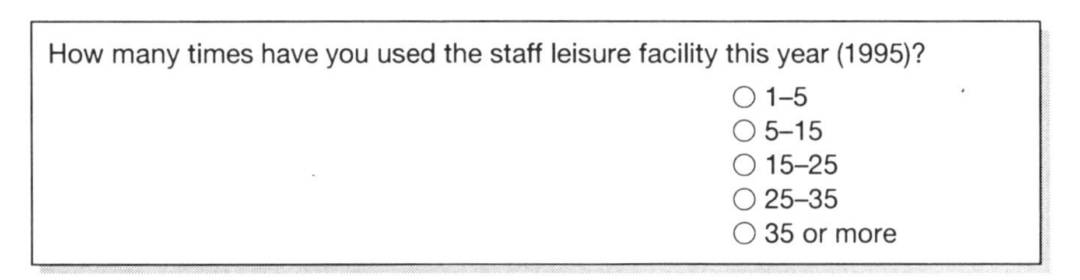
How many times have you used the staff leisure facility this year (1995)?

- ○ 1–5
- ○ 5–15
- ○ 15–25
- ○ 25–35
- ○ 35 or more

Fig. 3.7 Overlapping ranges

Impractical ranges of answers such as those given in Fig. 3.7 simply confuse the respondent and show that you have not been paying attention when you created the question. What happens if you have used the facility five times, 15, 25 or 35 times? You immediately fall on the 'cusp' and cannot easily make a choice.

What do you mean by . . .?

When dry-running a questionnaire, the response from one of your testers may well be, 'What do you mean by . . .?' It tells you that there is a lack of precision in the way in which your question has been asked or in the options for answering which you have made available. At that point changes need to be made to the question or its answer options. You will discover what those changes are by elaborating on your intentions with the tester. For example:

> 'When do you have your staff appraisal?'

Do you mean when *last* did you have an appraisal? Or at what frequency, or at what time, day, month?

> 'How old are you?'

Do you mean *exactly* how old in years, months, days? Or how old last birthday?

> 'When did you visit SainsCo?'

Do you mean, 'Have you *ever* visited SainsCo?', 'When *last* did you visit SainsCo?' or perhaps you are seeking for more specific detail and would be better asking 'How frequently do you visit SainsCo?' In this case a range of options may be the best way of ensuring that your respondent answers appropriately – *the answer is in the question*! The style of response will naturally depend upon the type of data you wish to collect.

> 'Have you used Washo?'

Have you used it recently? Have you used it ever? Have you used it once and rejected it? Again, the set of responses will help the respondent to understand your intention.

However, *beware the adverb*! Consider the following question:

> Do you *often* go to SainsCo?

Sometimes, a good deal? Interpretation of this sort of question will always be personal: to some people once a month is too often! Your idea of what is the benchmark for frequency will need to be made explicit in both question and answer. Since the word 'often' is subjective, choose a more suitable way of asking the question which will help the respondent match their answer to your criteria (Fig. 3.8).

Do you go to SainsCo . . .

- ○ More than once a week?
- ○ Once a week?
- ○ More than once a month but less than once a week?
- ○ Once a month?
- ○ Less than once a month?
- ○ Never

Fig. 3.8 Avoid subjective phrases

Alternatively, the question:

Do you go to SainsCo . . .

- ○ Regularly?
- ○ Not regularly?
- ○ Never?

can be linked to a question which then investigates frequency, if it is relevant.

Avoiding misunderstanding

Apart from making your question clearer by framing the question, testing it and then refining it, there are techniques which will ensure that you can direct the question straight to the nub of the matter. Putting the ball into the respondent's court is the best method since it involves them actively taking the response and quantifying it. Questions which begin 'When', 'Have you ever', 'Do you', all encourage the respondent to think in terms of generalities. 'Do you buy Katkins Katfood?' might be answered with a yes, no, sometimes, never, once or any non-specific variant.

Making the respondent quantify their answer will not only give more useful data, it will ensure that they are clear about your meaning. It may be necessary, for clarity, to ask the question in two stages: 'Do you buy Katkins Katfood?' 'How often do you buy the product?'. Alternatively, with the type of question you are about to ask it may be better to home straight in with 'How often do you buy Katkins Katfood?' and give a set of sensible intervals as possible responses.

How often, how many, what exactly, where exactly, when exactly – all contribute to precision of intention and help your respondent to focus.

Always seek simplicity and conciseness

In order to avoid the above traps two main qualities should be sought:

- simplicity
- conciseness.

Simplicity can be achieved by keeping to the KISS rule: Keep It Simple, Stupid! That entails an awareness of situations where the question is becoming entangled in its own complexity. If you feel that you are having difficulty framing the question to meet your other criteria, it may well be that it needs to be divided into two or more separate questions for the sake of simplicity and clarity.

Conciseness has to do with simplicity but essentially means:

- Don't ask questions that don't need asking – ones that are irrelevant to the subject.
- Don't ask questions whose answers you don't need – ones that are irrelevant to the analysis.
- Don't make your questions more involved than necessary – ones that are full of irrelevant detail or complexity.

Conciseness does not come easily. The tendency of questionnaire compilers is to try to include all factors that may possibly influence any given situation. In practice it is better to focus more fully on one or two of those factors and deal with them – concisely!

Lack of bias

Expectation of a particular result is the single most common reason for bias in questionnaires. Avoiding it is always tricky because the questionnaire compiler always has one eye on an outcome which they really feel, deep down, will probably result. Detaching oneself from privately held opinions is not easy, yet it is essential if your questionnaire is to look objectively at all the issues, apparent or hidden, which affect the problem you are attempting to tackle.

Bias can come into your questions in a number of ways: through the questions themselves, through the answer options you give, and through the order in which questions and/or answers are presented. Bias reveals itself when the question pushes the respondent towards the answer which the compiler expects. It also is there when there is a wilful desire to warp the outcome.

BIASED QUESTIONS

A biased question might be quite explicit by giving prominence to one aspect of a topic while leaving another aspect in shadow. Or it may be that it will not allow sufficient range of choice for expression of opinion. There are two aspects of bias in the silly question shown in Fig. 3.9. The first is that the question promotes the product and implants the idea of its excellence in the respondent's mind. The second is that there is little opportunity for the respondent to criticise the product in the range of answers.

How well does Washo, the leading hi-tech biological cleansing solution, compare with Blue-It in whitening your whites?

- ○ Superbly
- ○ Well
- ○ Satisfactorily
- ○ Poorly

Fig. 3.9 Bias resulting from lack of opportunity to criticise

How often have you seen an hotel customer satisfaction questionnaire which really allowed you to say those things you felt about that aspect of the service which was lacking? Naturally, no-one is going to give you the opportunity to express such an extreme opinion as that in Fig. 3.10 about how *bad* their service is, yet will always include superlatives such as *excellent* at the other end of the spectrum. If in undertaking your questionnaire you need to have a true spectrum of opinion your scales of comment must reflect truly all aspects from complimentary through to abusive!

How good was the service in the restaurant?

- ○ Excellent
- ○ Good
- ○ Satisfactory
- ○ Poor
- ○ Awful
- ○ Beyond Belief

Fig. 3.10 Allow a full range of expression

LEADING QUESTIONS

The leading question is typical of bias built in by lack of thought, for instance:

> Do you think that Washo is the best solution to washday needs ever sold to the public?

> In your opinion is the new career structure available to all hard-working staff a valuable incentive?

> Do you agree that the hospital's revised appointment system reflects an overall improvement in customer care in Countyshire Hospital?

IMPOSSIBLE QUESTIONS

My all-time favourite impossible question has little to do with surveys:

> If God is all powerful, can he create a ditch which is too wide for him to jump across?

In the context of a questionnaire, an impossible question is one which is incapable of being answered in an objective fashion or whose parameters are contradictory in some way. For example, Fig. 3.11 shows two questions which a respondent will find impossible to answer unless they are *equally* satisfied with the two parameters being judged: price and quality in the first question and range and availability in the second.

10. I think the price and quality of goods at Handy DIY is . . .	❍ Excellent ❍ Good ❍ Poor	11. I think the range and availability of goods at Handy DIY is . . .	❍ Excellent ❍ Good ❍ Poor

Fig. 3.11 Impossible questions

WHAT INFORMATION WILL YOU GAIN FROM ASKING

As has been mentioned several times previously, it is important to understand what you will gain from asking any particular question, either in terms of the validity and usefulness of the information you will collect, or in terms of the type of data and its ability to be analysed in the ways you wish. A number of factors emerge which have a bearing on this subject and these sum up the relevance of the questionnaire as far as the compiler, rather than the respondent, is concerned.

Open-ended questions

Open-ended questions (free text in which one is at liberty to write what one wishes) are notoriously difficult to analyse. Consequently, the amount of data which can be gained from them is limited without expensive coding (see '*Coding frames*' , p. 83, for details on coding open-ended questions). The first response in creating a questionnaire is for most people to write a number of open-ended, textual response questions such as:

What do you think about the proposed ring road?

Why do you like or dislike OiLea Margarine?

What is your opinion of TripleX Beer?

Although the information that people will write here may be interesting, it will not be easy to extract any data from it without a good deal of work. It should also be noted that people tend to fall into one of two categories when answering this type of question, depending on their mood. If they feel neutral about the issue, unsure of your intentions or simply have not warmed up yet they will provide little information. However, someone who is angry about the topic or delighted with it will do just the opposite. Sifting out the useful data will take some time and is a skilled task.

Personal information

Collecting personal information as part of a survey can be counterproductive for a number of reasons. Apart from any other consideration, you should ask yourself whether the information is necessary to your analysis. If there is no intention to contact respondents again in order to ask for additional information then personal details should be left out. Requests for personal information can:

- Inhibit the respondent who knows that their answers may be 'traced'.
- Make the researcher liable to the terms of the Data Protection Act in the United Kingdom.

- Suppress other aspects of the respondent's willingness to co-operate.

On the other hand, the benefits can be that:

- The subset of respondents may be identified and therefore further divided by classifying people by sex, age, postcode, marital status, etc., if those are likely to give a significance to the analysis.
- Respondents can be asked for further information.

Inclusion or otherwise depends totally on circumstances. It is likely to be totally unnecessary in the context of a shopfloor survey of staff or an internal audit of services. On the other hand, a customer satisfaction survey where an individual has highlighted a problem which you wish to investigate further would benefit from having collected the respondent's name and address.

Too many questions

A frequent fault is to try to capture the essence of life, the universe and everything in a questionnaire. Apart from the boredom factor which sets in somewhere after page five and has become terminal around page seven, a long questionnaire is probably that way because it is attempting to tackle many subjects at the same time. Although major market research agencies will have huge 'omnibus' questionnaires which are administered by interview and take a couple of hours to complete, most business and institutional questionnaire compilers will be well advised to keep their surveys brief, focused and to the point.

If you find your questionnaire is becoming too long, examine its reason for being so:

- Have you determined the objectives clearly?
- Do the questions focus on those objectives?
- Is there repetition or redundancy in the content of the questions?

Too few questions

It is less likely that you will have problems with too few questions. It can be frustrating for the respondent, however, if the questions introduce a topic about which they have strong feelings and yet allows them little or no opportunity to express their opinion. If your questionnaire is falling foul of this problem it is likely that you have insufficient knowledge of the subject you are tackling and you should listen carefully to your questionnaire test group.

Having asked for date of birth do you need to ask age?

Another aspect which can make questionnaires too long is redundancy – asking for information which has already been collected, is available from elsewhere or may be inferred or calculated from the data you have already. A good example of this is date of birth and age. Having asked for a person's date of birth there is no need to collect the age data as well. Modern data systems will happily calculate such information for you automatically.

Similarly, calculations about the number of days' stay at an hotel may be calculated from the dates of arrival and departure; the productivity per employee of a company may be calculated by reference to the number of the workforce and the annual turnover; the address of an individual may be derived from the postcode/zipcode (by access to the relevant database) and even their social grouping can be reasonably reliably predicted from that information.

The clue is, if the information may be *derived* from the respondent's answers then save yourself space in the questionnaire and time in data entry.

QUESTION PURPOSES (QUESTIONS AND THE TYPE OF ANSWERS TO EXPECT)

Choosing the correct question type determines how your respondent answers, the way in which the answer is collected and how that influences all the aspects which might be hidden in a phrase or word. Framing the answer type comes later; here we look at some of the reasons for asking questions. Questions are asked for a number of reasons and most can be categorised into one of the four groups illustrated below. Although there may be some uncertainty about where any particular question may fit, studying its nature and the type of response that it will elicit will help you to get the data you need.

To evaluate satisfaction or measure performance

Whereas a question can measure your opinion or attitude about a subject, it may not derive information about how pleased or displeased you were with that situation. That tends to be made up of many, much more specific, opinions about levels of service, quality of goods, response times and so on. Opinion and attitude questions might deal with generalities, but the satisfaction question will home in on particular issues. Opinion and attitude questions are subjective whereas it might be argued that satisfaction questions are more objective. The same principles might be applied equally to an hotel's facilities as to a student's continuous assessment or an employee's performance appraisal.

HOW WELL DID HE/SHE/WE DO?

This type of question asks the respondent to give a rating or a score for performance. In a customer satisfaction survey that might mean evaluating the quality of technical support, how rapidly the company responded to a ringing telephone, or any of the facets of the organisation's activity which the questionnaire compiler has decided are likely to be important indicators of customer satisfaction. Equally the score may be based on a quantifiable performance – a time taken to run 100 metres, a score in a Standard Attainment Target school test or the number of widgets fitted to crowmungles per hour by an operative.

In each case, an appropriate means of trapping the data must be decided. If we look at the ever-present hotel survey, the questions of Fig. 3.12 are answered by choice from a list. The Excellent/Poor type of response will not be appropriate, however, where we are measuring in units, although the intention is the same – to see how well the person/organisation did. In a simple health monitoring survey the performance of the individual in each of the physical tasks will render a numerical value (Fig. 3.13). That value provides a different type of profile according to how and when it is used. In the example shown (Fig. 3.13) a single value is taken for the heart rate after one minute's exercise at each of the predetermined speeds. This single value can then be measured against profiles of 'normal' results.

OUR SERVICE

How would you rate our service?

In the Restaurant	Excellent	Good	Fair	Poor
Anticipating your needs	1 ☐	2 ☐	3 ☐	4 ☐
Breakfast service	1 ☐	2 ☐	3 ☐	4 ☐
Quality of food and beverages	1 ☐	2 ☐	3 ☐	4 ☐
Quality of service	1 ☐	2 ☐	3 ☐	4 ☐
Ambience/decor	1 ☐	2 ☐	3 ☐	4 ☐

Fig. 3.12 Evaluating restaurant services

Heart rate at rest	☐ per minute	Each value measured after one minute duration of exercise
Heart rate at slow walk	☐ per minute	
Heart rate at fast walk	☐ per minute	
Heart rate at jog	☐ per minute	
Heart rate at run	☐ per minute	

Fig. 3.13 Health survey

However, a numerical value may be collected as a continuous stream of data – again, if we take the example above, the continuous path of change from heart rate at rest, rising to heart rate when running can be plotted against time. Rather than a single result (a snapshot) we now have a full motion video: a profile of the continuous change mapped second by second against a time line. This type of profile might be used when collecting information about any situation where there is ebb and flow: stocks and shares, profit and loss, population growth, productivity per person and so on.

WHERE CAN HE/SHE/WE IMPROVE?

This open-ended question is asked as a consequence of focusing the thoughts of your respondent on previous questions about the company or individual's performance. It may be possible to constrain the responses into groups or ask for general areas where improvement is necessary. However, this will to a certain extent predetermine the outcome. This type of question is an invitation for suggestions and should not, therefore, be directed by the questioner more than is absolutely necessary.

Questions of this type might begin by asking:

Which aspects of our service could be improved?

This could be followed by a checklist, but remember 'Other – please specify' when you do so. However, bearing in mind that it is unfettered opinion that you want, it is probably better to leave it wide open. Then constrain the responses you receive with a *coding frame* (see p. 83).

Follow the question by another open question – this time with the opportunity to elaborate:

In what ways could improvements be made?

As in open-ended questions of any type, the better you prepare the way into the question the more constructive and relevant will be the responses you obtain. Therefore, ask these questions after you have explored the measurable areas with questions that require a fixed answer before letting the respondent loose.

HOW DO WE MATCH UP TO THE COMPETITION?

Any question which invites comparison immediately assumes that you have quantified the service or goods against which the opposition is being measured. The respondent must have a clear picture of their own opinion, derived from careful questioning, before they can hope to comment objectively on the other element. A questionnaire which begins: 'Do you think *Sudso* is better than *Washo*?' is rather doomed if the respondent's first answer is 'No!'

In the light of previous questions (and it is worth drawing the respondent's attention to what they have already said), the question will compare two similar goods or services. On the basis that one can only compare like with like, it is patently nonsense to ask for comparisons between two products that are not similar. Questions might be phrased in these terms:

> Which do you prefer . . .?

> In your experience, is X more effective/expensive/rapid than Y?

> Do you feel that service in the staff canteen at the Birmingham site is better than the service in the staff canteen at the Dudley site?

To classify

Classification enables the researcher to group people by any one of a number of criteria. The purpose of this grouping may be in order to find a particular sample from the entire 'population' being surveyed. It may also be for the purposes of identifying trends which are defined by people's origins, sex, financial status or the area in which they live. For example, there may be a need to discover whether the purchasing preference of white males under 30 years of age, living in the south-east and in the £30,000–40,000 a year earnings bracket is for cabriolet or saloon cars.

That requirement constrains very much the data which is being collected and the population which is being addressed.

Similarly, in a hospital, for example, there may be a need to draw out factors which are influenced by the age group, disability, illness, mobility or other classification groups in order to examine trends. These questions need to be asked to enable the researcher to group responses at the analysis stage, and illustrate the characteristics of one or more classifications in reference to the subject being addressed.

Classification of individuals may be made by age, sex, household status, social grouping, marital status, work, income, housing, area of country, size and composition of household, and education. There are predefined standard classifications which may be used. These are to be found in more detail in the Market Research Society's *Standardised Questions* booklet. Not all of them would meet with approval when examined in the light of today's supposedly classless and equal society. Therefore care and sensitivity should be exercised when using them. They are reproduced here in summary, courtesy of the Market Research Society.

Sex: male or female

Household status: head of household, housewife, other adult

Marital status: single, married, widowed, divorced, separated

Age: 15–24, 25–34, 35–44, 45–54, 55–64, 65+

Social class: A (higher managerial administrative or professional)
B (Intermediate managerial administrative or professional)
C1 (Supervisory, clerical, junior administrative or professional)
C2 (Skilled manual workers)
D (Semi-skilled and unskilled manual workers)
E (State pensioners, widows, casual and lowest grade earners)
(For most practical purposes they are grouped into four: AB, C1, C2 and DE, or into two:
ABC1 (middle class) and C2DE (working class))

Occupation: divides into four separate functions: activity, industry, size of firm, degree of responsibility:

- Activity
  - working full-time (over 30 hours per week)
  - working part-time (8–30 hours per week)
  - housewife (full-time)
  - student (full-time)
  - temporarily unemployed (but actively seeking work)
  - retired
  - other permanently unemployed (e.g. chronically sick, independent means)

Continued overleaf

- Industry
  - primary (farming, fishing, mining, etc.)
  - manufacturing
  - selling, distribution and retail
  - finance and banking
  - transportation
  - other service industries
  - Civil Service and local government
  - Armed Forces
  - professions in private practice
  - education
- Size of firm (number of full-time employees) 0–9, 10–24, 25–99, 100–249, 250+
- Degree of responsibility
  - self-employed
  - senior manager or director (total responsibility)
  - junior manager (wide responsibility)
  - supervisor (limited responsibility)
  - no responsibility for other people

Income: difficult to use as a classification medium because of variations in ways in which people are paid – weekly, monthly, on commission and so on.

Terminal education age: using a question which asks 'At what age did you finish full–time education?'

16
17
18
19
20
21+
Still studying

Size and composition of household: subdivides into questions about:

- Number in household
  1
  2
  3
  4+ (using any suitable extension to this series that is appropriate)
- Number aged
  0–1
  2–4
  5–15
  16–20
  21+

Accommodation: asking specific questions dependent upon the information required:

- Type of accommodation:
  - detached house/bungalow
  - semi-detached house/bungalow
  - terraced house
  - flat/maisonette (self-contained)
  - flat/rooms (not self-contained)
  - other
- Number of rooms of which the occupier and family have exclusive use (number answer)
- Ownership or rental
  - owner/occupier (owning)
  - owner/occupier (buying on mortgage or loan)
  - rental from Council
  - rental privately unfurnished
  - rental privately furnished
  - rent-free/tied
  - other
- Age of building (using appropriate ranges for the sample)

Classification may also be made of the regions in which people live. This is now done using sophisticated systems which can describe the type of accommodation, the social grouping of the inhabitants and a wealth of other information by postcode area. Naturally, this material is commercially valuable and therefore is not readily reproduced here.

To gain information on habits and behaviour

It could be argued that the classification description could be fitted to accommodate nearly every question. When one collects information about people's habits and behaviour, however, it is likely that individual characteristics are not so important. The objective is to find a *profile*, be it of attitude to buying from hypermarkets or opinion about new procedures implemented in the company. Profiling people's habits or behaviour may be either domestic or work related. Domestically, such things as smoking and drinking, preferences for types of food and so on all are important indicators of future buying for market researchers. For instance:

- *Have you ever . . .?*

Have you ever considered making a will?	❑ Yes ❑ No
Have you ever wanted to give up smoking?	❑ Yes ❑ No
Have you ever visited the Harlow office?	❑ Yes ❑ No

- *When did you last . . .?*

When did you last use the public amenity refuse tip in Cawthorpe Road?

❍ In the last three months
❍ Between three and six months ago
❍ Between a year and six months ago
❍ More than a year ago
❍ Never

- *Do you own . . .?*

Do you own, or have you ever owned, a Ford motor car? ❍ Yes ❍ No

- *Will you . . .?*

Will you be updating your house contents insurance in the near future

❍ Yes
❍ No

In the company or institutional context the profile is much more finely attuned to the needs of the survey and the behaviour that relates to the task in hand, (Fig. 3.14).

To gauge attitude, opinion or preference

This type of question may be asked in a number of ways, each with its own peculiarities and facilities.

NUMBER SCALE

The number scale will allow the respondent to represent numerically where they stand upon a particular issue. The scale may be any number range (from 1 to 10, from 1 to 5, from 1 to 100 (although large scales show little better resolution than small ones), and the ends of the scale show the

(a)

Do you ever feel dizzy or weak?	❍ Yes ❍ No
Do you ever feel yourself trembling?	❍ Yes ❍ No

(b)

When did you last attend a career counselling session?

❍ In the last three months
❍ Between three and six months ago
❍ Between a year and six months ago
❍ More than a year ago

Fig. 3.14 Fine tuning the profile

extremes of a state of agreement/disagreement or satisfaction/dissatisfaction. For example:

Please read the following statement:

The company has a satisfactory incentive scheme for employees on the shop floor.

On the scale below please mark where your opinion lies by circling one number only:

Agree								Disagree	
1	2	3	4	5	6	7	8	9	10

SEMANTIC SCALE

The same question might have been rendered using a semantic scale, however (Fig. 3.15). It is also worth noting that, because there is an even number of options, there is no opportunity for the respondent to sit on the fence. It could be argued in this instance that perhaps there should be an option, 'No opinion' (see the section on Answer types (p. 53) for more detail on these question types).

Please read the following statement:

The company has a satisfactory incentive scheme for employees on the shop floor.

On the scale below please mark where your opinion lies by choosing an option:

Agree totally Agree broadly Agree slightly Disagree slightly Disagree broadly Disagree totally

Fig. 3.15 Using a semantic scale

MORE ABOUT FREE TEXT QUESTIONS

In asking questions about people's attitudes, their opinions or their preferences for particular options the questionnaire compiler is likely to open flood gates of response, particularly if the question hits close to the heart of a matter upon which the respondent has strong views. Interviewers can interpret the responses to render the information they need, but if a questionnaire is being filled out by a respondent with no other guidance, then questions such as 'What do you think about X?' with the option to enter ten lines of text will render a volume of response which is both unmanageable and, more importantly, very difficult to quantify and interpret. For that reason the question should guide the respondent into a particular area of the subject:

- Do you agree that . . .?
- Do you believe . . .?
- If x happened would you . . .?
- Given a choice between x and y, which would you choose?

The question 'Why?' might follow any of these, but the floodgates would once again open! Questions about attitude, opinion or preference should aim to dissect the issue in an informed way, allow the respondent scope in which to address the parts of the subject which are important to them and, above all, control the flow of opinion so that it may be measured.

There is, as ever, a caveat. Guiding the respondent in addressing a topic can also guide them into the answer for which you are looking rather than obtaining their true opinion. For example: 'Do you agree that Maclean's bread tastes better than any other wholemeal loaf?' is a loaded and leading question. Whereas, after a brief statement outlining the company policy on equal opportunity, the question 'Do you believe this policy to be fair?' gives a balanced opportunity to the respondent. Further probing about the reason for their answer may reveal a good deal of other information, (see the section on '*bias*', p. 66).

When is an answer not an answer?

As you write questions and decide upon answer types you may fall foul of a variety of common mistakes, some of which are dealt with more fully under the Answer types section. One of the most common for new compilers is to treat every question as a conversation piece – ask a question and expect a piece of text in response. Apart from being very limiting in style, this technique, or lack of it, will also limit the amount of data interrogation that can be performed afterwards.

Similarly, those who are unskilled in asking appropriate questions choose the wrong answer types from the range available. A multiple choice answer with an inappropriate range of answers is worse than useless. As is one with a set of answers which cannot be constrained to work for the sample answering the question.

Choose an appropriate answer style not only for the sake of the question being asked but also for the sake of having data that is useful

Answer types – some examples and their context

Text (open-ended)

A free text question is one which invites words as a response. The answer may be a single word or it may be pages of text. Single words are usually a response to a request for a fixed piece of specific information; for example:

- What is your surname?
- Please enter your place of birth (town)
- Please enter your nationality

A fuller response will be given when the respondent is given the opportunity to wax lyrical:

- Please add any further comments that you may have about XXXXXXX:
- Please state any further ways in which the local authority could help you:
- If you wish to add any further information to support your application please do so here:

This information is generally incapable of analysis. That being the case, it is rarely worth entering the data onto a computer system for the simple reason that it will fill up your datafile with little added value as far as analysis is concerned. However, such information may be tracked by using the process of *coding*. This is discussed in this section on p. 83.

Free choice

Since a text question gives the respondent free choice to say what they want you must be certain that you have:

- Made your requirements clear.
- Made clear the style of answer you expect.
- Given an appropriate space in which to respond.

If you ask for people's opinions, don't be surprised if you get them, particularly if the questionnaire is anonymous! Similarly, if you do not make clear the type of response required, do not be surprised if you find that the information comes back in a wide variety of styles all of which require interpretation at the data entry stage:

- What colour is your hair?
- Which would you say was your favourite alcoholic drink?
- When do you visit the staff recreation facility?
- How often do you visit the doctor?

None of these questions will reward you with sensible replies, simply because they are too free. Depending upon your view the response to the hair colour question could be '*brown*', '*chestnut*', '*auburn*', '*mousy*', '*grey*', '*silver*', '*white*'. The drink question does not specify whether it is looking for brand names, generic types of drink or something more specific than '*A nice pint*!' The last two invite responses from '*Thursdays*', through to '*Once a month*' or including '*4 o'clock*' and '*I don't*'! How you record that sort of data sensibly really depends upon what you want to do with it. To constrain the answer that you get you must give the respondent some guidelines either by making this into a multiple choice (range) question (as for the hair colour question) or by laying out the instructions for the type of response required:

Which would you say was your favourite alcoholic drink?
(spirits, beer, lager, red wine, white wine . . .?)

When do you visit the staff recreation facility? (Please state a day of the week)

How frequently per year do you visit the doctor? (once, twice, three times, etc.)

Should it have a closed option as well?

One way of making sure you guide the respondent is to split the question into two, beginning with a closed question which will focus the mind:

Which of the following do you drink most frequently: spirits, beer, lager, red wine, white wine

Which **brand** of this type of drink do you prefer?

The second question allows respondents to elaborate freely about the brand (you would not be able to make a multiple choice to catch all the possible variants in this instance) but you have collected important behaviour data from the first question which may be cross-referenced with the second. Making two questions from one is often a good idea, if space and time permit.

Coding frames

A coding frame allows you to put some structure onto unstructured responses. When you ask a question such as 'Please add any further comments . . .', you are inviting the respondent to write as much as they can fit into the space you have provided. You may even wish to offer them the option to continue on another sheet of paper. As was mentioned earlier, this data cannot sensibly be interpreted by any system which addresses the text directly. Consequently, the only way to extract data is to look for the instances of:

- particular words or phrases
- specific opinions
- specific suggestions.

These must be decided before you begin entering and analysing the data. Do this by scanning the forms that have been returned in order to get an impression of the type of response being given. Then set up a coding frame where each response for which you are looking has a separate tick box. When using software this means making a multiple choice question with numbered boxes representing each type of statement.

As you progress through the responses you may well find ones for which you have not legislated. Add new boxes representing these as they occur, until at the end you will have a data set containing abstracts from the comments, all presented in a form which is capable of analysis (Fig. 3.16).

Please enter any general comments in the section below:	For office use only
______________________________	☐ A1
______________________________	☐ A2
______________________________	☐ A3
______________________________	☐ A4
______________________________	☐ A5
______________________________	☐ A6

Fig. 3.16 Use of coding frames

It is worth remembering that the use of coding frames in this way means that you then have no need to enter the data from the comments answers in full – the abstract is the part for which you are looking. For the rest, refer back to the original forms if you wish to read the comments in full.

Preparing the way – constructive guidance to focus the subject's mind when answering very open questions

Open-ended questions are open to the misinterpretation which comes with imprecision. Counteracting that is a task which must be undertaken in the instruction part of any question. Give your respondent guidance about your intentions and the type of information you require otherwise they will either ramble on aimlessly, ploughing their own particular furrow, or fail to respond at all. Let them know:

- that they are free to speak their minds
- that you need to find out their opinions of X and Y
- that, more precisely, you need these aspects of X and Y to be discussed.

To help your respondent to give you the information needed you should give them:

- *Information:* Outline to them the types of response you are expecting, for example:

> Please add any further comments that you may have about the proposed bypass (Include your opinion of the project as a whole, the campaigns which have been waged on either side, and any suggestions you may have for a solution which will relieve the congestion in the town whilst minimising the distress to other people involved):

Here you have made it clear that you are not interested in invective, but in constructive information which can move the debate forward.

- *Statements:* A statement of objectives will help people to realise the direction which the questionnaire is taking. Although this tends to be made more commonly at the beginning of the questionnaire, it is worth reiterating that information at least in part at the point where people are being given an opportunity to stand on their soap-box.
- *Preparatory questions:* By the very nature of the questions which you ask before you give the respondent opportunity for free comment, you will mentally line them up on the runway which takes them in the direction you want. A series of questions which ask for details of their opinion about a number of specifics is then logically followed by another which allows them freedom to build on their earlier responses.

NUMERIC

Numeric answers are the response to questions requiring numeric values for calculation and analytical purposes. A numeric answer may take many forms and there are numerous pitfalls of which the questionnaire compiler should be aware. Numerics will be in one of the following forms:

Integers:	*123*
Decimals:	*123.456*
Numeric with leading characters:	*£123.45*
Numeric with trailing characters:	*123.45 years*
Negative numeric:	*–123.45*

There is a danger of asking for information in an inappropriate form with numerics, e.g.

Please enter your age: ________

This question makes it unclear whether this is years, years and months, decimal years. Therefore showing the format of the answer (a picture of what you require) is a good idea in order to constrain the respondent to reply correctly:

Please enter your age: ______ years ________ months

Please enter the price paid for the radio: £____.__ (inc. VAT)

At the point of data entry it is important to ensure that only values within the range which are allowed are entered in the data. This is done by setting a *valid range* which may or may not be made explicit on the questionnaire form itself. Entering data into a datafile using appropriate software will allow the compiler to set the range of legal values so that nothing outside that range can be entered, avoiding idiocies such as people's ages being rendered as 234 because of a typing error, a missed decimal point or some other error.

BINARY

Binary answers are those for which there is a two-state answer – either Yes or No, On or Off, Up or Down, Male or Female. Typically this type of question is a two-choice multiple choice question although it does have other characteristics. Once again, there are some inherent dangers in using this type of question. For instance:

Do you visit the chiropodist frequently? Yes/No

Quite properly might be answered by 'Sometimes', which is a happy compromise that is needed because of the imprecision of *frequently* in the question. In addition, I might choose not to answer at all because I consider it is none of the researcher's business. Having made that choice there is no way of expressing it on the form which makes any sense for analytical purposes. There is an argument which states that you should always have an *'Other'* option in any multiple choice question – or in this case, a *'Don't know / Won't say'* option.

MULTIPLE CHOICE

The multiple choice question allows the researcher to specify a precoded range of responses into which the respondent is expected to fit their opinions. It is vital, unsurprisingly, that the ranges should be suitable to the task (see comments on ranges later in this chapter, p. 93). Typically a multiple choice answer will allow the respondent to make either:

- *a single response:* Here only one option may be chosen from a list – usually this is obvious, but it is occasionally worth the effort to point it out to the respondent:

In which age range does your age appear? (Choose one only) ☐ Under 25 ☐ 25–34 ☐ 35–44 ☐ 45–54 ☐ 55–64 ☐ Over 65

- *or a multiple response*: In this case the respondent may be asked to tick any of the options which apply to them (Fig. 3.17).

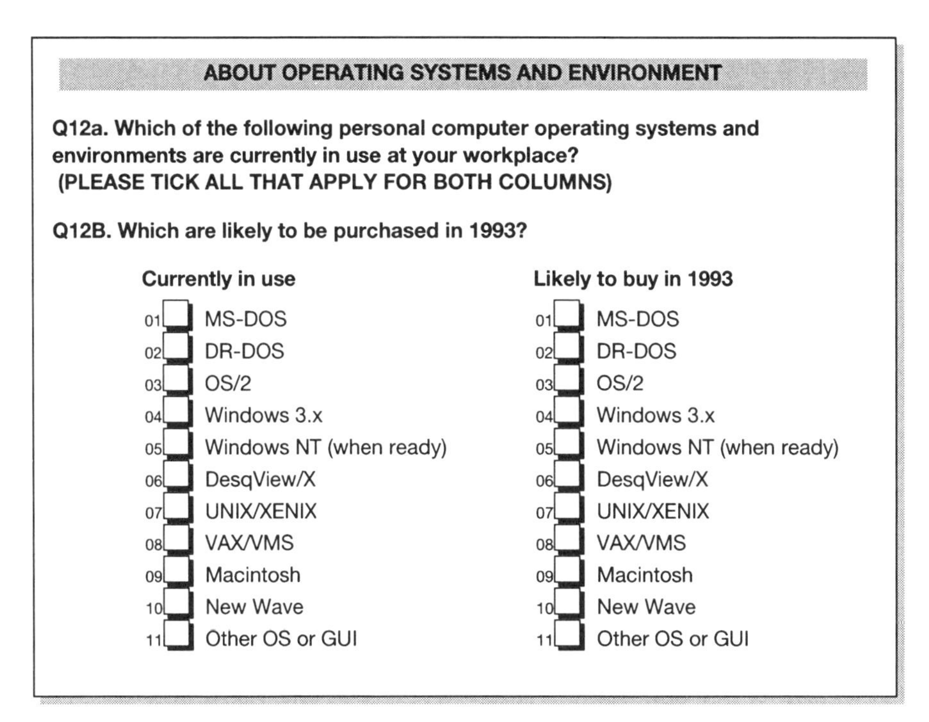

ABOUT OPERATING SYSTEMS AND ENVIRONMENT

Q12a. Which of the following personal computer operating systems and environments are currently in use at your workplace?
(PLEASE TICK ALL THAT APPLY FOR BOTH COLUMNS)

Q12B. Which are likely to be purchased in 1993?

Currently in use	Likely to buy in 1993
01 ☐ MS-DOS	01 ☐ MS-DOS
02 ☐ DR-DOS	02 ☐ DR-DOS
03 ☐ OS/2	03 ☐ OS/2
04 ☐ Windows 3.x	04 ☐ Windows 3.x
05 ☐ Windows NT (when ready)	05 ☐ Windows NT (when ready)
06 ☐ DesqView/X	06 ☐ DesqView/X
07 ☐ UNIX/XENIX	07 ☐ UNIX/XENIX
08 ☐ VAX/VMS	08 ☐ VAX/VMS
09 ☐ Macintosh	09 ☐ Macintosh
10 ☐ New Wave	10 ☐ New Wave
11 ☐ Other OS or GUI	11 ☐ Other OS or GUI

Fig. 3.17 Multiple response possible to question

Consequences for analysis

It is worth noting that whereas the single response answer is easy to analyse, the multiple response answer has inherent difficulties which may cause problems at the analysis stage (see Chapter 7 on data analysis for further discussion).

Prompted (with danger of putting the idea into their heads)

One of the problems that come with multiple choice questions is that of predetermining the outcome. For this reason some research agencies use interviews rather than paper questionnaires wherever possible and present ranges of options in multiple choice questions verbally in a varying order so that they minimise distortion that comes from having a particular brand name or other variable at the top or bottom of the list all the time. Prompted questioning allows the interviewer to ask about a person's perception of a particular product or range without influencing them unduly.

Unprompted (but noted against a 'private' list)

To minimise the weighting effect further, but also to produce a different type of result, is the unprompted question. Here the interviewer has a list of responses, multiple choice style, but these are never revealed to the interviewee. In response to the question:

Which soap powders are familiar to you?

the respondent may reply with a very different set of answers from those which would come up in a question where the possible answers were displayed. Use unprompted questions in interview or on paper if you wish the respondent to be completely uninfluenced in their choice of answers. The limitation is that your answer set may suffer from their lapses of memory. Multiple choice responses are an *aide-mémoire* which may, if used incorrectly, bias the result of your survey.

Need for 'Other, please specify'

As was mentioned earlier in this section, there is a need in any multiple choice question to allow the respondent whose opinions do not fit into any of your predetermined categories to express their view. For this reason the '*Other, please specify*' option is found in many questionnaires. Without it the respondent may be frustrated if they are continually omitted from the range of available options.

When this option is provided there needs to be space for the respondent to fill in the relevant detail. At its simplest level, there is

Please select your favourite colour

- ❏ Red
- ❏ Blue
- ❏ Green
- ❏ Other (please specify) ________________

Consequences for analysis

Using this technique does have consequences for the way in which you analyse your data. Assuming that 50 per cent of your respondents ticked '*Other*' and then wrote in another colour, you would be missing 50 per cent of the data in the analysis when you came to doing your statistics and graphs. Although '*Other*' would appear (probably as the largest bar in a graph) it would not show the range and distribution of answers that half your respondents had made. Therefore, it is a good idea to use software which will allow you to integrate these answers as new multiple choice options after the event, even when data are in the system.

Don't know

A similar rule applies to the '*Don't know*' brigade. They are an important element and should not be dismissed as airheads in your analysis. If someone doesn't know the answer it is worth asking why. Is the reason in fact something to do with the organisation or promotion which is being researched? Is '*Don't know*' in fact a very clear and positive indicator in this survey?

Won't answer

As with '*Don't know*', the response '*Won't answer*' can shed a particular light on the situation being investigated. It is worth following further those people who won't answer particular questions if it is thought that they may hold a key to the problem. '*Don't know*' and '*Won't answer*' are often put together as a single response type. It is worth considering whether this will be adequate for your needs.

Don't care

Finally in this section, the '*Don't care*' lobby. This will never be a part of the actual questionnaire but it is likely that you will be able to see the difference between those who will not answer because of lack of knowledge, a refusal to answer or apathy.

SCORED

This variant on multiple choice questions gives a weighting to the responses being offered. So, for example, in a customer satisfaction survey where respondents choose Excellent, Good or Poor for a variety of services, the response '*Excellent*' might be given a score of 2, '*Good*' a score of 1 and '*Poor*' a score of 0.

These scores might be given arbitrarily just as in popular magazines the '*How sexy are you?*' survey gives numeric values to your answers in order to tell you your rating. The validity of such games is dubious but in a serious survey the weighting of responses in order to highlight excellence or deficiencies in a particular area of service can be a useful analytical tool. Similarly, it may be that the scoring of answers is used to provide a scale for assessment of need, of success of training or other indicator where a person's rating entitles them or otherwise to certification, to insurance cover (are they a good risk), to eligibility for any other financial service or simply to show they have passed a profiling test of some sort (see also the section on ordered or ranked choice answers below).

RANKED (ORDERED CHOICE)

A question which asks for ranking or scoring is different from a multiple choice question which has been given a score or *weighting*. Ranking is the process whereby the respondent is asked to put a list into an order of preference, scoring 1 for the best and *X* for the last where *X* is the same as the total number of options being given. For example:

> Please rank the following programmes in order of preference, scoring 1 for your favourite down to 5 for your least favourite
>
> ☐ Brookside
> ☐ EastEnders
> ☐ Coronation Street
> ☐ The Bill
> ☐ Neighbours

Naturally there will be those who wish to score two or more of the options equally. This is quite acceptable as long as the list of responses remains complete. Therefore a respondent may put:

> Brookside – 3, EastEnders – 1, Coronation Street – 4, The Bill – 1, Neighbours – 5

Here we have a joint first place but no second place.

At the analysis stage this type of answer is scored inversely – that is to say, where the choice is '*1*' the score for analysis purposes is 5; '*2*' scores 4; '*3*' scores 3; '*4* 'scores 2 and '*5*' scores 1. When the scores of a number of respondents are added up for each programme there will then be a clear indicator of popularity for all the programmes being surveyed.

DATE

Quite simply a date answer is one where a date is entered! The date may refer to some event gone past such as a birthdate, but it is often an item of information collected to show when the survey was administered – today's date. Some systems will automatically date every record at the point of data entry. That may not, in fact, be the date when the information was collected. Be sure to differentiate if that is important to your analysis.

Dates can confuse – bear in mind that the way in which a date is entered can be ambiguous, particularly if you are using software. UK dates are usually entered (numerically) as day/month/year in a variety of formats from dd/mm/yy to dddddddd/mmmmmmmmm/yyyy. However,

US dates reverse the first two elements: month/day/year. If your computer is configured for United States rather than UK you may find that there are inconsistencies in your date data.

CALCULATED

A calculated answer is one which is derived from one or more other answers or some arithmetic or logical function. It is information which is extrapolated from the data you have already been given and in effect can be used to give an instant analysis of some factor as the data are entered on a computer. For instance, in a customer satisfaction survey, a set of scored multiple choice questions may be used whose scores are then combined in a calculated answer in order to provide an immediate result.

Similarly the results of the answers might be read by the system:

> If answer A is 'Excellent' and answer B is 'Excellent' then print 'Satisfactory performance'

Calculated answers do not have to be numeric in nature and it should be possible for you to calculate ages from dates of birth, levels of preference from multiple choice answers and overall ability from a combination of a variety of test questions. Another function is to sum scores attributed to multiple choice questions.

More general information on questions and answer types

In the previous part of this section (Question Purposes) the question was answered by explaining the various answer types in terms of the sorts of data which are collected. Here we look at the type of answer which is being given by the respondent to some less specific types of question and which of the above answer types might be used to store and retrieve it in a sensible fashion.

AN OPINION OR STATEMENT OF HABIT

In questioning a respondent one is often asking them their opinion: 'What do you think of . . .' 'Do you agree that . . .' 'How often do you . . .' 'How do you feel about . . .' and so on. This type of question type may be treated as open-ended unless you wish to constrain the respondent into a particular group of answers, focusing their minds on specific topics which need to be addressed. You might do this in one of the following ways:

- *Text:* Ask them for a set of free text comments, bearing in mind the limits of this style of data

- *Range:* Ask them to choose one or more from a range of predetermined answers, bearing in mind that they may be 'led' by the answers you have offered. Alternatively, ask them the question blind – do not show them the answers but have your own private checklist against which you mark their responses
- *Ranking:* Ask them to put a number of factors into order of priority. Ensure that you make clear in which direction the scale works – is 1 the top or the bottom?
- *Score:* Ask them to give a score to certain predetermined answers. This might be by actually collecting a numeric answer here (I think that your service rates 8) or it might more easily be by using a weighted multiple choice answer.

A NUMERIC VALUE

When collecting values one is asking for accurate numeric data – that is, assuming that the respondent has access to that information. In collecting this type of answer one is asking questions such as 'How much . . .' 'How many . . .' 'What is the cost of . . .' 'How old . . .'.

Numbers

In response one expects a numeric value that may be simply integers (123) or decimals (123.45) or either format with trailing or leading characters (£123.45, 123 years). Numbers on their own mean very little apart from as single 'bites' of information. It is when they are used in combination that they begin to give a new dimension to the data which you are collecting. Using software it is possible to have immediate results from every questionnaire form you enter on your system, simply by performing one or more processes automatically as the data are entered.

Collapsing raw data into groups

Raw data can be grouped together to produce outcomes. For example, when collecting information about a company:

- Number in labour force.
- Number of middle managers.
- Number of senior managers and directors.

It is then possible to calculate the total workforce by adding the three items together. If one then also has the annual turnover of the company, a simple division sum will give you the average productivity per employee – simple, but effective and the result is with you immediately. In the same way, insurance firms, mortgage brokers or any other financial institution can obtain instant quotations based upon the raw data typed into the system.

Class intervals

At the point of analysis the range of values entered as responses to a particular question over say 100 questionnaires can be enormous. Just in terms of asking for someone's age in years one can easily envisage a range from 18 through to 80 and perhaps even wider. In order to handle that sort of data, particularly at the graphing stage, it is sensible to group it into easily managed units. This process is called 'binning' and involves separating the data into class intervals at the data analysis stage, much as one might have grouped ages into ranges in a multiple choice question at the question design stage.

Retrospectively then, one looks at the range of data (the two extremes) and selects a sensible grouping interval. In the above case, an interval of 10 would give us six bands in which the data might appear. The data thereafter is represented in those bands on the charts which are plotted.

Not using numerics at all!

Of course it may well be that you should not have used a numeric at all. Choosing an inappropriate data type is a common enough error and it is often only when one comes to analysis that the problem is revealed. Perhaps you would have been better off with a range.

Ranges

A range will represent numeric data quite happily. Just as in the *binning* process one groups people into sets which represent particular intervals in a numeric (or any other) range. So, for example, at its simplest we have:

How old are you? 15–25, 26–35, etc.

However, beware the problem that comes with setting ranges. If your sample falls mainly into one group, unbeknown to you at the point of creating the questionnaire, your data will appear to be heavily biased towards one end of the spectrum when you come to analysis. Therefore, indulge in a little sample research before coming up with the final specification. The Market Research Society booklet *Standardised Questions* shows the ranges most commonly used in a number of situations.

A SIMPLE PIECE OF INFORMATION

After all, this is what questionnaires are all about – collecting pieces of information. Such information tends to be the underlying facts which describe the person, the situation or events. When you ask for name, address, postcode, date of birth you are requesting personal information – much of which many research agencies would shun as being detrimental to a satisfactory outcome in a survey.

That simple piece of information may relate to the person's behaviour or their way of life. It may classify them, but in the end it will fall into one of the following categories

- text
- number
- date.

A CALCULATION

A calculation allows you to derive data from that which you have already collected. It can equally be a simple message which tells you the consequence of the answers you have given.

Consequential data

Consequential data may be on the level of 'Because you answered 'Yes' to question 2 and 'No' to Question 3 then the answer to Question 4 must be 'Yes'. This type of *routing* and *skipping and filling* of questions is an automatic procedure used to verify answers and to save data entry clerks a good deal of time.

Message

The consequence of answering in a given way to a number of questions may simply be that you are not eligible for a mortgage, that you are a good risk for insurance, that you qualify for a Grade 'D' or that you are no longer entitled to benefit! Any, or indeed all of these, are calculated information provided thanks to a computerised system which can scan the data as it is entered. The computer performs the calculations, juxtaposing the responses you have made and taking into account any conditions which the compiler has set.

CODED

The information collected in codes is that which you have sifted from your respondents' ramblings. The codes are your creation, not theirs, and they represent the essence of the statements made by the respondent. Coded answers are also those which are multiple choice or ranked since the only difference is that the respondent sees the 'answers' in advance!

Validation of answers

How exactly can you ensure that your respondent gives you the answer you require and also that the data input operator transcribes it correctly? Two very difficult questions! To a certain extent the first has been answered by what has gone before and what follows in the rest of this book – careful design of a questionnaire, taking into account all the factors that might warp your data, is the only road to happiness. Add to that some sensible trialling with an informed group of respondents and you are nearer to Nirvana than ever!

Checking up on your respondent might seem a little sneaky but it has to be admitted that many will lie through their teeth rather than say something which will discredit them, get them in trouble or make them look less macho than their office image.

USING REPEATED QUESTIONS

Questions which ask the same thing in a number of different ways have been around a long while. Early and more recent intelligence and aptitude tests ask variants on questions throughout the test to check that you are actually being consistent. In a simple way it is possible to do the same in your questionnaire, although beware of insulting your respondent.

Rephrase

The question may be rephrased to hide the fact that you have actually asked it before. Having asked:

Have you ever contributed to charities which support the hungry overseas?

and having collected the answer, you may then like a little later to ask:

When did you last contribute to Oxfam?

Cross-correlation

You might also ask two sides of the same question in order to check validity of data. For example, asking someone's date of birth at an early part of the questionnaire and then their age later on allows the data operator to check that the two match. If you feel that it is necessary to check someone's story in a particular instance, this technique allows you to show inconsistencies.

USING DATA CHECKING

Turning to the data and the person who is entering it, it is important to ensure that they are typing in the correct answers. Data entry errors can account for a huge proportion of statistical error in your data and, if the data cannot be relied on with a high degree of confidence then you can have even less confidence in the conclusions you draw from it. Constraining data is the simplest and best way of ensuring that your operator cannot make mistakes too easily. Fixed answers, specified ranges and also a clear understanding by the operator of what the data means will all help.

Numeric ranges

Use numeric ranges either in multiple choice format or by setting a range of valid answers beyond which the system will not go when specifying your data structure. Most software will allow you to do something along these lines. So, for example, when asking a question about the weekly throughput of a plant or the number of patients seen by a consultant or the number of visitors to the theme park, pick sensible upper and lower limits which are not likely to be exceeded:

How many visitors have there been to this branch of Slipshod Shoes during the last seven days (Valid range 25–1,000)

Keyboard errors which turn 500 into 5,000 or 50 into –50 can be eliminated with this simple technique.

Closed questions

Similarly, use closed questions which offer a limited range of choices in order to minimise the typing fatigue error or simply the variance with which people describe something as simple as hair colour, flavours of yoghurt or the name of the current Prime Minister, e.g.

John Major	Major	Rt. Hon John Major	John Major MP

Giving people the choice from which to select keeps all the answers the same, but beware the possibility of bias in your results (see earlier section on this subject, p. 66).

Dates

Use a date format data entry system which will not only ensure that you cannot put 15 for the month, but will also clean up all the 29/02/91 type dates (invalid because 1991 was not a leap year and the 31/06/1995 mistake when June, as we all remember, has only 30 days.

4

Example questionnaires – you, the judge

- **In this section you are invited to criticise a questionnaire**
- **You will then be able to look at 'real-life' questionnaires in order to gain ideas, try your critical expertise and generally apply what has been discussed so far**

In this section you can examine a series of questionnaires which are offered as candidates for criticism. The first has been criticised along the lines of all the philosophy and 'good practice' which has been outlined in this book so far. Following it is a revised version – improved as a result of the criticisms and offered for your thoughts. It is *not* offered as a perfect model of a questionnaire since there is really no such thing. Any questionnaire's validity will depend upon

- its objectives
- its context
- its content
- its audience.

When these variables are taken into account, the same questionnaire may be inappropriate for a given situation and yet be perfectly acceptable and useful in another. That is always assuming that fundamental design rules have been adhered to:

- Conciseness
- Clarity
- Objectivity

As you work through these questionnaires it is worth noting how often you have noticed a problem and how often it has only been realised as a result of prompting. You may then measure to what extent you have soaked up the information in this book.

AN EXERCISE IN CRITICISM

The questionnaire in Fig. 4.1 is not, at first, obviously flawed. It is part of a project being undertaken on behalf of a hardware store in a medium-sized town (50,000 population). The shop's sales are falling and the management wants to know why. The researcher has looked at possible causes, talked to a variety of potential customers and has decided to field trial the questionnaire which follows. The questionnaire will be sent to a sample of 500 homes in the town with a coupon as a gift which is redeemable in the store to recompense the respondent.

The objective of the survey is to gain a profile of potential customers and their opinions about the store and how it compares with other similar stores in the area. It is intended that the results will influence the way in which the store presents itself and the range of products it sells, according to the survey's outcome.

Questions to ask yourself

- How successful do you feel the questionnaire will be as a tool for measuring the features which have been identified in the objectives?
- What analyses would be appropriate for this type of work, and will this questionnaire provide the right data for the purpose?
- Where has the compiler succeeded in addressing the real issues and where have they been missed?
- Indeed, what *are* the real issues?
- How well structured are: the introduction, the question order, the questions themselves, the responses?
- How would *you* respond if you were to be asked to complete the questionnaire – try it out for yourself

So how did you fare? It is likely, since your thoughts have been focusing on this type of issue, that you have found many faults which will not be annotated here below. This summary is intended to guide you in criticising your own work rather than being a definitive statement of what is or is not right.

Although seeming at first sight to fulfil some of its objectives, the Handy DIY survey shows some of its faults as soon as you try to complete it. This questionnaire has never been test-driven and, if it hit an unsuspecting public, would immediately give an impression that Handy DIY did not know what they were about, even though the questionnaire has been designed and executed by Kirkby Konsultants!

Handy DIY Survey ✓

As a previous customer of Handy DIY your opinions are of value to us. We need to understand how you feel about the store, what you like and dislike and your thoughts about our competitors. Please take a little time to consider the following questions. They will only take a few minutes to complete. As a 'Thank you' from us, we would like you to accept the voucher enclosed which may be redeemed as part of any purchase from our store, whether you complete the questionnaire or not!

In the questionnaire, we need your honest opinions about service, our product range and whether we achieve our objective of providing excellent value for money. When you have completed the survey, simply fold it up and place it in the reply-paid envelope which accompanies the form.

Thank you for your assistance and for your valued custom, both past and future.

Yours sincerely

R Digby - Managing Director, Handy DIY

Any communications regarding this survey should be made with Kirkby Konsultants on (0)123 456789

1a. Your Name ____________________

1b. Your Address ____________________

1c. Your postcode __________

2. I most recently visited Handy DIY . . .
   - ❍ In the last week
   - ❍ In the last month
   - ❍ In the last year
   - ❍ Never

3. On average I visit Handy DIY . . .
   - ❍ Once a week
   - ❍ Once a month
   - ❍ Once a year
   - ❍ Only when you have a sale

4. I have taken advantage of your special offers . . .
   - ❍ Frequently
   - ❍ Occasionally
   - ❍ Once
   - ❍ Never

5. Handy DIY prices are . . .
   - ❍ Similar to other DIY stores
   - ❍ Lower than other DIY stores
   - ❍ Higher than other DIY stores

6. I have noticed adverts for Handy DIY . . .
   - ❍ On the television
   - ❍ On the radio
   - ❍ In the newspapers
   - ❍ I don't notice advertisements

7. When shopping for DIY goods I generally shop at . . .
   - ❍ Handy DIY
   - ❍ Robertson's Hardware
   - ❍ SuperSave DIY
   - ❍ Nuts 'n' Bolts
   - ❍ Other

8. I choose the DIY store with the best . . .
   - ❍ Prices
   - ❍ Goods
   - ❍ Discount offers
   - ❍ Staff
   - ❍ Parking

9. When I shop at Handy DIY I find all that I need . . .
   - ❍ Every time
   - ❍ Nearly always
   - ❍ Sometimes
   - ❍ Not very often

10. I think the price and quality of goods at Handy DIY is . . .
    - ❍ Excellent
    - ❍ Good
    - ❍ Poor

11. I think the range and availability of goods at Handy DIY is . . .
    - ❍ Excellent
    - ❍ Good
    - ❍ Poor

12. I live in a . . .
    - ❍ Detached house
    - ❍ Semi-detached house
    - ❍ Flat
    - ❍ Maisonette

13. My house has . . .
    - ❍ One bedroom
    - ❍ Two bedrooms
    - ❍ Three bedrooms
    - ❍ Four bedrooms
    - ❍ More

Fig. 4.1 Survey for a hardware store

14. I shop at Handy DIY for . . .
- All my DIY needs
- Hardware
- Garden goods
- Decorating materials
- Timber
- Building materials
- Other

15. Handy DIY is excellent for . . .
- All my DIY needs
- Hardware
- Garden goods
- Decorating materials
- Timber
- Building materials
- Other

16. At Handy DIY I would like to change . . . ______________________________

17. Handy DIY is poorest for . . .
- All my DIY needs
- Hardware
- Garden goods
- Decorating materials
- Timber
- Building materials
- Other

18. I would use Handy DIY more if you stocked:

____
____
____
____

19. I read . . .
- The Guardian
- The Times
- The Telegraph
- The Mail
- The Sun
- The Mirror
- Today

20. I am . . .
- Single
- Married no children
- Married with chidren
- Retired

21. The distance from Handy DIY to my house is . . .
- Less than a mile
- More than a mile
- More than two miles
- More than five miles

Thank you for completing this survey!

Please return the completed survey in the reply paid envelope which accompanied it.

And remember . . .

Handy DIY is Handy for all your DIY Needs!

Let us examine the form in general terms before moving to the specifics.

General

There is an argument that would suggest that this survey would be better carried out without reference to Handy DIY at all. Naturally that would mean that few of the questions about Handy DIY's performance could be asked, but it would enable the compiler to profile customers of different stores and the attributes they look for. In asking them to relate all their answers to the store they use most frequently, the compiler would collect responses that came from Handy DIY shoppers as well as from other stores. The focus would not be so much on Handy DIY and therefore the respondent might feel more able to comment impartially since they do not need to 'please' the sponsor of the survey. However, many stores undertaking surveys wish their respondents to know from whom the questions originate because they use them as a means of raising their profile.

The advertisement slogan at the end of the questionnaire rather takes the objectivity out of the task. If a slogan is printed on the form or publicity materials accompany the questionnaire then it is likely that they may skew the answers in favour of the store. Maybe that is the objective?

The respondents are being encouraged to complete the form and place it in the reply paid envelope. If they have lost the envelope what should they do then? There is no address on the form and they are unlikely to want to go to the store in order to hand it in.

The voucher may be an incentive for people to respond, but only if they are likely to shop there anyway. This may mean that the respondents are simply going to be the store's existing customers who are committed rather than the more 'interesting' malcontents. One survey company in the United States sends its surveys with a dollar bill attached. In the UK respondents are sometimes encouraged with a 20p piece or the gift of a pen! This independence of 'currency' means that the respondent benefits, whatever their stance and may feel more obliged to respond.

Layout

Despite the fact that there is a good deal of white space at the end of the form, the questions on the first page are bunched up and quite difficult to separate. They would benefit from better spacing, perhaps not on a two-column basis?

The introduction is over long. Although friendly and informative, the introduction takes up a significant part of the first page and adds little to the proceedings – introductions should tell about your intentions and objectives

There is no logical route through the questions – should one answer down the first column and then down the next or traverse from side to side? This links in with the lack of order in grouping questions discussed below.

The questions

The questions are not grouped in any logical sequence – there are questions about the respondent, their opinions, their behaviour, all mixed in together. They would be better separated as follows:

- Information about the respondent.
- Their frequency and purpose for visiting Handy DIY.
- Their expectations of a DIY store.
- How well their expectations are fulfilled at Handy DIY.

There are no instructions accompanying the questions, some of which patently need additional information such as 'Tick one choice only' in order for people to answer consistently.

The questions which are not asked are as important as those which are. If the objectives are to gain an insight into what appeals to customers about the other DIY stores, causing them to shop there rather than at Handy DIY, it might be better to group people in a more logical way. The divisions of such behaviour may relate to the respondent's sex, their age or their socioeconomic group. Isolating one or more of those as a determining factor against which the other variables could initially be cross-tabulated would help you to observe trends by age group or sex, location or social class. All of which begs the question: 'What do you *need* to know about your respondent?'

Question 1: Do you *need* to know their name and address? Stating your name and address is guaranteed to affect the way in which you reply. Anonymous surveys get more valid results.

Question 2: Since this questionnaire is intended for delivery only to those people who previously visited the store, there seems little point in the 'Never' option.

Question 3: This question mixes two types of answer. The first three are to do with timescales whereas the 'Only when you have a sale' is a *reason* for visiting the store and should more properly be asked as part of Question 14.

Question 4: This question does not mention what these special offers might be – if you shop there infrequently then you will have no idea.

Moreover, might it not be a good idea to make this question a 'double-header' (one which tackles two things simultaneously) by asking 'Which of these special offers have you taken advantage of . . .' followed by a list of recent promotions? In this way you gather from the same question, the fact that, yes they do take advantage of special offers, *and* which ones.

Question 5: Are you asking here for a fact, or an opinion? If it's a fact then how do they know? Have they researched the market? It is more likely that you want an opinion, an impression, an idea of the way they *feel* about the store so a better way to ask the question may be 'I believe that Handy DIY prices are . . .' or 'I have the impression that Handy DIY prices are . . .'.

Question 6: This question has no clear instruction. Should the respondent tick only one option or more? If more, then why have the instructions not been made clear? This applies to several multiple response multiple choice questions in this survey: 6, 8, 14, 15, 17, 19

This is a 'So what?' question. What benefit will you gather from knowing this information? Would it not be better to ask them if they have seen a specific campaign or simply ask an open-ended question asking which advertisements they have noticed. This could still be coded in the way the question has been asked, but would allow you to gain more impression from comments like 'I saw the ad with cartoon men climbing ladders' (which was actually for a competing store!).

Question 7: This question needs an 'Other – please specify' since you should know where they are going if they are not going to the people you *think* are your competitors.

What does 'generally' mean? 'Under all normal circumstances'? If so, what circumstances cause the respondent to shop at Handy DIY?

The dots leading from the question lead the eye straight to 'Robertson's'!

Question 8: This question attempts to clarify what it is that drives people to shop at a particular place. Thus it is another candidate for 'Other – please specify' which would haul out many interesting variants.

What does the word 'goods' mean? If the intention is to isolate the indicators which govern where someone shops then this aspect of the question needs asking separately with a question which states: 'I choose the DIY store whose goods have the best: selection; range; value; price; quality'.

Should the respondent tick one or more (see comments on multiple response as in Question 6 above).

Question 9: A linguist might argue with 'all that I need . . .' but the general intention of the question should be clear.

Question 10: This question is impossible to answer because it has two variables in the question – price *and* quality. If you believe the price is good but the quality is poor then you cannot answer. This should be asked as two separate questions.

Couldn't this question be amalgamated with Question 5?

Question 11: The comments on Question 10 also apply here.

Question 12: And what happens if you live in a bungalow, a bedsitter, a tent, a hostel or hotel, a mansion, a palace? Is this question a good indicator of *anything*?

Question 13: This may give you an idea of people's socioeconomic grouping, or it may not. The little old lady left as a penniless widow in a large house is not representative. The question also assumes the respondent lives in a house.

Question 14: The options in this question are repetitive. For example, 'All my DIY needs' embraces all the other options. 'Building materials' embraces Hardware and Timber.

There are also many omissions from the list of options. Electrical, plumbing, kitchen, bathroom, tiling goods could all be included (and probably many more).

Question 15: This question implies some bias with the use of the word 'excellent'. This might be better expressed as 'Handy DIY's best department is . . .'.

The same omissions have been made as in Question 14.

Question 16: You would like to change . . . what? Your socks? The saucepans you bought last week? The intention should be made more clear: 'The thing about Handy DIY which I would most like to change is . . .'.

Question 17: The same set of answers as for Questions 14 and 15 cannot really be reused here. 'All my DIY needs' is patently absurd and is begging to be ticked! This would be a good opportunity to collect information about the *service* aspect of the store, rather than labouring the departments and/or products, which have largely been done to death at this point.

Since we have had little in the way of satisfaction scales, this might be a good opportunity for including one, addressing such features as 'Service', 'atmosphere', 'length of time in queues', 'parking facilities', 'cleanliness', 'ancillary services, e.g. catering', 'toilets', etc.

Question 18: What is this question looking for? Is it the goods or the brands? The instructions need to be made clearer.

Question 19: This question is very ill thought out. There is no 'Other – please specify' option. There is no instruction regarding multiple responses. The names are incorrect – for example, *The Telegraph* is actually *The Daily Telegraph* if we are talking about the national dailies. *The Telegraph* is a name for many regional newspapers and could be misleading. The question allows no response relating to local papers at all, yet this might be where most advertising for this store is sited.

It has to be asked whether this question is a determinant of anything useful in the survey process. In this instance it seems unlikely. Since it is so unwieldy, it would be better out! A more apposite question might be one relating to television channels viewed with the idea of tracking whether television advertising campaigns have been seen.

Question 20: So many people fall through the gaps in this question that it is probably useless. If you are a single parent, a widow or widower, divorcee, or unmarried couple with children you will not be accommodated. A widow with a 40-year-old son still living at home would be hard pressed to answer this question!

Question 21: The options in this question make no sense. The compiler was becoming bored! If you live six miles away you could legitimately tick the last three options. The options need to read 'less than a mile', 'between one and two miles', 'more than two miles away'.

If this question is being asked as a determinant of how accessible the store is to respondents it is worth considering whether two linear miles is actually a short distance or not. If you have a Mercedes, can afford taxis, have a bus route outside your door, then it is not far. If the journey involves two changes of bus or can only be undertaken on foot or by car or bike, then it is more arduous. A more useful question (perhaps ancillary) is 'How easy is it for you to get to Handy DIY?'

After revision

Figure 4.2 is my attempt to put some sense into the Handy DIY questionnaire. I am putting it there to be shot at! No questionnaire is perfect, after all.

When you examine questionnaires from a linguistic and analytical point of view, it rapidly becomes apparent that there is no such thing as a 'correct' or definitive questionnaire. The governing factors, in order, have to be:

- The objectives – what you want out.
- The audience – who will respond.
- The method – how they will respond.
- The content – what they will be asked.

Handy DIY Survey

As a previous customer of Handy DIY your options are of value to us. Please take a little time to consider the following questions, giving as honest answers as possible. The form will only take a few minutes to complete. As a 'Thank You', we would like you to accept the voucher enclosed which may be redeemed as part of any purchase from our store.

When you have completed the survey, simply fold it up and place it in the reply-paid envelope which accompanies the form or return it to our store in Haymarket, Kirkby.

Any communications regarding this survey should be made with Kirkby Konsultants on (0)123 456 789

Questions About You

1. My marital status (tick all which apply)
   - ❍ Single
   - ❍ Married
   - ❍ Divorced or separated
   - ❍ Widow or widower
   - ❍ I have children

2. I read . . .
   - ❍ The Guardian
   - ❍ The Times
   - ❍ The Daily Telegraph
   - ❍ The Daily Mail
   - ❍ The Sun
   - ❍ The Daily Mirror
   - ❍ Today
   - ❍ Other National Papers

3. My age . . .
   - ❍ Under 25
   - ❍ 25–34
   - ❍ 35–44
   - ❍ 45–54
   - ❍ 55–64
   - ❍ Over 65

4. My sex . . .
   - ❍ Male
   - ❍ Female

Questions About Your Home

5. My home has . . .
   - ❍ One bedroom
   - ❍ Two bedrooms
   - ❍ Three bedrooms
   - ❍ Four bedrooms
   - ❍ More

6. I live in a . . .
   - ❍ Detached house
   - ❍ Semi-detached house
   - ❍ Terraced house
   - ❍ Maisonette
   - ❍ Apartment
   - ❍ Bungalow
   - ❍ Bed-sitter
   - ❍ Other (please specify)

7. The distance from Handy DIY to my house is . . .
   - ❍ Less than a mile
   - ❍ Between one and two miles
   - ❍ Between two and five miles
   - ❍ More than five miles

Questions About Your Use of Handy DIY Store

8. I most recently visited Handy DIY . . .
   - ❍ In the last week
   - ❍ In the last month
   - ❍ In the last year

9. On average I visit Handy DIY . . .
   - ❍ Once a week
   - ❍ Once a month
   - ❍ Once every three months
   - ❍ Once a year
   - ❍ Less than once a year

10. Which of these special offers did you take up? (Tick all which apply)
   - ❍ £5 discount voucher in local press (Jan '94)
   - ❍ 'Two for One' promotion on plants (May '94)
   - ❍ Late Night Opening (June — July '94)
   - ❍ Christmas Bonanza Discount Sheet (December '94)

11. Our recent advertising campaign on local radio(Central FM) featured the voice of Simon Stardust. Do you remember which of these offers it was promoting?
   - ❍ Discount vouchers in local press
   - ❍ Free cup of tea for OAPs
   - ❍ Special on Bedding Plants and Vegetables
   - ❍ Grand Sale
   - ❍ I did not hear the advertisement at all

Fig. 4.2 Revised hardware store survey

Questions About What You Expect From A DIY Store

12. I choose the DIY store with the best . . .
- ❍ Prices
- ❍ Discount offers
- ❍ Staff
- ❍ Parking
- ❍ Other (Please specify)

13. I choose the DIY store whose goods have the best . . .
- ❍ Selection
- ❍ Range
- ❍ Price
- ❍ Value
- ❍ Quality
- ❍ Other (Please specify)

14. When shopping for DIY goods I usually shop at . . .
- ❍ Handy DIY
- ❍ Robertson's Hardware
- ❍ SuperSave DIY
- ❍ Nuts 'n' Bolts
- ❍ Other (Please specify)

Questions About How Well We Serve You

15. When I shop at Handy DIY I find all that I need . . .
- ❍ Every time
- ❍ Nearly always
- ❍ Sometimes
- ❍ Not very often

16. I believe that Handy DIY prices are . . .
- ❍ Similar to other DIY stores
- ❍ Lower than other DIY stores
- ❍ Higher than other DIY stores

17. I think the price of goods at Handy DIY is . . .
- ❍ Excellent
- ❍ Good
- ❍ Poor

18. I think the range of goods at Handy DIY is . . .
- ❍ Excellent
- ❍ Good
- ❍ Poor

19. I think the quality of goods at Handy DIY is . . .
- ❍ Excellent
- ❍ Good
- ❍ Poor

20. I think the availability of goods at Handy DIY is . . .
- ❍ Excellent
- ❍ Good
- ❍ Poor

21. I shop at Handy DIY for . . . (Tick all which apply)
- ❍ Gardening goods
- ❍ Hardware
- ❍ Electrical
- ❍ Decorating materials
- ❍ Building materials
- ❍ Plumbing
- ❍ Kitchen and bathroom goods
- ❍ Tiling materials
- ❍ Other (please specify)

22. I would use Handy DIY more if you stocked . . . ____________________

23. At Handy DIY I would like to change . . . ____________________

Thank you for completing this survey!

Please return the completed survey in the reply-paid envelope which accompanied it or drop it into the box in our Haymarket Store in Kirkby

The following examples from a range of contexts will give you some food for thought. If you wish to handle them and try to modify them the following questionnaires all appear as examples on the *PinPoint 3 for Windows* demonstration disk (see '*Technology Tools*', Chapter 10, for details on how to obtain this).

SAMPLE QUESTIONNAIRES

Quality Assurance and TQM

NONCONFORMANCE REPORT FORM

NCR Number: ___

Date Raised: / / ____

Section A - Problem

Raised by: ______________

Source		**Department**		**Problem Type**	
Internal	☐	Sales	☐	Production Fault	☐
Audit	☐	Purchasing	☐	Delivery Time	☐
Customer	☐	Production	☐	Delivery Condition	☐
Supplier	☐	Inspection	☐	Other	☐
Previous NCR	☐	Despatch	☐		

Description of Problem

Section B - Remedy

Proposed Remedial Action

Responsibility for Remedy

- Purchase Manager ☐
- Production Manager ☐
- Administration Manager ☐

Correction Status

- Accept with Concession ☐
- Repair with Concession ☐
- Rework to Specification ☐
- Scrap & Replace ☐
- Not Applicable ☐

Target Completion Date: / / ____

Action Check

- Accept ☐
- Reject ☐
- Further Action ☐

Section C - Improvement

Proposed Improvement Action

Responsibility for Improvement

- Purchase Manager ☐
- Production Manager ☐
- Administration Manager ☐
- Quality Manager ☐

Proposed Improvements

- Provide Training ☐
- Revise Procedure(s) ☐
- Re-engineer Production ☐
- Other ☐

Target Completion Date: / / ____

Action Check

- Accept ☐
- Reject ☐
- Further Action ☐

Section D - Close-Out

Closure Comment

Closure Date: / / ____

- Accept ☐
- Reject ☐
- Further NCR ___

Note that this is not a questionnaire, simply a form. Yet the rules governing the creation and administration of forms are generally similar to those for questionnaires.

Internal audit

THE PINBUYER COMPANY LTD

Number

PURCHASE ORDER

Date

Supplier

Delivery Address

Delivery Date

Item	Quantity	Unit Cost	Item Cost
		£ .	£ .
		£ .	£ .
		£ .	£ .
		£ .	£ .

Total Cost	£ .
+ VAT @ 17.5%	£ .
Total Payable	£ .

Approved (sign/date) ____________________

One function of internal audit is to track transactions. These might be of any type, but the order, invoice, payment trail needs to be monitored with efficiently designed forms.

Understanding your customers' needs

This questionnaire collects details of the requirements that customers have from the service offered by a mailing house. It is an intelligent attempt to find out how the business can better be configured to meet the needs of the market.

ITIS Information Services Limited

1. ABOUT YOU AND YOUR COMPANY - your address details

Are the details on your label correct ?

If not, use the box below the label to correct them:

Mr/Mrs/Ms/Miss ______ Forename ______ Surname ______

Job Title ______ Company ______

Address

______

______

Post Town ______ County ______ Postcode ______

Is there anyone else in your company who needs to know about our services ?

Name	Job Title
______	______
______	______
______	______

2. ABOUT YOU AND YOUR COMPANY - Mailing Lists

How much do you expect your use of mailing lists to increase or decrease over the next two years?

Rented Prospect Lists	Customer Database Use
☐ Decrease by 20%	☐ Decrease by 20%
☐ Stay the same	☐ Stay the same
☐ Increase by 20%	☐ Increase by 20%
☐ Increase by 50%	☐ Increase by 50%
☐ More than 50%	☐ More than 50%

Tick the boxes which match the level of expenditure you plan to make on mailing lists over the next 12 months.

Rented Prospect Lists	Customer Database Use
☐ Less than £2K	☐ Less than £2K
☐ £2K – £5K	☐ £2K – £5K
☐ £5K – £10K	☐ £5K – £10K
☐ £10K – £25K	☐ £10K – £25K
☐ £25K +	☐ £25K +

3. ABOUT YOU AND YOUR COMPANY - Your Mailings

If you don't use direct mail at present turn to Question 4.

How often do you carry out your mailings ?

- ☐ Once a year
- ☐ Twice a year
- ☐ Quarterly
- ☐ Once every month
- ☐ More often than once a month

Tick the box which matches the total size of mailings you expect to make over the next twelve months.

- ☐ Less than 10,000
- ☐ 10,000 to 20,000
- ☐ 20,000 to 50,000
- ☐ 50,000 to 100,000
- ☐ 100,000 to 250,000
- ☐ 250,000 plus

What proportion of your mailings go to consumers, as opposed to businesses ?
e.g. 50% / 50%

Consumers ___% Businesses ___%

What proportion of your mailings use an in-house list, as opposed to those rented from outside suppliers ?
e.g. 40% / 60%

In-house ___% Outside suppliers ___%

Who supplies your outside lists ?

- ☐ List brokers
- ☐ Agencies
- ☐ Mailing Houses
- ☐ List owners
- ☐ Consultants
- ☐ Others

4. ABOUT YOU AND YOUR COMPANY - What do you do ?

Briefly describe to us the activities of your company
e.g. Office equipment supplier - Direct response agency

5. ITIS DIRECT MAIL - Lists

Tick the boxes of those ITIS lists you use already or are interested in.

Use Now	Of interest
☐ UK Business Masterfile	☐
☐ European Business Lists	☐
☐ Worldwide Academic & Library File	☐
☐ International Managed	☐
☐ International Bookbuyers Masterfile	☐
☐ Euroschools	☐
☐ Other	☐

What other lists could we help you with ?

Indicate which attributes of a business list are most important to you – Rank the most important 1, the next 2 etc.

- ___ SIC (Industry) Selection
- ___ Named contacts
- ___ Selection by employee numbers
- ___ Selection by turnover
- ___ Low minimum order
- ___ Telephone numbers
- ___ Turnround time

What other selections would you use if made available on Business Lists ?
e.g. Industrial estate, Overseas, parent etc.

7. ITIS LETTERSHOP

Do you use a mailing house for the production and despatch of your mailings ?

☐ Yes ☐ No

Tick below those lettershop services you use now, and which also interest you.

Use now	Of interest
☐ Personalised letter	☐ Personalised letter
☐ Mailsort	☐ Mailsort
☐ Plastic Packaging	☐ Plastic Packaging
☐ Fulfilment	☐ Fulfilment
☐ Response analysis	☐ Response analysis
☐ Print management	☐ Print management

8. ITIS DATABASE SERVICES

Do you hold a file of your customers ?

☐ Yes ☐ No

If you do, what is the size of this file ?_______

Do you currently use this file in your marketing ?

☐ Yes ☐ No

How much do you know about your customers ?

- ☐ Size of company
- ☐ Industry Type
- ☐ Decision Maker Job Function

What else do you need to know about them ?

9. YOU AND ITIS DATABASE SERVICES

If you've used ITIS before, please indicate how pleased you've been with . . .

	Excellent	Very Good	Good	Fair	Poor
Quality of service	☐	☐	☐	☐	☐
Quality of information	☐	☐	☐	☐	☐
Results	☐	☐	☐	☐	☐
Speed of delivery	☐	☐	☐	☐	☐

The 'Persona' questionnaire is one devised by Corporate Communication Associates (CCA) for profiling companies in terms of their management style and culture. The sample of the questionnaire reproduced here generates a score according to the choice selected in each question. These scores are aggregated at the end of the questionnaire in order to provide ratings which are then interpreted from profile documentation. The average scores, which appear underneath the respondent's scores, are drawn from an accumulation of responses from other members of the same organisation being profiled.

Using profiling techniques such as these, professional consultants can build a picture of the structure, perceived culture and the underlying forces which govern a company's working practices. Authoritarian or open and participative cultures may be highlighted, and individuals' pictures of their place in the organisation help to build an overall image of the networks which make a company tick. Naturally, such analyses must be undertaken by professionals and, like any other survey, the results must have consequences for those being surveyed.

The system has been devised by CCA in line with psychological and organisational theories and any reader wishing to participate by completing one of these forms may do so by contacting CCA at the number listed at the end of this book.

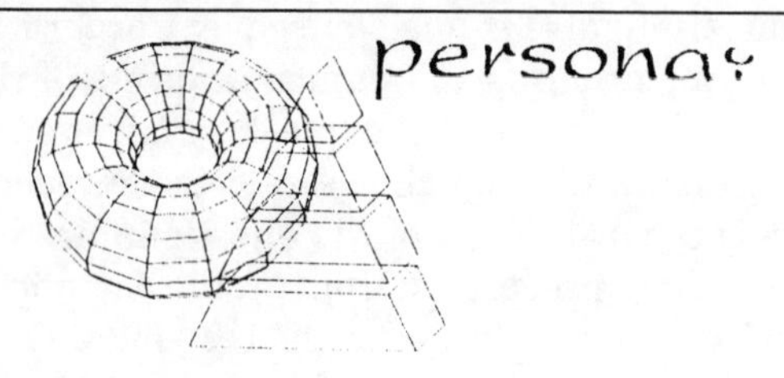

organisation culture survey

Please read each of the following statements and indicate, by ticking the appropriate box, how far you think it applies to your organisation.

	strongly agree	agree	no opinion	disagree	strongly disagree	
1.Top management usually takes employees' views into account before making major decisions.	☐	☐	☐	☐	☐	☐
2. The company is committed to equal opportunities.	☐	☐	☐	☐	☐	☐
3. The company is committed to increasing staff participation and involvement.	☐	☐	☐	☐	☐	☐
4. Most people feel free to express disagreement with their managers.	☐	☐	☐	☐	☐	☐
5. Communication between managers and staff is generally good.	☐	☐	☐	☐	☐	☐
6. Most of our managers recognise and praise good work.	☐	☐	☐	☐	☐	☐
7. A good manager is expected to supervise subordinates' work closely	☐	☐	☐	☐	☐	☐

	strongly agree	agree	no opinion	disagree	strongly disagree	
8. Wherever possible, the company gives individuals freedom to decide exactly how they should do their jobs.	☐	☐	☐	☐	☐	☐
9. There are few signs of people being under significant stress	☐	☐	☐	☐	☐	☐
10. Reasonable risk-taking is encouraged here.	☐	☐	☐	☐	☐	☐
11. Age is seldom a barrier to promotion here.	☐	☐	☐	☐	☐	☐
12. There is rarely any suspicion about the motives behind management decisions.	☐	☐	☐	☐	☐	☐

13. There are many rules and procedures governing the way people work here.	☐	☐	☐	☐	☐	☐
14. Company rules are strictly observed.	☐	☐	☐	☐	☐	☐
	strongly agree	**agree**	**no opinion**	**disagree**	**strongly disagree**	
15. Managers are able to use their intuition when making decisions.	☐	☐	☐	☐	☐	☐
16. The company has a clear vision of the kind of employer it aspires to be	☐	☐	☐	☐	☐	☐
17. You have to be a 'company-person' to succeed here.	☐	☐	☐	☐	☐	☐
18. Most employees in the company prefer to work in a large organisation.	☐	☐	☐	☐	☐	☐
19. Most of our people would prefer to work in a prestigious, successful company than one offering variety and adventure	☐	☐	☐	☐	☐	☐
20. There is mutual trust between managers and employees.	☐	☐	☐	☐	☐	☐
21. Most people are clear about what the company expects of them	☐	☐	☐	☐	☐	☐
	strongly agree	**agree**	**no opinion**	**disagree**	**strongly disagree**	
22. Most people here co-operate fully with one another.	☐	☐	☐	☐	☐	☐
23. Managers in this company enjoy a good deal of autonomy.	☐	☐	☐	☐	☐	☐
24. Job-holders are expected to be highly trained.	☐	☐	☐	☐	☐	☐
25. Individual decisions are generally regarded as superior to group decisions here.	☐	☐	☐	☐	☐	☐
26. Most people are committed to the idea of excellent customer service.	☐	☐	☐	☐	☐	☐
27. This company is very successful in financial terms.	☐	☐	☐	☐	☐	☐

Think of an ideal job for you (not necessarily your present job). Now read the following statements and indicate how important each of them would be to you personally.

I would like to	extremely important	important	slightly important	not important	
28. . . . have a challenging task which gives me a sense of achievement	☐	☐	☐	☐	☐
29. . . . work with pleasant, co-operative people.	☐	☐	☐	☐	☐
30. . . . have the freedom to determine my own approach to the job.	☐	☐	☐	☐	☐
31. . . . work for an organisation whose values I share.	☐	☐	☐	☐	☐
32. . . . have a good relationship with my manager.	☐	☐	☐	☐	☐
33. . . . have sufficient time for my family and personal life.	☐	☐	☐	☐	☐
34. . . . have a well defined job where the priorities are clear.	☐	☐	☐	☐	☐

Now, please indicate how far you agree with each of the following statements:

	strongly agree	agree	no opinion	disagree	strongly disagree	
35. A large proportion of employees in most companies avoid working hard.	☐	☐	☐	☐	☐	☐
36. A large company is generally better to work in than a small one.	☐	☐	☐	☐	☐	☐
37. A truly consultative manager will generally get the best results.	☐	☐	☐	☐	☐	☐
38. Most employees are trustworthy.	☐	☐	☐	☐	☐	☐
39. Subordinates should feel free to express disagreement with their managers.	☐	☐	☐	☐	☐	☐

40. Your name

41. Sex ☐ Female ☐ Male

42. Job title

43. Company/organisation

44. Approx no. of employees

45. Industry/nature of business

46. Address

47. Phone

Thank you for completing this questionnaire.

Cultural orientation

48. Mgt style (max 28) ☐
Average score 17

49. Tolerance of ambiguity (max 28) ☐
Average score 13

50. Reason-intuition (max 28) ☐
Average score 15

51. Teamworking (max 16) ☐
Average score 12

52. Customer orientation (max 4) ☐
Average score 3

53. Financial performance (max 4) ☐
Average score 3

54. Task preferences (max 28) ☐
Average score 15

55. Personal values (max 16) ☐
Average score 13

Understanding your customers' behaviour

The following questionnaire divides into a number of pages, each of which in the latter sections is dedicated only to a particular set of respondents. The routing through this questionnaire is critical to gaining a sensible set of responses and the compilers have attempted to indicate instructions clearly to the interviewer. It should be mentioned that this questionnaire would be administered by an interviewer rather than being filled in directly by the respondent.

Questionnaire No. ____

Date __/__/__

Interviewer's Name ______________________

Where did the interview take place?

1 ☐ At respondent's home
2 ☐ At respondent's work
3 ☐ In the street

Where was this? ☐

Respondent's details

Respondent is:
1 ☐ Male head of household
2 ☐ Female head of household
3 ☐ Not head of household

Currently employed
1 ☐ Yes
2 ☐ No

Occupation of respondent ______________________

Age ☐

Sex
1 ☐ Male
2 ☐ Female

Number of adults over 15 in household ☐

Q1. Do you ever read any daily newspapers, including evening papers?

1 ☐ Yes 2 ☐ No ***IF NO, END INTERVIEW***

Q2. Which papers do you read?

01 ☐ Times
02 ☐ Guardian
03 ☐ Independent
04 ☐ Telegraph
05 ☐ Mail
06 ☐ Express
07 ☐ Mirror
08 ☐ Sun
09 ☐ Star
10 ☐ Herald Post **GOTO Q3.**

11 ☐ Other (specify)____________________

IF HERALD POST NOT MENTIONED THEN ASK:

Q2a. Have you ever read the Herald Post?

☐ Yes

☐ No **IF NO, END INTERVIEW**

Q3. How often do you read the Herald Post during the week?

1 ☐ Every Day

2 ☐ Several times a week

3 ☐ At least once a week

4 ☐ Less than once a week

Q3a. And how about Saturdays?

1 ☐ Every Saturday

2 ☐ At least once a month

3 ☐ Less than once a month

4 ☐ Never

For office use only ____________________

Q4. Do you ever participate in Bingo, or any other competitions in the Paper?

1 ☐ Yes

2 ☐ No **GOTO Q5.**

Q4a. Which games in particular?

1 ☐ Bingo

2 ☐ Where's the Ball?

3 ☐ Other (specify)____________________

Q5. Do you have the Herald Post delivered?

1 ☐ Yes

2 ☐ No **GOTO Q6.**

Q5a. On which days do you have the Herald Post delivered?

1 ☐ Monday
2 ☐ Tuesday
3 ☐ Wednesday
4 ☐ Thursday
5 ☐ Friday
6 ☐ Saturday

WEEKDAY + SAT READERS GOTO Q8

SAT ONLY READERS GOTO Q9

WEEKDAY ONLY READERS GOTO Q5b

Q5b. If the Herald Post is not delivered on Saturday, why not?

____

____

____

______________________________ **GOTO Q7a**

Q6. When do you read the Herald Post:

1 ☐ Weekdays only **GOTO Q6g**
2 ☐ Saturdays only **GOTO Q6j**
3 ☐ Saturday and some weekdays **GOTO Q6a**

ASK ALL WHO READ WEEKDAYS AND SATURDAYS

Q6a. On weekdays, do you usually buy the Herald Post, or does another member of the household?

1 ☐ Someone else buys it
2 ☐ I buy it

Q6b. On weekdays, where is the Herald Post bought

1 ☐ On the way to/from work
2 ☐ Local shops
3 ☐ Other (specify)____________________

Q6c. At approximately what time? _______________

Q6d. On Saturdays, who buys the Herald Post?

1☐ I buy it

2☐ Someone else buys it

Q6e. Where is it bought? ______________________________

Q6f. At approximately what time? ______________

GOTO Q8.

ASK ALL WHO READ WEEKDAYS ONLY

Q6g. On weekdays, do you usually buy the Herald Post, or does another member of the household?

1☐ I buy it

2☐ Someone else buys it

Q6h. On weekdays, where is the Herald Post bought

1☐ On the way to/from work

2☐ Local shops

3☐ Other (specify) ______________________________

Q6i. At approximately what time? ______________

GOTO Q7

ASK ALL WHO ONLY BUY THE HERALD POST ON A SATURDAY

Q6j. On Saturdays, do you usually buy the Herald Post, or does another member of the household?

1☐ I buy it

2☐ Someone else buys it

Q6k. Where is the paper bought

1☐ On the way to/from work

2☐ Local shops

3☐ Other (specify) ______________________________

Q6l. At approximately what time? ______________

GOTO Q9

ASK ALL WHO READ THE HERALD POST, BUT NOT ON A SATURDAY

Q7. Are there any particular reasons why you do not buy or read the Herald Post on a Saturday?

____

____

____

____

Office use only ☐1 ☐2 ☐3 ☐4 ☐5

SHOW PAPER

Q7a. Here is a copy of the Saturday edition. How would rate the following features:

	Very Good	Good	Fair	Poor	Very Poor
Value for money	1☐	2☐	3☐	4☐	5☐
No. pages of news	1☐	2☐	3☐	4☐	5☐
No. pages of sport	1☐	2☐	3☐	4☐	5☐
TV Programmes	1☐	2☐	3☐	4☐	5☐
Classified Ads	1☐	2☐	3☐	4☐	5☐
Overall Style	1☐	2☐	3☐	4☐	5☐
Use of Colour	1☐	2☐	3☐	4☐	5☐

Q7b. Can you think of anything else you would like to see included in the paper that would tempt you to buy it?

____

____

____

____

Office use only ☐1 ☐2 ☐3 ☐4 ☐5

END INTERVIEW

ASK ALL WHO READ THE HERALD POST BOTH DURING THE WEEK AND ON SATURDAYS

Q8. How would you rate the value of the Saturday paper compared with the weekday editions?

1 ☐ As good as the weekday edition

2 ☐ Better than the weekday edition

3 ☐ Not such good value as the weekday edition

Q8a. In what way?

____

____

____

Office use only ☐1 ☐2 ☐3 ☐4 ☐5

ASK ALL SATURDAY READERS

Q9. Do you ever read any of the following articles in the paper?

Q9a. What do you think of the space allocated in the paper to the following?

	Read	Not Read	Unaware	Too Much	About Right	Too Little	Pass
TV Progs.	1☐	2☐	3☐	1☐	2☐	3☐	4☐
Sport	1☐	2☐	3☐	1☐	2☐	3☐	4☐
Style	1☐	2☐	3☐	1☐	2☐	3☐	4☐
Woman's Circle	1☐	2☐	3☐	1☐	2☐	3☐	4☐
Postal Club	1☐	2☐	3☐	1☐	2☐	3☐	4☐
News Pages	1☐	2☐	3☐	1☐	2☐	3☐	4☐
Entertainment	1☐	2☐	3☐	1☐	2☐	3☐	4☐
Classified Ads	1☐	2☐	3☐	1☐	2☐	3☐	4☐

Q10. From time to time, the Saturday edition contains a Home and Garden supplement. How do you rate this?

	Very	Not particularly	Not at all	Don't know
Interesting	1☐	2☐	3☐	4☐
Informative	1☐	2☐	3☐	4☐

END INTERVIEW

Measuring your customers' satisfaction

This questionnaire is a standard customer satisfaction survey, extensively used throughout this work. The key to this type of questionnaire is simplicity and clarity so that a busy visitor might feel inclined to fill it in as they dash for the door!

CROWN AND CASTLE HOTELS

At Crown and Castle Hotels, we aim to provide all our guests with the best possible service and facilities.

We are interested in obtaining our guests opinions on the service we offer, and would be extremely grateful if you could inform us of your thoughts on your stay with us on this occasion.

Thank you for choosing Crown and Castle Hotels and for taking the time to complete this questionnaire. We look forward to welcoming you back in the near future.

G.B Andrews, General Manager

Your Name ....

Your Address ______________

____

____

From __/ /__ **To** __/ /__

Room Number ____

Your age ☐ Under 25 ☐ 25–34 ☐ 35–44 ☐ 45–54 ☐ 55–64 ☐ Over 65

Your sex ☐ Male ☐ Female

What was the primary purpose of your visit ? ☐ Business ☐ Conference ☐ Pleasure ☐ Weekend Break ☐ Other

OUR PRODUCT

How well did we meet your expectations?	**Excellent**	**Good**	**Fair**	**Poor**
On Reservation				
accuracy of information	1☐	2☐	3☐	4☐
Your Welcome				
on arrival at reception	1☐	2☐	3☐	4☐
In Reception				
check-in speed	1☐	2☐	3☐	4☐
In the Bedroom				
cleanliness of room	1☐	2☐	3☐	4☐
overall comfort of room	1☐	2☐	3☐	4☐
general maintenance	1☐	2☐	3☐	4☐
In the Telephone Service				
staff telephone manner	1☐	2☐	3☐	4☐
speed of response	1☐	2☐	3☐	4☐

Further comments ?

OUR PEOPLE

How would you rate our staff in terms of:	Excellent	Good	Fair	Poor
Friendliness	1 ☐	2 ☐	3 ☐	4 ☐
Efficiency	1 ☐	2 ☐	3 ☐	4 ☐
Reliability	1 ☐	2 ☐	3 ☐	4 ☐
Anticipating your needs	1 ☐	2 ☐	3 ☐	4 ☐
Attending to your needs	1 ☐	2 ☐	3 ☐	4 ☐
Ability to resolve problems	1 ☐	2 ☐	3 ☐	4 ☐

Please name any member of staff who made your stay especially enjoyable ☐

OUR SERVICE

How would you rate our service ?

In the Restaurant	Excellent	Good	Fair	Poor
Anticipating your needs	1 ☐	2 ☐	3 ☐	4 ☐
Breakfast service	1 ☐	2 ☐	3 ☐	4 ☐
Quality of food and beverages	1 ☐	2 ☐	3 ☐	4 ☐
Quality of service	1 ☐	2 ☐	3 ☐	4 ☐
Ambience/decor	1 ☐	2 ☐	3 ☐	4 ☐

Further comments ?

In the Lounge or Bar	Excellent	Good	Fair	Poor
Anticipating your needs	1 ☐	2 ☐	3 ☐	4 ☐
Quality of service	1 ☐	2 ☐	3 ☐	4 ☐
Quality of food and beverages	1 ☐	2 ☐	3 ☐	4 ☐
Ambience/decor	1 ☐	2 ☐	3 ☐	4 ☐

Further comments ?

What did you like most about our Hotel ? ☐

What did you like least about our Hotel ? ☐

How would you rate our Hotel in terms of value for money ? ☐ Excellent ☐ Good ☐ Fair ☐ Poor

Thank you for taking the time to complete this questionnaire

The next questionnaire is a simple survey of student satisfaction in a college. The emphasis is on gaining graded opinions relating to aspects of their course, the amenities and the quality of life generally in the institution. This type of questionnaire could be profiled using a scoring technique to gain an overall 'score' per student. Since this type of survey is conducted on a regular basis in our institutions the possibility to compare opinions as students pass through their courses is significant. As changes occur, which they surely will, it is then necessary to pinpoint the causes.

Student Survey
Programme Evaluation 2
Academic Year 1992/3

The college aims to provide quality in our advice, education, training and level of service provided to you. Please help us in this by answering the following simple questions about getting on the course and your experiences as a new student.
We do not ask you to give your name, and we will treat any information you give us in strictest confidence.

Section 1. Yourself

Please enter course code ____ College Centre: ☐ One ☐ Two ☐ Three

Are you . . . ☐ Male ☐ Female Are you . . . ☐ 16–18 ☐ 19–22 ☐ 23–29 ☐ 30–45 ☐ 46–65

Section 2. The College

What do you think of the following features of the college? Please tick one box for each statement.

The buildings from the outside	☐ Good	☐ Acceptable	☐ Below standard	☐ Poor
The condition of the classrooms	☐ Good	☐ Acceptable	☐ Below standard	☐ Poor
The condition of specialist rooms, e.g. laboratories, workshops, etc.	☐ Good	☐ Acceptable	☐ Below standard	☐ Poor
The extent and quality of computer facilities	☐ Good	☐ Acceptable	☐ Below standard	☐ Poor
The extent and quality of library services	☐ Good	☐ Acceptable	☐ Below standard	☐ Poor
The extent and quality of private study areas	☐ Good	☐ Acceptable	☐ Below standard	☐ Poor
The extent and quality of refectory and canteen services	☐ Good	☐ Acceptable	☐ Below standard	☐ Poor
The extent and quality of social areas, e.g. student common room	☐ Good	☐ Acceptable	☐ Below standard	☐ Poor
The extent and quality of toilet and washing facilities	☐ Good	☐ Acceptable	☐ Below standard	☐ Poor

If you would like to make any further comments about lighting, heating, furniture or any other aspect of the college facilities, please do so below:

____
____
____
____

Section 3. Course Organisation
What do you think about the organisation of your course? Please tick one box for each statement.

The amount of work is . . .	❑ Too much	❑ About right	❑ Too little
The level of work is . . .	❑ Too high	❑ About right	❑ Too low
The amount of time spent in the classroom is . . .	❑ Too long	❑ About right	❑ Too short
The amount of timetabled private study is . . .	❑ Too much	❑ About right	❑ Too little
The amount of tutorial time is . . .	❑ Too much	❑ About right	❑ Too little
The length of the college day is . . .	❑ Too long	❑ About right	❑ Too short
The number of breaks throughout the day is . . .	❑ Too many	❑ About right	❑ Too few
The duration of breaks is . . .	❑ Too long	❑ About right	❑ Too short
The information you were given initially about the course proved to be . . .	❑ Very useful	❑ Adequate	❑ Inadequate
The information you were given initially about the college proved to be . . .	❑ Very useful	❑ Adequate	❑ Inadequate

If you would like to make any further comments about the organisation of your course, please do so below:

____
____
____
____

Section 4. Course Content
What do you think about your course? Please tick one box for each statement.

The teaching materials used, e.g. handouts, textbooks, etc, are . . .	❑ Good	❑ Acceptable	❑ Below standard	❑ Poor
The equipment used for practical skills work is . . .	❑ Good	❑ Acceptable	❑ Below standard	❑ Poor
The amount of support/feedback you receive as part of your course is . . .	❑ Good	❑ Acceptable	❑ Below standard	❑ Poor

If you would like to make any further comments about the content of your course, please do so below:

____
____
____
____

Section 5. Client Satisfaction

Is the course proving to be what you expected when you first started? ❑ Better than expected ❑ What you expected ❑ Disappointing

Would you recommend the course to a friend? ❑ Yes ❑ No ❑ Undecided

Thank you for your help in completing this questionnaire

Surveying a community

The following brief survey examines a random sample of cyclists and polls their opinions about specific issues and also allows them freedom to have their say about provision for cyclists. Interestingly, the version of this questionnaire used by West Sussex was distributed by handing it out to cyclists and even by fixing it to parked bikes chained up at the railway station!

West Sussex County Council

Chichester Cycle Questionnaire

MAY 1994

To help us to carry out our policy to improve conditions for cyclists in Chichester we would be grateful if you would complete this questionnaire and mark in your route on the map overleaf. A pre-paid envelope is attached.

Thank you.

Q1. About you

Q1a. What sex are you? ☐ Male ☐ Female

Q1b. Age ☐ 0–16 ☐ 17–24 ☐ 25–34 ☐ 35–44 ☐ 45–59 ☐ 60 plus

Q1c. How long have you been cycling regularly in Chichester? ⎵⎵ years

Q1d. How long have you been cycling altogether? ⎵⎵ years

Q2. About your journey

Q2a. What address did you cycle from before receiving this questionnaire?

Street ______________________ Postcode ______

Q2b. At what address did you or will you finish your cycle journey?

Street ______________________ Postcode ______

Q2c. How far have you cycled? ☐ . kms Q2d. How long did it take you? ☐ mins

Q2e. What is the purpose of your journey?

1 ☐ Work 2 ☐ Education 3 ☐ Shopping 4 ☐ Leisure 5 ☐ Other 6 ☐ Not stated

Q2f. Other (please specify) ______________________

____

Q2g. How many days a week do you cycle? ⎵ days

Q3. Have you ever had an accident? ☐ Yes ☐ No ☐ Not Stated

Q4. Accident Details

Q4a. Was another vehicle involved? ☐ Yes ☐ No

Q4b. Did the last accident involve any damage ☐ To bike ☐ To Person

Q4c. Was it reported to the police? ☐ Yes ☐ No

Q5. Your Opinion

Q5a. Where do you/would you like to park your bicycle?

____

____

____

Q5b. What other improvements do you think the council should make?

____

____

____

____

Training Needs Analysis

The following lengthy questionnaire is designed to create a profile of an individual's needs and set them against the tasks that they perform. The results from this survey would help to generate individually tailored training plans as well as giving the researcher a profile of the state of skills across the organisation. Once again, this type of questionnaire might be used on a reasonably regular basis to give a profile of the effects of training schemes upon the company and its staff.

Skills Audit Questionnaire

Page: 1

Name ☐
Division ☐
Department ☐
Job Family ☐ Level ☐ Length of time in this job (years) ☐

1. Into which category does your job fit?

- Editorial, Publishing ☐
- Sales, Promotion, Marketing ☐
- Contracts, Rights ☐
- Finance, Accounting Services ☐
- Design, Production ☐
- Administration ☐
- Customer Services, Direct Mail ☐
- Distribution, Stock Control, Warehouse ☐
- Office Services, HR, LIS ☐
- Other (please specify) ☐

Other job category ☐

2. Which computer types do you use?

- Don't have access to any machine ☐
- Apple Mac ☐
- IBM compatible PC ☐
- Workstation terminal ☐
- Other - please specify below ☐

3. Other computer type ☐

4. If you have no access to a computer, do you need it?
Yes ☐ No ☐

5. How would this access help in your job? ____________________

6. How are Information Technology (IT) and/or computers used in your job?

- Not used at all ☐
- Reference ☐
- Feed information in ☐
- Used to monitor processes ☐
- Output used in job for decision making ☐
- Partially integrated into job function ☐
- Largely integrated into job function ☐
- Other (please specify)
- Other use of IT ☐

____

7. Do you update or enter any of the following groups of data into ANY computer system? Please tick all relevant boxes.

- None ☐
- Customer data ☐
- Product data ☐
- Scheduling data ☐
- Customer orders ☐
- Customer dues ☐
- Customer credits ☐
- Customer returns ☐
- Sales data ☐
- Purchasing data ☐
- Costing data ☐
- Stock data ☐
- Financial data ☐
- Marketing data ☐

8. What IT functions do you have available to help with your job? If none, go to Question 10.

- None ☐
- Database system ☐
- Workstation enquiries ☐
- Desktop publishing ☐
- Other Workstation systems ☐
- Electronic mail ☐
- Workstation downloading ☐
- Executive information systems ☐
- Spreadsheet system ☐
- Group diaries ☐
- Word processing ☐
- End user reporting tools ☐

9. Other IT functions available to you in your job.

____

____

Skills Audit Questionnaire

Page: 2

10. What IT functions do you think you need in your job but do not have? If none, please tick none and go to Question 13.

- None ☐
- Workstation enquiries ☐
- Other Workstation systems ☐
- Workstation downloading ☐
- Spreadsheet system ☐
- Word processing ☐
- Database system ☐
- Desktop publishing ☐
- Electronic mail ☐
- Executive information systems ☐
- Group diaries ☐
- End user reporting tools ☐
- Other (please specify to right) ☐

11. Other IT functions required

____

____

____

____

12. How could the items to the left or above help you achieve your agreed objectives?

____

____

____

____

13. How would you describe your keyboard skills? Use ONE entry ONLY.

- Touch typing ☐
- Numeric pad best ☐
- One or two fingers only ☐

14. Do you need better keyboard skills?

- Yes ☐
- No ☐

15. Which Workstation enquiries do you use? If none, please tick none and go to Question 18.

- None ☐
- Title and customer ☐
- Sales/purchase/nominal ledgers ☐
- Production Costing ☐
- Sales analysis ☐
- Subscriptions ☐
- Invoice archive ☐
- Systems reference file ☐
- Inspection copies ☐
- Mailing ☐
- Royalties/Authors ledger ☐

16. Understanding Workstation enquiries. Please tick the boxes for facilities you can use.

- Able to find customer and/or title data, and use mnemonics to display it on a screen. Able to print data displayed. ☐
- Able to find invoices in the archives. ☐
- Able to display sales analysis data for customers and/or titles, and use mnemonics to display it. ☐
- Able to enquire into sales and/or purchase ledgers, or production costing and interpret the data displayed. ☐
- Able to retrieve and interpret mailing or royalty data. ☐
- Able to use the Systems Reference file to find and interpret codes. ☐

17. How did you learn your Worstation enquiries? Please tick the most appropriate box.

- Self-taught. ☐
- Taught by someone else at your desk or terminal. ☐
- Formal off-job training. ☐

Skills Audit Questionnaire Page: 3

18. Which Workstation systems do you use? If none, please tick none and go to Question 22.

- 01 None ☐
- 02 Customer order input ☐
- 03 Sales analysis ☐
- 04 Sales/purchase/nominal ledger input ☐
- 05 Production costing maintenance ☐
- 06 Subscription input & maintenance ☐
- 07 Royalty input & maintenance ☐
- 08 Stock management ☐
- 09 Shipping/dispatch ☐
- 10 Enquiries ☐
- 11 Other (please specify below) ☐
- 12 Title/customer maintenance ☐
- 13 Downloading ☐

Other Vista systems

____

____

____

19. Which Workstation system do you know best? Please enter the line number from the list above. ☐

20. What are you confident of doing on your Workstation? Please tick the relevant boxes.

- Able to perform file maintenance, e.g. adding and/or amending information to for example, customers, titles, production impressions. ☐
- Able to input data for processing by the system, e.g. customer orders/payments, supplier invoices, allocating costs to impressions. ☐
- Able to specify and submit requests for sales analysis reports. ☐

21. How did you learn your Workstation system? Please tick the most appropriate box.

- Self-taught. ☐
- Taught by someone else at your desk or terminal. ☐
- Formal off-job training. ☐

22. Could you be more productive if you had more Workstation training? Yes ☐ No ☐

23. Can you use a mouse attached to a PC or Mac? Yes ☐ No ☐

24. How well do you understand a windows environment? Please tick the relevant boxes. If you do not use a windows environment, please tick no knowledge and go to Question 26.

- No knowledge. ☐
- Able to use Icons and maximise or minimise a window. ☐
- Able to move from one window to another. ☐
- Able to modify the appearance of the screen. ☐
- Able to devise or amend own start-up routine. ☐
- Able to manage files and to secure data, or open new folders/directories. ☐
- Able to move between folders/directories. ☐
- Able to set up new applications/printers. ☐

25. How did you learn to use a windows environment?

- Self-taught. ☐
- Taught by someone else at place of work. ☐
- Formal off-job training. ☐

26. Do you need to know more about the windows environment? If no, tick no and go to Question 28. ☐ Yes ☐ No

27. How would knowing more about the windows environment help in your job?

____

____

____

____

Skills Audit Questionnaire Page: 4

28. Which spreadsheet system can you use? If none or don't know, please tick appropriate box and go to Question 33.

- None ☐
- Lotus ☐
- Excel ☐
- Other (please specify below) ☐
- Don't know what spreadsheet is ☐
- Microsoft ☐

29. Other spreadsheet ____________

30. How well do you know your spreadsheet system? Please tick the relevant boxes below.

- Able to load an existing spreadsheet file, input or change data, save and print. ☐
- Able to change format or presentation of an existing spreadsheet. ☐
- Able to add/delete columns/rows, and create new formulae to generate totals. ☐
- Able to design and create a new spreadsheet file to meet a specific requirement, including headings, column widths, formatting, presentation and creating formulae. ☐
- Able to consolidate two or more spreadsheet files. ☐
- Able to design and write macros. ☐
- Able to use graphics and other software 'add-ins' with a spreadsheet. ☐

31. Which spreadsheet do you know best?

- Lotus ☐
- Microsoft ☐
- Other (specify below) ☐

Other____________

32. How did you learn a spreadsheet system? Please tick the most appropriate box.

- Self-taught. ☐
- Taught by someone else at your place of work. ☐
- Formal off-job training. ☐

33. If you have none, do you need spreadsheet skills? If no, tick no and go to Question 35. Yes☐ No☐

34. If you have none, how would spreadsheet knowledge help in your job?

....

....

....

....

Skills Audit Questionnaire Page: 5

35. Which word processors can you use? If none, please tick none and go to Question 40.

- None ☐ 1
- Word ☐ 2
- Wordperfect ☐ 3
- Displaywrite ☐ 4
- Other (please specify below) ☐ 5

36. Other word processor ....

37. If you know a word processor, which do do you know best? Enter the box number from Q.35

☐

38. How well do you understand your word processor? Please tick the relevant boxes below.

Able to create and revise documents, editing and saving text. Printing. ☐

Able to use at least three of the following: dual column; maths; pagination; directories; spell check; headers/footers; mail/merge; change pitch/pointsize; line drawing. ☐

Knowledge of complete repertoire of the package, and having confidence to use most features if necessary. ☐

39. How did you learn word processing? Please tick the most appropriate box below.

- Self taught. ☐
- Taught by someone else at your place of work. ☐
- Formal off-job training. ☐

Answer no more questions.

40. If don't have a word processor, do you need one? If no, answer no more questions.

Yes ☐ No ☐

41. If you had a word processor, how would it help you achieve your objectives? ....

....

....

....

....

For office use only

☐ 1
☐ 2
☐ 3
☐ 4
☐ 5

Thank you for your cooperation. Please return the completed form to Room 202 'Personnel'.

Layout of a questionnaire

- **In this section you will be able to examine all the design elements which help to make your questionnaire more readable**
- **The subject of routing (guiding the respondent from one questionnaire to the next) will be examined and its importance for data entry will be discussed**
- **The final presentation of a questionnaire will be considered, up to the print stage**

This section deals with a number of issues including style, presentation and routing (illustrating the route through the questionnaire). Although few people creating questionnaires are professional designers there are simple ideas which will help keep your survey looking professional and neat. Do *not* use a typewriter! A good quality desktop publisher or word processor, or better still a dedicated questionnaire design system (see *'Technology tools'*, Chapter 10) will help to create the polished look that you require.

The way in which you present your questionnaire will determine in many ways how the respondent uses it. A shoddy looking questionnaire will elicit shoddy answers. If the respondent feels that you have not bothered to make the questionnaire easy to read, clean-looking and clear then they will have little confidence that you are going to look after their answers very well either.

FONTS AND POINT SIZES

The font (the typeface and its various styles) which you choose for your questionnaire will either help or hinder readability. First-time desktop publishers go wild with the fonts, having discovered that there are so many to play with. The end result looks like a seaside playbill! There are some simple rules to follow with fonts and styles, but first let's examine the variety of opportunity which typography offers us. In any piece of text you may have a style which is:

- sans serif
- serif
- underlined
- CAPITALISED
- **emboldened**
- *italicised*

Serif and sans-serif describe the generic nature of fonts. Those with serifs (the twirls and ornaments of a slightly more ornate font) are supposed to be easier to read in volume. Sans-serif is plainer and has a clean look but does not lead the eye so well – that is the theory. In the final analysis, personal preference and whichever you think suits the nature of your printed material must be the arbitrators.

As for the other ornaments (underline, bold and italics) these are all variants on the original style and may be used to highlight and to characterise particular aspects of your questionnaire. For example, some simple conventions make everyone at ease with the questionnaire because they know the rules:

- Plain text for the question itself.
- Italicised for the instructions to the respondent.
- Capitals for instructions to an interviewer.
- Bold to emphasise a difficult or easily missed factor such as '*Choose **one** option only*'.

The *point size* of text refers to the scale, measured in points used by typographers. Most text in books is usually 10 or 12 point, depending upon the font being used. This book is set largely in 10 point Century Schoolbook. Be consistent with the size of text used for:

- The title.
- Headings.
- Subheadings.
- Introductory text.
- Question text.
- Instruction text.

Decide in advance what all of these should be and set them up in your system before you begin. Do not choose too many different fonts, nor too many sizes. Use bold and italic to differentiate rather than having text zooming up and down in size like a typographer's nightmare.

The question

The layout of a question is critical to gaining a sensible answer. Economy of space must be traded off against legibility and ease of use. Although questions should not be cramped up together in an unreadable mass, nor should they be distributed three to a page unless the answer area warrants this. Not only is it hugely wasteful of paper and print, it is quite trying continually to have to turn the pages when the whole thing could have been fitted into a much smaller space.

The response area

Similarly, the response area for the question should be laid out in the most economical but effective manner. A set of multiple choice questions, all with the same set of responses need not be printed with their answer options aligned vertically but can be turned tidily into a table question which takes less space, is easier to read and much easier to data enter afterwards (Fig. 5.1).

(a)

In the Lounge or Bar

Anticipating your needs
☐ Excellent
☐ Good
☐ Fair
☐ Poor

Quality of food and beverage
☐ Excellent
☐ Good
☐ Fair
☐ Poor

Quality of service
☐ Excellent
☐ Good
☐ Fair
☐ Poor

Ambience/decor
☐ Excellent
☐ Good
☐ Fair
☐ Poor

Fig. 5.1 Layout (a) can be reduced to (b)

(b)

In the Lounge or Bar	Excellent	Good	Fair	Poor
Anticipating your needs	1 ☐	2 ☐	3 ☐	4 ☐
Quality of service	1 ☐	2 ☐	3 ☐	4 ☐
Quality of food and beverages	1 ☐	2 ☐	3 ☐	4 ☐
Ambience/decor	1 ☐	2 ☐	3 ☐	4 ☐

ALIGNMENT OF QUESTION AND ANSWER SPACES FOR CLARITY

All questions can suffer from the 'disassociation' effect: the question, tightly packed in with other questions in a block, that has its response frames across the other side of the page, for some reason best known to the compiler (Fig. 5.2). Not only is this tricky, when answering, for the respondent to choose the correct question box (never mind the correct response) it is even more difficult for the person entering data to be consistently accurate. Cross-correlation errors, particularly when entering data in a different format from that on the form, is sufficiently fraught with problems without the compiler introducing another element of chance into the equation.

Q3. How often do you read the Herald Post during the week?	
Every day	☐ 1
Several times a week	☐ 2
At least once a week	☐ 3
Less than once a week	☐ 4

Fig. 5.2 Disassociating response from options

If that spacing is really necessary, one solution is to introduce rulings across the sheet. They need only be feint, perhaps dotted lines, but they will allow the eye to travel comfortably from the question to the response frame without the need for a ruler. With large numbers of questions, however, this will look cluttered and messy. Notice in Fig. 5.3 how the response boxes are aligned left of the response in order to avoid this very problem.

2. ABOUT YOU AND YOUR COMPANY – Mailing Lists

How much do you expect your use of mailing lists to increase or decrease over the next two years?		Tick the boxes which match the level of expenditure you plan to make on mailing lists over the next 12 months.	
Rented Prospect Lists	**Customer Database Use**	**Rented Prospect Lists**	**Customer Database Use**
☐ Decrease by 20%	☐ Decrease by 20%	☐ Less than £2K	☐ Less than £2K
☐ Stay the same	☐ Stay the same	☐ £2K–£5K	☐ £2K–£5K
☐ Increase by 20%	☐ Increase by 20%	☐ £5K–£10K	☐ £5K–£10K
☐ Increase by 50%	☐ Increase by 50%	☐ £10K–25K	☐ £10K–£25K
☐ More than 50%	☐ More than 50%	☐ £25K +	☐ £25K +

Fig. 5.3 Avoiding disassociation

Aiming for a clean look, the most appropriate method is to move the elements together. It may be more sensible, for instance, to align the questions in two separate columns on the page, divided by a vertical rule or placed into a frame (see next section).

BOXES AND RULES

Boxes or frames surrounding questions can be used with great effect in order to section off parts of the questionnaire for particular purposes (Fig. 5.4). For instance, if there is a need on the form to collect the name and address of the respondent, this can be placed in a frame on one section of the page, followed by another frame for their opinions about the quality of rides at the theme park, then a section on how they travelled there, and lastly a section on their opinions about the catering facilities. With each set of questions in its own frame the questionnaire has logical grouping and looks more attractive.

Your Name ____________

Your Address ____________

____

____

From __/__/__ To __/__/__

Room Number ___

Your age ☐ Under 25 ☐ 25–34 ☐ 35–44 ☐ 45–54 ☐ 55–64 ☐ Over 65

Your sex ☐ Male ☐ Female

What was the primary purpose of your visit ? ☐ Business ☐ Conference ☐ Pleasure ☐ Weekend Break ☐ Other

Fig. 5.4 Boxes or frames can make a questionnaire more attractive

USE OF FRAMES, GRIDS, LINES AND COMBS FOR DATA ENTRY

The actual data entry area where the respondent writes their response, ticks the box, enters the ranking or whatever response is required, can have a variety of designs for different purposes. In its simplest form the question has a line or bracket on which the respondent enters an answer, for example:

Your Name -----------

This is fine for text and numerics but gives little indication of what sort of response is required. It may seem obvious, but it is important to give enough space for the response to be made. A short line to accommodate an 'Any other comments' response is unrealistic.

Similarly, a frame may be used to indicate where data is to be entered. A frame generally indicates that you would be writing a word or phrase or a number in a small space. That is, of course, unless you had made a large frame for 'Other comments' (Fig. 5.5).

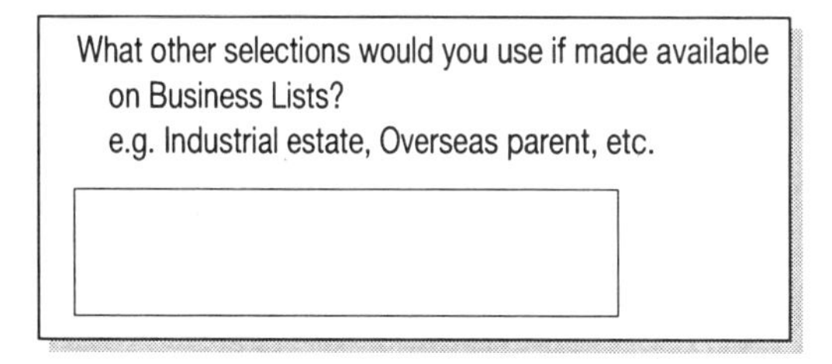

Fig. 5.5 A frame for 'Other comments'

The grid (prison bars!) is used to make people print separate letters, supposedly for clarity when data entering. My instinct is always to write freehand straight through these (which probably says something about me!) and my opinion is that if the respondent does not have the sense to write clearly in any case, then putting an obstruction to flow of response such as this type of frame is not going to improve matters. Apart from entering credit card numbers there seems little point (and why are there never enough boxes in the grid?). Since this system indicates how much space has been allocated in the data file for this information, it gives you an impression of what they want (below), and also the fact that they have not researched sufficiently carefully to see how much space is needed!

Q11. How many microcomputers are currently installed at your worksite? ☐☐☐☐☐☐ computers

Slightly less annoying is the comb (below). This does at least allow you to continue the flow of writing, but indicates how many characters are available for data entry. Interestingly, this is also the format commonly used for pen-based computers which recognise handwriting and that type of support is built into some software for questionnaires (see *'Technology tools'*, Chapter 10).

County Postcode

As mentioned throughout this section, the intention of many of these formats is to constrain the respondent to answer with an appropriate number of characters. A further technique which is additional to the formats above, is to make it very clear how the response is to be made, either by giving an example response to begin with or by constraining the format with a 'picture' which prevents the respondent from entering in any way other than that which you have chosen. For instance, numeric or monetary values can be constrained simply by providing a line with the necessary leading character and decimal point:

Total expenditure £

Whichever forms of entry area you use, they must be used consistently throughout your questionnaire. The respondent, the interviewer, the data entry clerk will all then recognise what is required at any given point simply because you have adhered to a simple set of conventions. For example:

- Text questions: a line –
- Numerics: a frame –
- Multiple choice: square shadowed tickbox - ❑ 1
- Ranked: short bracket – 1
- Further comments: large frame
- Dates: pictured line – / /

GROUPING AND ROUTING QUESTIONS

Grouping is all about structure, about thinking out beforehand how the questions are tied together naturally and the possible routes from one question or group to another. With that forethought you can indicate clearly to the respondent much about your intentions, about the nature of the data being collected and the style of answer required.

Natural groups of questions can give the respondent a feeling of having crossed hurdles, particularly in long questionnaires. They have reached the end of the section – it contains all the questions which are logically linked together and need continuity of thought. They now stop, make a cup of coffee, then return to finish the rest.

This effect can be achieved simply by using an outline box or by dividing the page off with horizontal rules between each section (see '*Boxes and rules*', p. 142). In a desktop publisher, word processor or a dedicated questionnaire system this effect is easy to achieve.

There is a further benefit from grouping questions when using questionnaire software. Not only may the respondent see the nature of the groups explicitly on the questionnaire form, but the data entry and analysis areas can also benefit from the ability to handle questions in blocks. Therefore, for instance, it may be possible to display just the 'Personal' or 'Satisfaction' questions and omit the others from the analysis. Equally it also means that in the design area, questions may be moved *en masse* and copied as a block from one form to another, enabling the use of archiving to save time at the design stage. If you always begin a questionnaire with this block of questions, you should only ever need to design them once!

The route through the questionnaire

You rarely need to print a route map to show where the respondent should go next when they have answered a question. The natural sequence of questions down columns, across boxes or following a numbered sequence is usually fine, provided that there are no 'skip' situations. It is important, however, that your questionnaire should cope with all contingencies. Every possible route that can be tracked should be tested to ensure that it:

- makes sense to the respondent
- includes all the necessary questions whichever way through you go
- gives ample opportunity for appropriate responses.

Routing from one question to another

The principle of routing has two variants – routing which explicitly moves you directly to another question, skipping other questions, as a result of your answer and secondly, hierarchical routing which takes you into another part of the questionnaire or even into another questionnaire altogether as a result of your answer. Although the two are similar, the first enables the compiler to keep tabs on the accuracy of answers and saves time and confusion in data entry whereas the second divides the questionnaire into major groups and points the respondent only into those areas which are relevant.

Explicit routing can be achieved in a number of ways. The questionnaire will begin with those questions which establish the subsequent route. The process should be natural and, like a flowchart, should be capable of being traced easily. A question may ask:

In which area of the company do you work?		
	Clerical	❑ 1
	Administrative	❑ 2
	Engineering	❑ 3
	Sales	❑ 4
	Marketing	❑ 5
	Accounts	❑ 6

The route from that question to further questions depends upon the answer being given. There is little point in someone in the engineering section answering the questions which are aimed at clerical staff. However, unless the question bears instructions which clearly indicate where the respondent goes next, they will try to answer every question!

Criminal Investigation Department

Quality of Service - Victim Satisfaction

Sub-Div : [ ] Month : [ ]

My name is and I am phoning you on behalf of Mid-Counties Police. I am contacting selected members of the public who had recently had cause to call upon us for our advice or assistance. I would like to ask you a few questions to measure your satisfaction with the service we provided.

Type of Crime :
- Burglary ☐
- Robbery ☐
- Auto Crime ☐
- Offence against the Person ☐
- Theft ☐
- Criminal Damage ☐

How satisfied or dissatisfied are you that the police responded quickly enough to your request for assistance ?
- Very satisfied ☐
- Satisfied ☐
- Neither satisfied nor dissatisfied ☐
- Dissatisfied ☐
- Very dissatisfied ☐

Have you received any further visits from specialised departments since your initial report ?
- Yes ☐
- No ☐

If 'YES' - who from ?
- C.I.D. ☐
- S.O.C.O. ☐
- Both ☐
- Uniform ☐

If 'NO' - would you have expected any visit from :
- C.I.D. ☐
- S.O.C.O. ☐
- Both ☐
- None ☐

Have you received any progress report on the investigation of your case ?
- Yes ☐
- No ☐

If 'YES', how were you contacted ?
- Personal Visit ☐
- Letter ☐
- Telephone ☐

If 'NO', would you have expected a progress report by now ?
- Yes ☐
- No ☐

Were you given AND would you have expected advice on the following:

	Given	Expected
Victim Support	Yes ☐ No ☐	Yes ☐ No ☐
Criminal Injuries	Yes ☐ No ☐	Yes ☐ No ☐
Insurance Claims	Yes ☐ No ☐	Yes ☐ No ☐
Crime Prevention	Yes ☐ No ☐	Yes ☐ No ☐
How the enquiry would progress	Yes ☐ No ☐	Yes ☐ No ☐

Did you expect your crime to be detected ? Yes ☐ No ☐

Reasons : ....

Do you know the name of the investigating officer ?
- Yes ☐
- No ☐

If 'NO', do you feel you should know ? Yes ☐ No ☐

Do you know your Crime Reference Number ? Yes ☐ No ☐

If 'NO', do you feel you should know ? Yes ☐ No ☐

What is your overall impression of Mid-Counties Police as a result of the way you were dealt with on this occasion ?
- Very Good ☐
- Good ☐
- Adequate ☐
- Poor ☐
- Very Poor ☐

What good or bad points influenced this impression ?

....

Is there anything further you wish to comment upon ?
(Please continue overleaf)

Fig. 5.6 Routing questions graphically

The route on Fig. 5.6 is illustrated graphically with arrows on the questionnaire and with instructions. The analogy with a flowchart might be made here. Frequently, instructions alone are not sufficient to ensure that answers are entered correctly. Bear in mind that people do not always have their brains switched on when filling out a questionnaire. The boxes and arrows in the example above can make things clearer although the overall appearance, if there are many such routes to be shown, will look messy and cluttered unless very well designed.

Routing from one section to another

Using general questions in one section which are elaborated upon in another is a technique by which you again are able to impose orderliness upon your questionnaire. It may be that your respondent is asked to complete some general replies about the nature of the technical support that they received from the company. If necessary (particularly if responses indicate dissatisfaction) the respondent may then be guided to a section which analyses their opinion and the causes for their dissatisfaction in more depth. Naturally, if they had not been dissatisfied then this section of the questionnaire would not have been relevant for them. The structure and the way in which these questions are designed will ensure that they do not need even to see them.

Beware of making your respondent dot around too much through the questionnaire. Where possible, keep the flow natural, but where relevant, jump out of the loop, answer additional relevant questions and then jump back in again.

Using specific questions which branch out to separate questionnaires

In the same way it may be that a single questionnaire is inadequate to the task of collecting the necessary responses. It is better to have two or three separate and clear questionnaires than to have a massive, daunting book full of questions which, although they may not all need to be answered, will look like a mountain top climb as far as the respondent is concerned. Of course, if the questionnaire is being administered by an interviewer then there will be less difficulty. However, do not make any assumptions about the interviewer's understanding of the route through that questionnaire. They are just as likely as the respondent to be working on automatic pilot!

The response to a given question or group may split the respondent off onto another questionnaire sheet or booklet immediately. This type of questionnaire is called hierarchical and the nature of any route through the questionnaire excludes responses from the other routes. In other words, once you start down the hierarchical tree, you cannot jump across to another branch. This type of questionnaire is an end result of clear planning and structuring at the design stage. Hierarchical questionnaires are not born by accident!

The other type of routing out to separate questionnaires takes place at a later date, as a result of the collection and analysis of responses. For example, it may be that a public service such as a housing department have surveyed their customers about their housing needs in the next three years. Those people who have indicated that they have a need for new housing and that it applies to more than one member of the family (e.g. there are two brothers both of whom will require separate housing in the next three years) will receive a further questionnaire which asks for more details about the specific needs of those two individuals.

Naturally, this process could have been achieved upon a single questionnaire, but the complexity that it introduces as far as collection of responses is concerned might mean that it is more effective to tackle the issues separately.

OTHER ELEMENTS ON YOUR QUESTIONNAIRE

Apart from questions, response areas and instructions on your questionnaire form, you may decide to add other ornaments:

- to make it look attractive
- to identify the company through the house style
- to mark association with other companies or bodies.

The presentation of this type of material depends very much on how much importance you decide to give to it. Consider making a separate cover for your questionnaire which bears all the promotional information which you wish to communicate but keeps it separate from the content of the questionnaire. From the company's or organisation's point of view you may wish to include:

- Company logo.
- Company information.
- Statement of intent and principle.

The last of these is a statement of confidentiality and adherence to a code of practice. The Market Research Society has a standard form for this statement which is adopted by all its members. If you are not a member of the society (and membership is well worth considering) then the statement can be modified so that no reference to the society is made, but a statement of principle shows that you are following the standards of a code of practice. In addition you may wish to consider giving the respondent some reassurance about the confidential nature of the answers they give.

PRINTING

Creating a dazzlingly beautiful questionnaire is largely wasted effort if you then print it out on a tired and sloppy dot-matrix printer with a worn ribbon! Create a master plate from which the copies will be duplicated. If you have a laser printer this will be quite adequate to the task. If not, and in default of borrowing someone else's (remember you could take the disk to their machine), then a print bureau will be able to run off a copy of the questionnaire for you in any one of a number of formats, ready for printing. For short runs that will be made on a photocopier, a good quality laser print will be quite acceptable. If you are intending to undertake a print run then you will need to discover the medium in which your printer requires the master. Printshops should be able to run out a master copy on bromide or film at a reasonable cost.

The method for creating all the copies you need is best determined by looking at the quantity you require. A hundred or so single sheets will probably be reasonably economically done on a photocopier. Beyond that the cost of a professional print run becomes more attractive, particularly if the questionnaire is multi-page and requires stapling. The costs for print are very competitive with photocopying, even when using a short run at a High Street print shop. It is worth monitoring prices and examining where the photocopier becomes less viable – the cost per sheet can be quite staggeringly high, depending upon your contract.

It is also worth bearing in mind that a properly printed questionnaire looks much superior to a photocopy, particularly when paper other than standard 80 gram copier is used. Your survey of the chairmen of boards of the top 500 companies in the country is much more likely to be answered if it looks professional and crisp.

The key factors are:

- Design the questionnaire carefully for clarity.
- Be consistent with styles of text and ornaments.
- Do not crowd the page.
- Align elements consistently.

- Show routes through the questionnaire clearly.
- Consider print volume and . . .
- Create a master copy appropriately for . . .
- Relevant printing method.

Data entry and ambiguity

- **In this section data entry (putting responses into a data system) is examined**
- **Techniques and systems for data entry are reviewed**
- **Problems that occur with data entry are discussed**

'*There's many a slip 'twixt cup and lip*' as the old saying has it. Never was this more true than in surveys. Get the questionnaire right and the respondent may still misunderstand and give you invalid data. They misread the instructions. They misread the question. They misunderstand the type of answer required. Sometimes these problems are the fault of the questionnaire compiler and sometimes are because the respondent is paying no attention to what they are doing. Equally, interviewers who are presenting questions to respondents in the street or at their place of work or home, may misinterpret your intentions. For that reason you need to bolt down:

- The instructions – are they simple and clear. Do they *really* explain what is required (see the next two points).
- The question and its intention – is it clear what you mean, what you are asking?
- The answer and its specification – is it clear whether the respondent should write words, write numbers, tick one box, two boxes, tick as many boxes as they want, put all of the options into a ranked order . . . or what?

These topics are addressed elsewhere in the book but they stand reiteration. Without clear question design there will be no clear or accurate data.

Get valid data on the form and the data entry clerk may mistype, misinterpret or miscorrelate answers with questions unless you put in safeguards. Things can be expected to go wrong with data when the question is ambiguous either in its nature or in the form in which the respondent believes the answer should be presented. You would expect that someone would be able to enter it correctly though, wouldn't you? The answer, as ever, is yes and no. If it were you who was entering the data then it would be accurate to a large extent except for typographical errors and the odd slip. Someone who is paid to hammer as much data into a data system as they can over a seven-day period is not interested in data integrity. They are interested in getting to the end of another form. If it is not clear what they have to enter then they may make it up, ignore it or make misguided attempts to interpret it.

The phone rings, the coffee trolley arrives, the attractive man/woman from the next office walks by, the lunch break or the end of the day intervenes and the data entry process stops. If it picks up where it left off, accurately and without any slip that is a tribute to the organisational skills of the individual doing the work. More often you will be left with incomplete data on that record or a duplicate record, or no record of that dialogue at all. If one multiplies that over a number of staff all doing the same thing then the level of error in the data can become quite staggeringly high.

You can minimise these effects in the way in which you design your form and in the type of database management system you use. It is important to make life as easy as possible for those who enter data for you. If there are obstacles then the process becomes more unreliable. An obstacle may be:

- Unclear specification of answer type to enter.
- Poor form layout which has no logical route through it.
- Poor form layout which is difficult to read.
- Poor response quality – lots of written word in bad handwriting.
- Dissimilar form for the data system from the one used in the survey.
- Lack of motivation, especially when the number of forms is large.

Form design quality will govern the first three problems. Unless your operator instructions are clear then you may find data misentered or misinterpreted. If the route through the form is not obvious then answers for one question may become transposed with those for another. If the form is cramped up with too little space for the respondent to make their answers clear then you can expect a high rate of poor data. In the fourth problem you have made life difficult by insisting upon written answers. Are you sure that they need to be written? Can they not better be accommodated by ranges or ranked questions which are much easier and quicker to enter and have a higher degree of analysis capability? If there needs to be so much written word, have you assessed whether entering the data is actually a worthwhile occupation at all, particularly if this is all qualitative information rather than something that can be quantified.

The fifth problem has to do with the type of system used to collect the data. Many organisations create their surveys on desktop publishers, word processors or even typewriters. They enter data on a form in a database system which bears little resemblance to the structure of the questionnaire or, even worse, type the responses into the cells on a spreadsheet. Think of the problems inherent in this: you have a series of responses, all very similar, in a multiple choice question – we shall deal with the answers for only one question here. Each time you come to enter the answer for that question you must type it in full into the cell. This is not too much of a problem if the answer is 'Excellent' or 'Good', but if it is 'Prefer to stay at home and read the paper' it becomes arduous. One other aspect of the problem is that your typist may enter 'Excellent', 'Excelletn', 'excellent', 'Excellen' or any other variant, each of which has an unique characteristic which will be picked up on by the database system to show it as a separate and different response.

For this reason, most traditional systems insist on a numbered code next to each option so that you type in '2' instead of 'Good' or '1' instead of 'Excellent'. The data are then only readable by computers in effect because, in its codified form, it loses meaning. How much easier then to have an identical form on screen which will capture the data simply by means of the operator placing a mark in the relevant tick-box or choosing the correct option. This then places the data into the system without the need for typing. Simple? It is one of the features of *PinPoint for Windows* (available from Longman Logotron), whose demonstration disk may be obtained free of charge (contact the company at the address at the end of this book).

METHODS OF DATA ENTRY – THEIR BENEFITS AND PITFALLS

There are many ways in which data can be collected. How you do it largely depends upon the size of the questionnaire itself and how many responses you expect to handle. Naturally, your data collection method should be appropriate to your survey size.

By hand

Before the days of computers the only way in which survey data could be captured was by tallying and hand-calculated analysis. Not only is this laborious but it also missed the magic ingredient of experimentation (playing with the data) which computers are so good at. Hand-tallying of results is either a question of keeping a tally sheet record of the number of any given response or the summation of numeric values. Survey techniques have come to where they are now directly as a result of the information technology revolution. They allow analysis of large volumes of data with ease.

By keyboard

Hand-entered data will always suffer from the problems mentioned earlier. Keyboard data entry suffers from mistyping as well as misreading of data. Punching keys will always be a marginally random activity unless one is a highly proficient touch typist.

By optical mark reading (OMR)

Further refinements of information technology techniques for data entry are the optical mark reader and the scanner. These are machines which will, in conjunction with appropriate software, read forms automatically with no need for human intervention. The two techniques (OMR and scanning) are radically different and have different capabilities:

OMR (optical mark reading) is a system which works through a technique whereby the computer recognises patterns of marks in predetermined positions on the response form. An OMR form may simply be a matrix of numbered check boxes or it may take the form of a more traditional looking questionnaire with boxes next to all options for each question.

One of the limitations of this technology is that it constrains the questionnaire compiler to use only multiple choice (range) questions. This is because no textual data are entered by the system and statistics are based upon the frequency or the count of the marks made on the page. For this reason OMR is used for more traditional form-filling activities such as attendance registers or examination test papers.

HARDWARE NEEDED

The mark reading hardware is less sophisticated than that needed for scanning, but it is very sensitive, particularly to the standard stationery which is used for the forms. Attempts to use home-produced, desktop published forms result in a higher level of inaccuracy as the forms are scanned. The inconsistencies of scale between a computer-designed page and the output from a printer make it very difficult to guarantee the accuracy of the data. Since it is very difficult to know whether a form has been entered correctly or not, anything other than 100 per cent reliability is unacceptable.

BUREAU

Bureaux specialising in reading OMR forms exist and they also offer services for the design and publication of the forms for your purposes. Their facilities will be quite expensive but the quality of their equipment will guarantee a high degree of accuracy in data input.

By scanner

Scanners work in a different fashion from an OMR system. The scanner recognises a complete page photographically. Changes in the image of that page are recorded as data according to the criteria that the system has been 'taught'. For example, it may be that a page will contain a number of multiple choice tick boxes. The system can be taught to recognise the meaning of a tick in any given box. Similarly, the system can learn that certain areas contain text or numbers in a particular format. If the scanner system also contains an optical character recognition (OCR) system then it can make attempts to interpret the text that has been entered on the form. This will, of course, very much depend upon whether responses have been typed or hand written. In the latter case there is a larger requirement for intervention by human operators to check and validate the data.

HARDWARE NEEDED

Scanning hardware is available in an wide variety of configurations and prices. For high volume, high accuracy scanning including OCR there is a need for high specification scanners with sheet feeder. Low volume work without any OCR overhead is going to be tackled adequately by a much cheaper model of scanner. It is also likely that you will need a card to go in the back of your computer which will decode the signal from the scanner and turn it into the data format which your software can recognise. Not all scanners need this because some have that hardware on board already and send the finished data straight in through one of the ports on the back of your computer.

The problem with such hardware and software is that you may well use it once or twice a year, but what do you do with it for the rest of the time? For this reason, consider sharing resources with other departments in your business or institution, if that is a possibility. A three-way investment in a piece of kit such as a scanner can make budgets go much further.

WHEN THINGS GO WRONG IN DATA ENTRY

Data entry can go wrong for a number of reasons. Apart from the reasons mentioned earlier in this section (see above) there are data errors which are hidden deeper in the responses themselves, caused often by the respondent's misinterpretation of what is required or caused by unclear specification leading to confusion. To illustrate the latter instance, how would you answer the question:

Do you live in . . .		
	The Town	❑ 1
	The Country	❑ 2
	A Village	❑ 3
	A Hamlet	❑ 4

An apparently simple question requires more than one response if you live in a village in the country. The respondent's confusion may override instructions to tick one box only. Your data entry operator may well have been told to enter one response only. Which do they choose? Worse, if the system is an automatic scanner, what happens then?

Multi-response answers are allowable, of course, under some circumstances. You may wish people to tick as many responses as apply in a particular question, and your data entry system will be able to accommodate multiple responses – won't it? If you are entering data on a spreadsheet, how do you configure the cell containing the answer for the following question:

19. I read . . .	
	❍ The Guardian
	❍ The Times
	❍ The Telegraph
	❍ The Mail
	❍ The Sun
	❍ The Mirror
	❍ Today

A data cell on a spreadsheet or a single text field on a database will only accommodate a single response, unless of course you simply type this data (or its codes) in a long string into the one entry area. This makes analysis difficult, however, and cannot easily be overcome. What exactly do you want to do with the answers from this question? It is likely that you will simply be totalling the number of responses for any given newspaper in order to see which has been the most read, ever. In that case, each separate response really needs to be entered as a separate data 'bite' in a response area of its own. You may need, for example, to include a response area on your data system for perhaps up to three or four newspapers. In that case you may wish to change the question to:

Which three of the following newspapers have you read the most frequently?

Not answered, not asked and 0

In your collection of data ensure that you legislate for a variety of opt-outs: *'not answered'*, *'not asked'*, *'don't know/won't say'*. All of these have importance as a response (or lack of it) since it may tell you something about the state of mind of the respondent.

- *Not answered:* This simply means that the respondent failed to answer the question – or does it? Could it also mean that the interviewer failed to ask it or that the data entry operator skipped it accidentally. Cure the two problems by ensuring that interviewers clearly code questions which have not been put to the respondent as 'Not asked'. In the software on which your data are entered look for a part of the system which constrains an answer to any or all questions before the operator can move on to the next record in order to avoid the data entry 'misses'.
- *Not asked:* A positive entry by an interviewer in a face-to-face or telephone interviewer indicates that for reasons governed either by time, the nature of previous answers or the disposition of the respondent, the question was not put. A note about why the question was not asked, if not obvious, will help understanding of the circumstances.
- *Don't know/won't say:* If someone doesn't answer because they do not know the answer this tells you more about them or the situation than simply recording 'Not answered'. The 'Don't knows' may be in a majority and highlight a need for an information exercise on the part of management, steering committee or governing body.

Not answering – what does it mean?

When the respondent leaves the response blank, what exactly is the cause? Have they forgotten to put an answer? Are they insulted by the question? Did they have a heart attack at this point? Any one of a number of reasons can be responsible for empty answers and you need to have legislated for them if your data are to contain meaning in this area. A 'not answered' may be a positive response to a question in one of a number of ways:

- *Don't know:* The respondent simply has no idea of the answer and has left the space empty. Do you need to know that they don't know? Might it be significant in the analysis that 20 per cent of your respondents did not know whether they agree with the statement that 'A bypass will benefit our village'.

- *Won't say:* Quite different from 'Don't know' is 'Won't say', although the two are often lumped together as a single option for response. If someone will not say what they think that may be because they feel threatened by the situation – the bosses are spying on me; the tax officers are closing in; the paranoia which I have says that this is all a conspiracy. Some of these reasons are ones which you may need to uncover – Why does he/she feel threatened and why do they believe that the management would spy on them in this way? Is this symptomatic of another problem, apart from the usual 'us and them' scenario?
- *Missed it by accident:* If the two responses above are present and yet no response has been entered then you can assume that it was missed out by accident by the respondent or perhaps by the interviewer. A blank, provided you have offered the 'don't know/won't say' option, can then be interpreted as another item of data (it was missed) and therefore the question should be examined for sense and the interviewer's record for the number of misses can be tracked to see whether they are actually doing their job correctly.

ALSO MISSED THE 'NONE OF THE ABOVE' OPTION – THEREFORE THAT SHOULD BE TICKED?

A further possibility is that you have included 'None of the above' as an option to a multiple choice question. This is not a 'Don't know/Won't say' but a statement that your respondent's status or experience does not fall into that range of choices. Consequently, if the question is still left blank what happens then? Quite simply there should be a decision route which makes a consequential response – in Fig. 6.1, no tick was placed in any of the boxes therefore should 'None of the above' be checked? The argument centres around whether, with the respondent not answering, we can guess that:

- they don't buy charcoal at all
- they don't buy any of those brands of charcoal
- they do buy charcoal but they are not telling you
- they made a cup of tea and missed the question.

Do you buy any of these brands of barbecue charcoal?

	EasyLite	☐ 1
	Briquets	☐ 2
	Chunkies	☐ 3
	BarbieBricks	☐ 4
	None of the above	☐ 5
	Don't know/won't say	☐ 6

Fig. 6.1 No answer when 'None of the above' option given

The decision you make will depend on the type of question. Leaving the question unanswered is only an option if you are happy to have blanks in your data. Your data entry system may automatically generate a 'Not answered' response when you omit answers. If not, it may be worth considering adding a 'Not answered' option to your data entry form. Otherwise, give the operator clear instruction as to which answer should be used in any given circumstances – my choice for the previous example would be 'None of the above', but you could argue for hours about which would be most accurate. The only criterion is really what you intend to do with the answer afterwards.

A further problem can occur because the operator entering the data has skipped the question. This can be overcome simply in many data entry systems which work on a record-by-record (case-by-case) system where there can be a criterion built into the system which checks for an answer in particular questions before the user moves on to the next record. This 'Must be answered' option will prevent question skipping and will alert the operator to a blank in particular questions.

HOW DO YOU FILL AN UNANSWERED NUMERIC QUESTION?

If your questionnaire has asked for a number in answer to a question and the respondent has left it blank, what should go into the frame? How is that response interpreted by your analysis? The same questions arise here but there are different answers. Leaving the answer blank means that nothing is added to the analysis. However, in some data systems you will find that a blank numeric is automatically converted into a '0' (zero). Zero may, in terms of your analysis, be a positive answer whereas leaving a blank could be because of any of the reasons we mentioned earlier. Some systems are capable of rendering a 'not answered' option when a numeric question is left blank. If so, this should be used in preference to automatic zero.

Failing to follow routing

Your respondent was asked to answer 'Yes' or 'No' to Question 4. They have answered 'Yes' and the instructions say 'Now go to Question 7'. However, they have plodded on through Questions 5 and 6. What do you do? The data may well be contradictory. Consider this example:

Q4. Do you smoke cigarettes?	Yes
	No (Please go to Question 7)
Q5. How many cigarettes a day do you smoke on average?	
Q6. Please enter your usual brand of cigarettes	
Q7. Have you ever smoked as a habit in the past?	

It is fairly logical to assume that if someone has answered 'No' to Question 4 and then answered 5 and 6, that they really meant to answer 'Yes'. However, leaving the data as they have responded at the entry stage will make your results inaccurate. Your assumption that they meant 'yes' is a safe one when they tick the '100+ per day' box and write 'Capstan Full Strength'!

Automatic data systems can scan for that type of error and make the appropriate decision for you, provided that you have given a set of rules in the first instance. Where no such system exists there needs to be some error-checking built in through the routing of answers (see Chapter 5). You will not be able to rely on your data entry operator to perform this type of checking.

OVERCOMPLETE MARKING OF THE FORM

A similar problem occurs when the respondent has overmarked the form. Where a single option has been asked for, the respondent has ticked four. What do you do then? Take the first one, the last one, all of them, none of them? If you have asked for a single choice then you had your reasons. Your respondent may be expressing the fact that your question does not match his experience. The earlier example which asked respondents to say whether they lived in town, country, village or hamlet (p. 157) is a prime example of a situation where a respondent will overmark. It's not their fault! Your response must therefore be either to change the data structure to accommodate the overmarking because you recognise that the fault is yours, or you must discount overmarked questions.

Your respondent may simply not have been paying attention and therefore has failed to apply any thought to their responses. In this case it is likely that much of the rest of the form is inaccurate and, on an occasional basis, it is probably best to ditch that form. If the problem is consistent throughout the respondents however, the fault is definitely yours.

7

Getting out more than you put in

- In this section the analysis of data is considered
- Simple statistical measures and what they mean are discussed

Once you have collected your data you then need to analyse them. It is unlikely that you will derive all the information that is to be had, simply by looking at the data. The various statistical and analytical tools which are available to you will allow you to extract more from your data than might be apparent on the surface. In this chapter we look at putting data into sets by sorting or selecting, how some statistical tests work, what they mean and how much use they are to you, and finally, methods of presenting data as graphs, charts, cross-tabulations and tables. These tools are all related to tasks which you need to do. They are presented, not as a learned work on statistics, but in the context that, if you are not expert with statistics, you will want to make the most of the information you have in as clear and informative a way as possible. The clue here is, do not try to use any statistical tool which will mean nothing to you or to the person to whom you are presenting the information. For this reason, the more sophisticated statistical tests are omitted and the work concentrates on simpler tools.

ANALYSING INFORMATION

Analysis is the process whereby the information you have is presented in a way which extracts the most useful facts from it. In a survey of visitors to an hotel it may be that 500 people have completed the customer satisfaction questionnaire. Simply looking at the stack of returned forms is likely to yield little useful data. Once that information has been put into a structure in a computer system it is then possible to perform a number of analyses, depending upon how the questions were asked in the first place (see the section on Asking Questions)

Sorting

One of the simplest techniques for looking at trends and for gaining an impression of the way in which people are thinking and responding is to *sort* the records on any one of the answers that you have. For instance, on our hotel questionnaire, which we shall use widely in this section, we could sort the respondents by their ages and then see whether there were more people in any particular age group than in another. We could sort them by their postcodes to look and see whether more people were coming from one area of the country than another. Equally, we could sort them by their answers to one of our levels of satisfaction questions (How well did you rate the restaurant? Excellent? Good? Poor? Awful?) simply by sorting the forms on the basis of the answer to that question you could have a 'measure by eye' of the various levels of satisfaction.

All of this is quite crude, however, since we are simply grouping answers together in order to see how many fall into any particular group. The technique of sorting can be useful in preparing data for graphing, particularly if one wishes to present a graph whose labels follow a logical order. If the data are sorted already into that order then the graphing process should take that into account.

Selecting groups

The process of data selection is one where you specify certain conditions relating to parts of your data set in order to retrieve all the records (cases) which conform to those conditions. This is a data handling activity and, as such, is one with which many people are familiar. For example, out of a collection of survey records you may wish to isolate all those who are *female* or who come from *Birmingham* or who drive a *Ford*. By asking the right question of your data system you will be able to retrieve and display only those records which conform to one (or more) of those criteria.

WHY MAKE GROUPS?

Selecting or choosing groups of respondents in a survey gives you the opportunity to view their results in isolation. It also allows you then to compare their results with the whole set of data or with other *subsets* – parts of the full set of data.

The punchcard history

In the 'good old days' of punchcards, before the advent of computers, it used to be that records were kept by punching holes and slots in record cards so that, by pushing a needle through hole 56 one could isolate all those who had answered 'Yes' or '6' or 'Tuesday' or whatever the key response was, simply by then lifting the needle with all the relevant cards attached. The words 'hole count' and the use of punch numbers are still in market research practice today, although their application has changed somewhat!

SUBSETS

A subset is formed by asking a question of your data such as '*Select all records where* ***sex*** *includes* ***female***'. Such a question then results in the system finding and displaying a *subset* – a part of the full set of data, described by the criteria that selected it. When selecting subsets, the way in which criteria are framed can influence the outcome, particularly where more than one criterion is used for selection. Take, for example, the following criteria:

Select all records where
sex includes *female*
AND *Age* is greater than *35*

This is radically different from

Select all records where
sex includes *female*
OR *Age* is greater than *35*

The difference lies in the set of data which is being interrogated for each question. In the first, the '***sex*** *includes* ***female***' parameter is enacted, giving us the subset which includes *only* all the females. Then the second part of the interrogation clicks in: '***AND Age*** *is greater than* ***35***'. Now that 'female' subset is further searched against the criterion of age greater than 35, giving us the resultant *subset* of all females who are older than 35.

In the second instance, however, we are selecting all the females and then, instead of examining the 'female' subset for the next condition, we are saying 'examine the full set once more, this time to pull out all the people who are over 35'. The resultant subset which we have then comprises all the females and all the people over the age of 35 (regardless of whether they are male or female).

COMPARING GROUPS

For example, having isolated all the female respondents in your survey you may wish to compare and contrast their behaviour with that of the males. Isolating the females gives you the opportunity to examine their responses in isolation, graph them, cross-tabulate and statistically analyse them. Similarly, you may then wish to do the same with the data belonging to the male respondents. Thereafter it is interesting to superimpose the two sets of information and draw conclusions.

This process may, in your context, be to do with comparing the performance of salesmen in the North and the South, analysing the responses of those people who live on two very different council estates, assessing the training needs of workers from four different branches of the same company, or simply comparing the results of last year's survey with this year's.

EXAMINING TRENDS

By looking at a rolling set of data (the figures from two years ago, last year, this year) and comparing them, by overlaying bar charts, for instance, it is possible to see the movement of trends. For example, doctors and hospitals now monitor their patient population, not to see whether they are ill, but to measure their health and examine the impact of their services on the general health of the population. If their services are having an impact then the graphs should slowly progress in a favourable direction and the evidence should be quite explicit in the movement of the superimposed bars of a bar chart, year on year.

Equally, a company can measure the effects of efficiency measures, cost-cutting, improved work practices, change of supplier and so on, by examining the figures relating to the affected processes and comparing them on a regular basis with previous performance. Little in the way of statistical skill is needed here (although it helps for seeing the underlying trends) because there is either an effect on productivity, efficiency, profit (or whichever measure is being used) or there is not. If your sampling of data shows no change, or even a deterioration in performance, then that is the time for some countermeasures!

STATISTICS – EASY TO CALCULATE, BUT DIFFICULT TO UNDERSTAND, INTERPRET AND INFER FROM

What are statistics?

This book is not a statistics primer. You are probably not a statistician nor a market researcher. The author is not a statistician either. The information in the next few pages is designed to help you understand what some of the more common measures mean and how they are arrived at. The examples given here and the statistical methods described are by no means the whole story. This 'taster' of some of the analyses which may be derived from your data is to help you to get to grips with the output from your results. When you come to describe those results in ways other than simple totals you need to express them in a language which has a meaning not only to you, but also to those for whom the results are being prepared. Although this work touches upon *standard deviation*, *normal* and *skewed distributions* and a number of other statistical tools, they should only be used where they will be understood. For most purposes and most people, a graph will suffice. However, underlying the graph are probably interesting trends which can only be 'seen' through the power of statistics. Once you have the basics then it is time to look in more depth at the whole topic than this book can provide. There are other books in this series for that purpose.

A graph can provide a two-dimensional view of the data. The statistics go beyond that to add a third dimension which cannot be seen readily by the untrained eye. However, statistics only mean something if they mean something to you or to the person for whom you are preparing them. Statistics on their own are only useful to a statistician. For the untrained or inexpert it is important that all analyses are accompanied by a narrative which covers:

- What the statistics tell you – the results.
- What the statistics mean – the interpretation in relation to the sample.
- What the consequence is – how that affects your plans (the justification).

DESCRIPTIVE

Descriptive statistics simply tell you something more about the data which you have before you – they describe it. Simple measures such as mean, mode, sum all provide you with a simple description of *facts* about the set of data.

INFERENTIAL

Inferential statistics tell you something more about the data than can be actually described as fact. Inferences are assumptions made upon the best knowledge available. To infer something from a set of data one looks at the available evidence and then states 'It is likely that . . .'. Consequently, inferential statistics should be used with more care than descriptive statistics.

Do you need to work it out?

The question must be, do *you* need to sit and work out the statistics? The answer must be no. Spreadsheet systems, calculators and dedicated survey analysis software have all been designed to take the sweat out of statistics. All that you have to do is to understand what it means when the result appears on your screen or printer. Although sometimes an understanding of how a statistic is arrived at will help you understand its purpose, more often than not you will find that the maths gets in the way. Leave that to the computer or the calculator – understand the purpose, not the mechanics; understand the output, not the process.

What you can and cannot do with statistics

I shall not use the old chestnut about *'Lies, damned lies and statistics . . .'* (oh well!) It has been suggested that you can prove anything with statistics and to a certain extent this appears to be true. Data can be manipulated and massaged until they render up that for which you are seeking. This is just the same as slanting a survey to finding the expected results – it is dishonest, even when unintentional! Statistics cannot be used in isolation. They throw light on the situation being examined provided that they are used in an intelligent and, more importantly, a knowledgeable way. Statistics in the hands of an inexperienced amateur, and the results being shown to other inexperienced amateurs, can only end in grief.

It has been said earlier, only use statistical measures and tests when you understand what they describe and how you should interpret them. Statistics let you look at the props and supports that hold up the imaginary scenery which is the concept being examined. The underlying trends which are hidden to the 'naked eye' are revealed by statistical analysis. Dishonestly used, statistics can also hide those very same trends, as many a political party in opposition would claim. What you can do with statistics is:

- *Infer:* Take the information you have and make educated and reasonable guesses about what underlay the results. Inference is a practice which is made perfect with practice. Experienced statisticians will look at trends in the light of all the available evidence and *infer* the underlying causes. We lesser mortals must be satisfied with looking at the data and hoping to see a little below the murky surface using some simpler tools and less experience.
- *Abstract:* Allowing the user to see the wood for the trees is another function of statistics. By clearing away the 'noise' of surrounding information, statistics can allow the true nature of discrete features of the data to be shown in all their glory.
- *Elaborate (extend):* By taking a trend identified in a set of data, and extending it into the future, it is possible to gaze into the crystal ball. If a set of circumstances look set to continue, or to change according to the influence of another set of variables, then the interaction of these influences may be plotted from the historical past into an imaginary future.

- *Correlate:* Statistics also allow you to see how one set of variables influence another. Although these influences may not immediately be evident, one can either uncover them or, more often, confirm the suspicion that they were there in the first place. For example, proving that there is a link between juvenile crime and school holidays might seem to be quite a self-evident truth. Yet the influences could also be an influx of visitors into the town during holidays, improved weather bringing out all types, a natural peak that has some influence other than holiday times, and so on. The hypothesis may be proved or disproved by correct sampling and statistical techniques.

Before you begin statistical analysis

It is not simply a matter of saying, 'here's a set of numbers, let's try some statistics on them'. Statistics, as has been said *ad nauseam* so far, depend upon interpretation and context. First, *you must have data which is capable of statistical analysis.*

You cannot perform statistical analyses on questions which ask for name and address, for example. The data will be numeric in origin *or* it will consist of frequency counts or percentages of incidence of a particular answer choice in a multiple choice or ranked question. These used to have to be coded numerically but with modern software this is no longer necessary. Data which uses codes representing some feature of the sample being surveyed (region, political party, etc.) let the number stand for a particular answer in the questionnaire: Excellent (1), Good (2), and so on. These numbers have no value other than as pointers to a reference table which the researcher is using. As such they *represent* text.

However, if you try to perform analyses on text-based answers in a spreadsheet, for example, you will find that it cannot deal with that type of answer (see *'Technology tools*, Chapter 10, for some suggestions of ways round this problem).

Second, *you should group the data into the categories you wish to measure.*

For example, in a customer satisfaction survey you may wish to profile the opinions of two contrasting groups and see how they match each other and whether the correlation between them is significant. In order to do that you will first need to isolate each group as a *subset* (see previous section) and then perform your analysis on each one in order that they may be compared.

Tools such as cross-tabulation enable you to cross-reference data which are drawn from very different sources and then measure whether there is correlation between the elements being cross-referenced. This exercise automatically isolates the subsets of the questions involved because each answer element is displayed with its count of responses in the table.

The most commonly used measures and what they can tell you

SOME TERMINOLOGY

Values: the numbers collected in relation to any particular area of information. Values are often numeric but can also be textual – words such as 'Excellent', Good', Poor' which are then counted for frequency.
Series: a set of *values*, all relating to the same *variable.*
Average: the result derived when all the values in a series are added together and then divided by the number of values.
Total: the sum, the result, the outcome of performing an analysis or a mathematical operation.
Percentage: the proportion of the series being described, expressed as a fraction of 100.
Square: the result when a number is multiplied by itself.
Square root: the result when the process of squaring is reversed – not quite so easy!
Case: one respondent's data.

In the following examples it is necessary to work out some mathematics. If you are not a mathematician, do not give up! There is nothing here that you cannot achieve with a pencil and paper at worst or with a calculator or spreadsheet. Since a spreadsheet is very much a universal tool, this section will work examples in spreadsheet format, showing the processes and enabling you to see how they operate. Of course there are many instances where the working out can be done with a simple formula from your spreadsheet's library of functions. That route is the way you would do it normally but, for the purposes of the book, all working will be shown and functions will not be used except where unavoidable.

SIMPLE MEASURES

At the risk of stating the obvious, and for the sake of completeness, this section looks at some of the simplest statistical measures. They require little in the way of calculation, yet are important indicators, particularly when examined in conjunction with some of their more complex kin.
Minimum: The lowest value in a range of numbers.
Maximum: The highest value in a range of numbers.
Sum: The total of all the values in a range of numbers when added together.

MEASURES CALCULATING A TYPICAL VALUE

What is *typical* about the range of numbers in a series? How far can the range of values be said to be close to the central value in the range? If the range of numbers is all very similar, how similar are they? The *mean*, *median* and *mode* all aim to tell you something about your numerical information, but each must be used with an understanding of its limitations.

Mean

The mean is the calculation of the *average* value, created by adding up all the values in the series and then dividing it by the total number of values in the series. The mean aims to tell you the midpoint, the centre, the most likely value for another instance of a value occurring in the series. It is an estimate based upon the best available knowledge – the information you already have. For example, you may wish to predict how likely it is that you will achieve a sales target with a particular product. You know the buying behaviour of your current customers and can find the mean level of purchase. It is not unreasonable to assume that, given another set of people with similar characteristics you would be able to predict that their average level of purchase would be the same. In some circumstances the mean succeeds in its aim. Unfortunately, there are some circumstances where it totally fails to do so.

Consider a survey which collects data about people's spending on alcohol. Out of 12 people in the sample the following were the weekly totals for spending on all alcohol (wine, beer and spirits):

A	B	C	D	E	F
£2.30	£1.79	£18.81	£25.00	£7.60	£91.10
G	H	I	J	K	L
£13.03	£0.00	£25.000	£6.45	£28.71	£5.95

If we convert that to a columnar format for ease of analysis, we get Fig. 7.1(a). Putting the columns into ascending order (Fig. 7.1(b)) we can see that there is a wide range of spending in this set. In fact, if we add up all the values and then divide by the total number of values (12):

(a)

Case	Spend
A	£2.30
B	£1.79
C	£18.81
D	£25.00
E	£7.60
F	£91.10
G	£13.03
H	£0.00
I	£25.00
J	£6.45
K	£28.71
L	£5.95

(b)

Case	Spend
H	£0.00
B	£1.79
A	£2.30
L	£5.95
J	£6.45
E	£7.60
G	£13.03
C	£18.81
D	£25.00
I	£25.00
K	£28.71
F	£91.10

Fig. 7.1 The mean of a data set

we derive the mean value of this set of data which could be thought of, if you were not looking at the constituent figures, as being fairly representative of the spending of the group.

Total	Mean spend
£225.74 divided by 12 =	**£18.81**

However, it is obvious even to a non-statistician that something is adrift. A spend of £18.81 is not representative of the group at all, although one member of the group sits right on the mean. In fact it is towards the top end of the spending range. If one were to project this value onto another sample market one might have a very inflated idea of likely returns from a sales campaign.

The *outlier* (the value of £91.10 for case F) is the thing which *skewed* the set of data. (An outlier is a value or set of values which are outside the normal range – an exception.) It may be a perfectly valid datum (piece of information – the singular of data) but its effect on the rest of the set in analysis is to distort the calculation. Tackling outliers is always a thorny issue in research, particularly if they are valid. One technique is to take them out of the calculations since they have an adverse effect on the data, but to report them separately, or even to provide two sets of statistics, one containing the outliers and the other omitting them.

An outlier could be defined as being a piece of information which is so far outside the normal range of data as to be exceptional. If we omit the outlier from our calculations then we have a very different picture

(Fig. 7.2). Remove it and the mean makes more sense, although it is worth noticing that those values which lie near the mean are few in number. Perhaps these data are not so happily analysed by this method? To deal with the above data it might be better to look at the median.

Case	Spend	
H	£0.00	
B	£1.79	
A	£2.30	
L	£5.95	
J	£6.45	
E	£7.60	
G	£13.03	
C	£18.81	
D	£25.00	
I	£25.00	
K	£28.71	
F		
	£134.64 Total	**£11.22** Mean

Fig. 7.2 Removing outliers from determination of mean

Median

The median is simply the midpoint marker of a set of numerical data. In Fig. 7.2 we now have 11 sets of values since we removed value F. Therefore the midpoint (the median) is E £7.60 since it stands halfway through the set of data. What would have happened had we left in value F and therefore had an even number of values and consequently no midpoint? Quite simply we would have taken the two values which straddle the midpoint (in this case E and G at £7.60 and £13.03 respectively) added them together (£20.63) and found their mean by dividing them in two which would have given a median of £10.31 (rounded down).

How representative does our original median, omitting the outlier, look at £7.60? (Bear in mind that statistics is not mindless – one should apply common sense to the data and decide whether the result you are calculating is really representative or not.) It certainly seems more representative than the mean of £11.22 because we, as sales/marketing people, do not want to be too optimistic in case we have our fingers burned! It is worth remembering that the median can be misleading when the range of data is small, particularly when extremes occur either side of it. As for whether it represents this group or not (would any value represent any section of this set of data fairly), it is so widely scattered? Yes, in fact there is a simple measure which may indicate behaviour quite reliably for this group, provided we apply a little common sense with statistics.

Mode

The mode is the value which occurs most often in the range of data. It can only be fairly applied when the data are grouped into clusters and may even have more than one value. For example, a range of data which had a cluster of five instances of 30 as a value and another cluster of four instances of 80 could be described as having two modes: *bi-modal*. In our sample table of data we have two cases of £25 (values D and I) and they represent the mode, which incidentally means exactly what it sounds like: the most fashionable, the most popular value. Once again this statistic can be misleading when the range of data is small but when used intelligently can give a perspective on your information that is not available from other statistics.

MEASURES SHOWING THE WAY IN WHICH VALUES ARE DISTRIBUTED

These measures are usually called measures of dispersal because they indicate the way in which the values in a set of data are distributed relative to, for example, the mean. If the values are nearly all distributed to one side or other of the mean then the data can be described as *skewed*. This will sometimes happen where outliers are having a serious effect on the data, but can just as easily be a consequence of the nature of the data.

Range

The range shows the difference between the highest and lowest values in a set of data. It is calculated simply by subtracting one from the other. It shows how far apart the two extremes of the data set are and therefore allows you to judge whether other statistics, such as the *mean*, are representative of a 'universe' from which this set of data was derived. By comparing ranges from two apparently similar data sets we can see how widely spread the scores are (the higher the range value, the wider the distribution) and therefore have an indication whether their similarity is true or only apparent.

In our sample set of data the range is calculated by subtracting value H from value F (not a difficult problem!) giving a range of 91.10. This is a wide dispersal for such a small set of data and must make us question how well the data might predict other similar groups and whether other statistics we have derived are appropriate or not.

Like other statistics described here, the range can be distorted by extremes which are not truly typical of the rest of the set. If we remove the outlier (value F) then the range of the data becomes 28.71 which, although quite large, is more acceptable in the context. It is worth noting that so far we have ignored the value for H of £0.00 which is itself an outlier. An argument could be mounted for removing this value since, after all, this is a data set about people's habits in purchasing alcoholic drink. If the spend of case H is £0.00 then they do not buy alcohol. The study is presumably not interested in those who do *not* buy, but in those who *do*. In itself one could surmise that perhaps around one in 12 people drink no alcohol – and how reliable is that information? Given the size of the set, probably not very.

Mean or average deviation

The *mean deviation* or *average deviation* is a measure of the average amount by which scores deviate from the mean! Confused? Think about it. It is the amount by which each single value differs from the mean or average value, all totalled up and then averaged by dividing by the number of scores. It is the average deviation from the average. The higher the value of the mean deviation, the more that the results are dispersed across the range. Using our example table, Fig. 7.3(a), we decided the mean was £18.81, skewed rather by the outlier in case F. We then measure each value against the mean of £18.81 (Fig. 7.3(b)).

(a)

Case	Spend
H	£0.00
B	£1.79
A	£2.30
L	£5.95
J	£6.45
E	£7.60
G	£13.03
C	***£18.81***
D	£25.00
I	£25.00
K	£28.71
F	£91.10

(b)

Case	Spend	Calculation	Deviation from 18.81
H	£0.00	=18.81 – 0	18.81
B	£1.79	=18.81 – 1.79	17.02
A	£2.30	=18.81 – 2.30	16.51
L	£5.95	=18.81 – 5.95	12.86
J	£6.45	=18.81 – 6.45	12.36
E	£7.60	=18.81 – 7.60	11.21
G	£13.03	=18.81 – 13.03	5.78
C	***£18.81***	=18.81 – 18.81	0.00
D	£25.00	=25.00 – 18.81	6.19
I	£25.00	=25.00 – 18.81	6.19
K	£28.71	=28.71 – 18.81	9.90
F	£91.10	=91.10 – 18.81	72.29

Fig. 7.3 Finding the mean deviation

Did you notice the sleight of hand at work in the table above? If you are a mathematician you will have jumped on it instantly. In this table we are simply noting the difference between the mean (£18.81) and all the other values. We start by subtracting the values H, B, A, L, J, E, G and C from 18.81 and then, magically begin subtracting 18.81 from the values D, I, K and F. That is because we are ignoring whether the values give us a positive or negative result. We are ignoring the plus and minus signs, something of which mathematicians would disapprove. The result, however, is to give us a measure of deviation which ignores mathematics but can be quite handy none the less. It is calculated now by totalling the deviations, giving us a total of 189.11. Then we divide that total by the number of cases, in this instance it is 12 and we have

189.12/12= 15.75

This represents the *average* amount by which each value *deviates* from the *mean*. This figure is quite high and shows therefore that since on average each value deviates from the mean by 15.75 there is little consistency in the figures we have here. The larger the result of the calculation, the greater is the dispersion of values across the range.

Standard deviation

The *standard deviation* is a similar measure to average deviation but more accurate mathematically because it takes into account the plus and minus signs which may have so offended some of you! Standard deviation gives you a view of how far, on average, all scores deviate from the mean. It achieves this with a little bit of mathematical jiggery-pokery: if you take any minus (negative) value and square it (multiply it by itself) then the result is a positive number. Provided you return to the unsquared value afterwards all will be well.

Worked example

In the spreadsheet (shown in Fig. 7.4) the following process has taken place:

- First, a true difference from the mean has been calculated in the column marked 'Calculation'. This shows that for the first value (case H) the difference between the mean (18.81) and case H's value is –18.81. The minus sign is of importance.
- Second, each of the values derived from the calculation has been squared (multiplied by itself) so that in case H we have –18.81 multiplied by –18.81 which gives 353.88 as a result.
- Third, that column of squared deviations is now added up to give the *sum of squares*.
- Fourth, the *variance* is calculated by dividing the sum of squares by 12 (the number of cases).

- And finally the *square root* of the variance gives the final *standard deviation*.

Case	Spend	Calculation	Deviation from 18.81 Squared	
H	£0.00	–£18.81	£353.88	
B	£1.79	–£17.02	£289.74	
A	£2.30	–£16.51	£272.64	
L	£5.95	–£12.86	£165.42	
J	£6.45	–£12.36	£152.81	
E	£7.60	–£11.21	£125.70	
G	£13.03	–£5.78	£33.43	
C	£18.81	£0.00	£0.00	
D	£25.00	£6.19	£38.30	
I	£25.00	£6.19	£38.30	
K	£28.71	£9.90	£97.98	
F	£91.10	£72.29	£5,225.60	
Total	£225.74	£0.00	£6,793.78	Sum of squares
Average	£18.81		566.1487139	Variance (sum divided by 12)
				Square root of variance gives
			23.79387976	Standard deviation

Fig. 7.4 Determining standard deviation

It is worth remembering that all the process could have been done quite transparently on your spreadsheet simply by entering the STDEV function and specifying the range of numbers to be dealt with.

Once again, the higher the figure the larger the distribution. It is worth comparing with the mean to see how well or badly the mean represents the truth. You will notice that we now have three separate measures of distribution and each is radically different for the same set of figures:

Range: 91.10
Mean distribution: 15.75
Standard distribution: 23.79

Since each is a different technique, each must be demonstrating something different about the data. Standard deviation is used as the most common measure for looking at the way in which particular scores deviate from a mean score. To understand how this is done, it is first of all necessary to understand distribution.

SO WHAT IS DISTRIBUTION?

Distribution is a way of describing how scores are disposed on a graph. Take, for example, a survey of shoppers at a local supermarket. As the shoppers pass through the checkout an automatic system logs the amount they have spent. The values have been grouped into ranges in order to make our graph simpler. For each value of spend we have had a tally count so that, for the £30 range there were four customers who spent in that range:

Spend	£10	£20	£30	£40	£50	£60	£70	£80	£90
Tally	1	2	4	6	7	6	4	2	1

To simplify how that result looks a little more we can represent it diagrammatically (Fig. 7.5). Now you can see that each column represents the number of cases in each group. Our statistical analysis of the spending of the people in the store is based upon the total amount spent related to the number of cases we have. Distributing them in the fashion of Fig. 7.5 is bringing us nearer to a chart which represents the figures graphically, converting them from numbers on a calculator into a picture. The numbers at the base of each column represent the total spend for each range, so our £30 range of four customers naturally made a total spend of £120. The way these figures are distributed gives us some simple calculations for mean, median and mode.

				£50				
			£40	£50	£60			
			£40	£50	£60			
		£30	£40	£50	£60	£70		
		£30	£40	£50	£60	£70		
	£20	£30	£40	£50	£60	£70	£80	
£10	£20	£30	£40	£50	£60	£70	£80	£90
£10	***£40***	***£120***	***£240***	***£350***	***£360***	***£280***	***£160***	***£90***

Fig. 7.5 Diagrammatic form of spending distribution

They all turn out the same because our set of data conforms to what is called a *normal distribution*. This frequently occurring style of distribution of results is characteristic of many sets of statistical data. As its name suggests, it is the type of distribution of results which you might expect under normal circumstances when dealing with a stable set of variables. It is characterised by low tally counts in the extreme regions of the scale (as with our £10 and £90 spenders above) but a bulging of counts towards the centre. The whole shape of the curve describes a bell (Fig. 7.6) and is the subject of the rest of this section.

Total:	£1,650
No. of cases:	33
Mean:	£50
Median:	£50
Mode:	£50

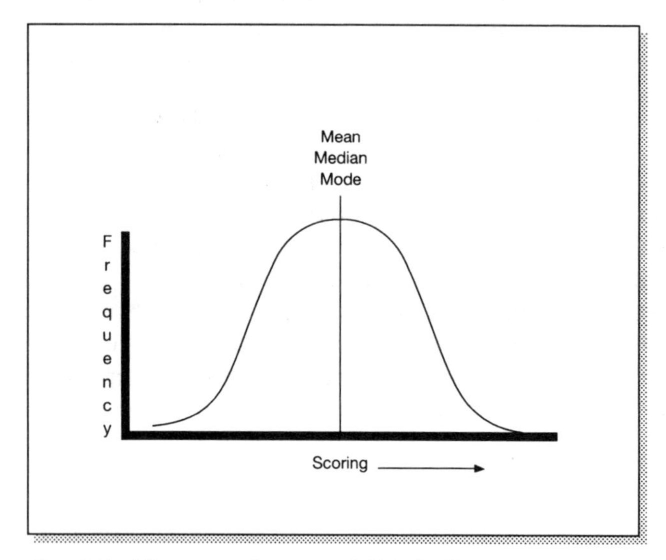

Fig. 7.6 The normal curve of distribution

THE NORMAL DISTRIBUTION

Typically, the normal curve will be characterised by the fact that mean, median and mode all fall in roughly the same place. A normal distribution also allows you to state categorically some statistical facts about the set of data without having to resort to your calculator. Since the mean, median and mode are all at the halfway point, it follows that 50 per cent of the results must be down the scale and 50 per cent up the scale. If the data are so evenly distributed it must therefore be easy to plot other markers on the graph and state the percentage of people who lie above or below those marks. Not quite as easy as you might think since the percentages are not to do with measuring, say, 25 per cent of the way up the scale to find 25 per cent of the population. It is to do with the area under the curve. As the curve rises one side and descends the other the area bounded by it becomes smaller and it becomes more difficult to identify how individual scores and percentages relate to each other. Predefined marks on the chart can show where percentages for any sample which conforms to the normal curve, will fall. These percentages are invariable *if the curve is of normal distribution.*

So where does *standard deviation* come into all this? 'Standard deviation gives you a view of how far, on average, all scores deviate from the mean', we said earlier. If we perform our standard deviation test on the figures above we get a standard deviation (SD) of 18.7 (rounded). The useful characteristic of the SD is that we can then plot this onto a graph to indicate one or more standard deviations above or below the mean and, more importantly, this tells us something about the proportion of sample which lies inside the area marked.

If you mark 18.7 onto either side of the mean you have now bounded between 31.3 and 68.7 on the graph. (Bear in mind that our customers probably did not spend whole units of £10 so the figures are likely to fall into these fractions in any case. In addition, the larger the sample, the finer the resolution of the scale can be.) An interesting fact also to notice is that roughly one-third of all the sample lies in a sector described by one standard deviation from the mean. As a rough rule of thumb this is a useful measure. As a consequence, since we have now accounted for two-thirds of our sample within the scope of two standard deviations, the remaining third must be those people who lie in the regions beyond.

However, if the distribution were to be skewed in one direction or another the characteristics of the sample would be different and this would be reflected in the standard deviation which would reflect the skew in its score.

Why would you want to know?

Imagine a survey of throughput by machine line operators who were constructing electronic components. The factory rotates the workforce around each of the tasks on a weekly basis in order to avoid problems of boredom. There are 68 in the workforce altogether and the survey is conducted retrospectively over a period of three months by collating the data from piecework figures. Ignoring the question of quality of construction for a moment, it is a simple process to work out the mean score from the workforce's productivity and thereby derive the standard deviation.

Perhaps the mean level worked out to be 60 components constructed per day and the standard deviation of those scores was 8. This tells us (bearing in mind that around one-third of all of our sample lies within one standard deviation from the mean), that two-thirds of our workforce will be producing between 52 and 68 components per day – this is what we can expect (Fig. 7.7). It is no longer sufficient to say 'Your output is above average' if we can plainly see that at least one-third of the sample falls in that first standard deviation above the mean – and there are others above them!

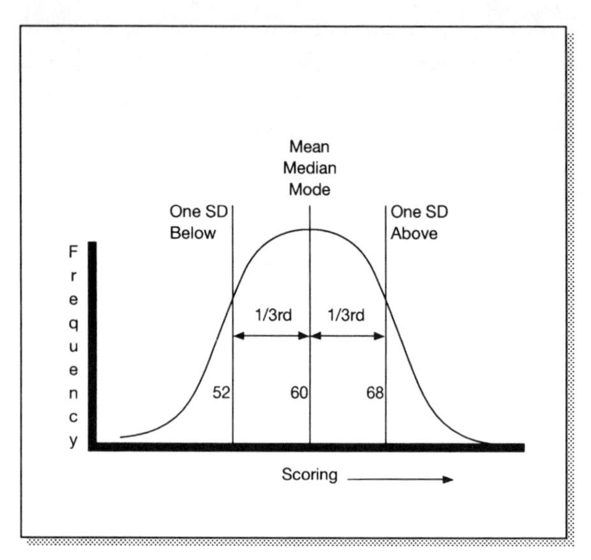

Fig. 7.7 Workforce productivity

If a worker therefore had a productivity level of 68 components per day, they are likely to be around five-sixths of the way up the productivity scale of achievement! Whereas 68 might not have seemed so high in isolation, when looked at in comparison to the bulk of other figures it shows itself to be a considerable level of performance.

Remember that:

- The characteristics of normal curves are constant.
- Standard deviation applies only to normal curves.
- Fixed percentages of a population in a normal distribution may be predicted for any part of the curve.

SKEWED DISTRIBUTIONS

However, what happens when distributions are not normal? For example, if you are a gambler you are interested in the likelihood of a particular event happening as predicted. The roll of a pair of dice may be influenced by all types of factors to do with the accuracy of the dice and the distribution of their weight which make a particular value more likely to occur than others. The only way of discovering this is to plot the frequency of each value (the numbers 2 to 12) and see whether the *distribution* is weighted towards a particular value. Under normal circumstances, the more frequently that one throws the dice the more the curve should tend towards a normal distribution. However, weighted dice will skew that distribution to one side or another.

Skewed distributions still allow you to predict behaviour and to look at trends. Although they are not *normal* in the statistical sense of the word, they are still consistent – the data are not random. They merely point up the fact that the data are skewed to one end of the scale or another (Fig. 7.8). When this happens it has an interesting effect upon mean, median and mode.

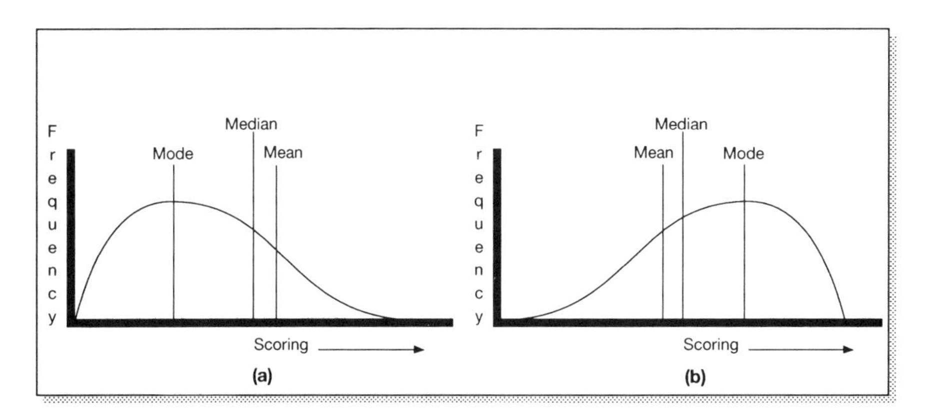

Fig. 7.8 Skewed distributions: (a) positively skewed, (b) negatively skewed

The median, since it is the midpoint of the data, stays halfway along the horizontal axis. The mode, however, since it is the most 'popular' score, appears where the curve peaks. The mean, meanwhile, has disappeared off to the opposite end of the scale from the mode. For this reason it is usual to quote all three of these statistics when dealing with skewed distribution since each is telling us something different about the data:

- The median – where the halfway point lies.
- The mode – which is the most frequently occurring score.
- The mean – the average score for the whole set of data.

A BRIEF LOOK AT MEASURES OF ASSOCIATION

When it comes to analysing the type of data above, it is obvious that we cannot apply the rules of the standard deviation and normal curve – because it is not *normal*! Consequently, other tests must be applied – ones which compare the distribution we have with the distribution of a similar or related set of data. These tests are often called *goodness of fit* tests and work by comparing one set of data with another in order to highlight differences and provide a measure of correlation. First we need to look at the vehicle (cross-tabulation) for one of the most common measures of association – Chi-squared.

Chi-squared and cross-tabulation

One of the most common tests of association is *chi-squared* (pronounced *ky* to rhyme with *sky*). The name derives from the Greek symbol 'χ'. This test works on the basis of comparing what might be expected from a distribution of data with what actually is there. It can be used in comparing one set of data with another *control* set (a set of data drawn from a group used as a stable reference point). Alternatively, it may be used in comparing the relationship between two sets of dissimilar but related data in order to find out whether one factor is having an influence on another. For example, in our imaginary hotel customer satisfaction survey, we might wish to compare customers' satisfaction in the cleanliness of the hotel against their age ranges. This would be in order to see whether age correlated with satisfaction in any way (for instance, we may uncover the fact that the older age group tend to be more critical of cleanliness). This may lead us on to do further comparisons, finding that they are particularly critical of cleanliness in the restaurant.

The most common method for tackling chi-squared is using *cross-tabulation*. A cross-tabulation allows you to plot one set of responses to a question against the responses for a totally different question (or questions) in order to observe any patterns which might emerge. Chi-squared simply tells you how high that correlation is – whether, in other words, it is *significant*. In common with other statistical measures of this sort, the figure which is derived from chi-squared tells you nothing about the actual population which you are measuring – it tells you about the mathematical relationships between the data, not any fact about that group of people.

Taking our hotel example as a model, in a survey there are certain levels at which one might expect people to respond. Looking at the table below (a cross-tabulation of *quality of service* against age) we could predict that, all things being equal, each cell in the table would have a similar number of respondents from our sample of 100 – however, all things never are equal!

	18–25 years	*26–35 years*	*36–45 years*	*46–55 years*	*55+ years*	*Totals*
Excellent	5	5	5	5	5	25
Good	5	5	5	5	5	25
Quite good	5	5	5	5	5	25
Poor	5	5	5	5	5	25
Totals	20	20	20	20	20	100

Since the data is likely to be either random or in a pattern, we need to establish whether there actually *is* a pattern. This is done by evaluating how closely the data conform to any sort of distribution. In the example of Fig. 7.9 the data are definitely bunched. Here the chi-squared measure indicates that there is a high level of difference between the groups, that is to say, the age of the respondents *does* affect the way they respond about the facility being measured. Looking at the table more closely, it is worth drawing out the component features. The *primary question* or *rows question* is that to do with the customers' satisfaction with the facility. Each category of answer is displayed and the cells in the table indicate the frequency for each response, matched with those in the *secondary* or *column* question.

Cleanliness counts % columns	**Age** Under 25	25–34	35–44	45–54	55–64	Over 65	Total
Excellent	4 22%	4 25%	2 25%	0 0%	0 0%	4 20%	14 14%
Good	10 56%	6 38%	0 0%	16 50%	0 0%	14 70%	46 46%
Fair	4 22%	6 38%	6 75%	12 38%	4 67%	2 10%	34 34%
Poor	0 0%	0 0%	0 0%	4 12%	2 33%	0 0%	6 6%
Total	18	16	8	32	6	20	100
Chi-Square						42.020	
X2 probability						0.000	

Fig. 7.9 Bunched data

The secondary question is plotted against the primary question and the results are measured in the columns in this instance. That is to say, the totals and percentages shown in each cell relate to the *column* question's relationship to the *primary* question. So, for example, in the 65+ column, 20 per cent of the respondents voted that the facility was '*Excellent*' and 70 per cent voted that it was '*Good*'. The remaining 10 per cent voted '*Fair*' bringing the total to 100 per cent.

Even by 'eye' it is apparent that there is significant grouping of the data in this set of information. However, in research things are not usually so clear cut. A set of data may exhibit 'bunching' but the level to which this is significant can only be obtained by applying a test. Chi-squared correlates the data you have collected and compares it with what might be expected.

8

Presenting information

- **In this section the methods for presenting your findings are discussed**
- **The sensible use of graphs, charts, tables and cross-tabulations in combination with appropriate text and other information is examined**
- **A structure for a report is suggested**

When you have completed your survey, collected your data, performed the various analyses and tests you wish to try, you will then need to present the data to other people as a record of your efforts. 'Spoiling the ship for a ha'p'orth of tar' is often the case when people come to presentation. The material to be included in your presentation is likely to comprise three elements:

- Statistics.
- Graphs, charts, tables, cross-tabulations.
- Narrative.

Those three elements are interdependent and indispensable. The following section examines how graphical output can be used and explains the need for interpretation.

WHO IS YOUR AUDIENCE?

Your audience is likely to be a person or set of people who have no idea what it is that you have been trying to do. As a result of that fact, a bald presentation of data or graphs or statistics is going to mean little to them. They need to see the broad picture, understand what you were trying to achieve, how you set about it, the instruments which you used and finally, what you discovered.

Evidence is the key. You need to provide evidence to confirm your findings. A heap of questionnaire forms placed on the boardroom table with the comment, 'Well, they certainly seem to show that people are buying more Bradshaw's Jam than they used to' is unlikely to convince anyone. You have a hypothesis, you explain it. You needed proof, gathered it, analysed it and concluded from it. Now you must explain it.

The report is the opportunity to present everything in summary, clearly, concisely and with references to any sources which may allow the curious to find out more. Your audience need to be treated in an appropriate fashion for their status. Statement of the obvious is sometimes necessary to get your point across (as you may have noticed in this book!) but your audience is known to you so you must present your information in a form appropriate to their skills.

WHAT MAKES A PRESENTATION?

A presentation should consist of a combination of the elements above, but showing a progression:

- The objective (mission statement) of the research.
- A brief overview of the method – population, sample, area, questionnaire techniques.
- A graphical overview of the outcome.
- A brief outline of any significant statistics relating to the graphs.
- A summary of the results as implications for your business.
- A summary of the results as action points.

It may be that some of these elements will be part of a verbal presentation to a board of directors or managers, but a printed summary will allow them to chew over your findings at their leisure. A variety of presentation systems are available to us.

Report

You may decide that a printed report is the most appropriate medium to deliver your results. This has the advantage of permanence and should contain a complete record of all that went on during the project – in a digestible form. A report must beg to be read; if it does not then your work is wasted. The factors which persuade people to read on are:

- Good presentation and layout.
- Lively and clear graphical presentations.
- Light, concise and informative text.

Sometimes the material being handled does not lend itself to a light treatment. Consider breaking it up into a number of separate elements (chapters if you like) each of which tackles a particular aspect of the project and which, combined, give an overview of the whole.

Overhead projector (OHP)

An OHP presentation uses transparencies which are projected and form the visual part of an audio-visual presentation. The key to OHP work is:

- low text
- high graphical content
- plenty of colour
- one point or issue per slide.

In making each slide a discrete topic it is possible to elaborate individual areas of data by looking at the graphical detail but explaining at length and perhaps with questions, verbally.

35mm slide

Although used less nowadays than other methods, 35mm slide presentations are still popular with those people who have not yet graduated to OHP or, more recently, to computer-based presentation systems

PowerPoint (or similar) sequence

PowerPoint is Microsoft's computer-based presentation manager which allows the user to create sequences of screens containing text, graphics, sounds, backgrounds in a clear and consistent fashion. Such presentations can be created very simply and, particularly with the graphing capability in PowerPoint, it is possible easily to create dramatic graphs and charts which will bring your data to life.

These presentations may form the backbone of a lecture/presentation or may be delivered as a final report although this is likely to need further detail presented in paper report format.

USING PICTURES AS WELL AS WORDS OR NUMBERS

'A picture has been said to be something between a thing and a thought' (Samuel Palmer)

Every picture tells a story. One picture is worth a thousand words. Pictures are a means of communication. By representing things in images a whole range of information can be communicated which would otherwise take many words. In our present context, the graphical representation of data helps the user to understand the data and its structure, as well as illustrating trends and influences – if those have been built into the picture.

In reporting your findings it will often be the case that those to whom they are to be presented need to see the nub of the matter quickly and are not interested in an exegesis of the why and wherefores. 'What is the cause? What is the consequence? What is the remedy?' might well sum up what most people want from your presentation. Giving them that in a concise fashion will help your case, regardless of whether detail information which *you* understand has been skipped.

Graphs, charts, tables and cross-tabulations – what do they show?

A graph will turn your numbers into pictures, enable you to see trends and to pick out deficiencies simply through an examination of the image. Graphing gives you the ability to realise the data in a way which may make further analyses unnecessary. For example, if a profit line is seen to be rapidly falling, while on the same graph the costs and overheads line is soaring there is little need for a genius to work out that the company is in financial trouble. Similarly, if the results from the last two surveys, plotted as bars, have shown an increase in student satisfaction with union facilities, then the third survey, plotted on top of the other two and confirming the trend, is clear evidence that your policies have been successful.

Graphs and charts can represent your data in two or three dimensions. In two dimensions, a pie chart, for example, can illustrate the proportions of people who visit a tourist attraction, by age range. Each segment of the pie represents a group of people and the area of the segment gives an indication of how many there are in that segment. The two dimensions in this example are the ages of the visitors and the percentage of each group which attended the attraction (Fig. 8.1).

If you are a 'numbers person' then the table will delight you because it speaks to you in your language. However, if like me, you are a 'picture person', you will instantly elaborate more meaning from the pie chart. Yet this and the table are representations of the same data.

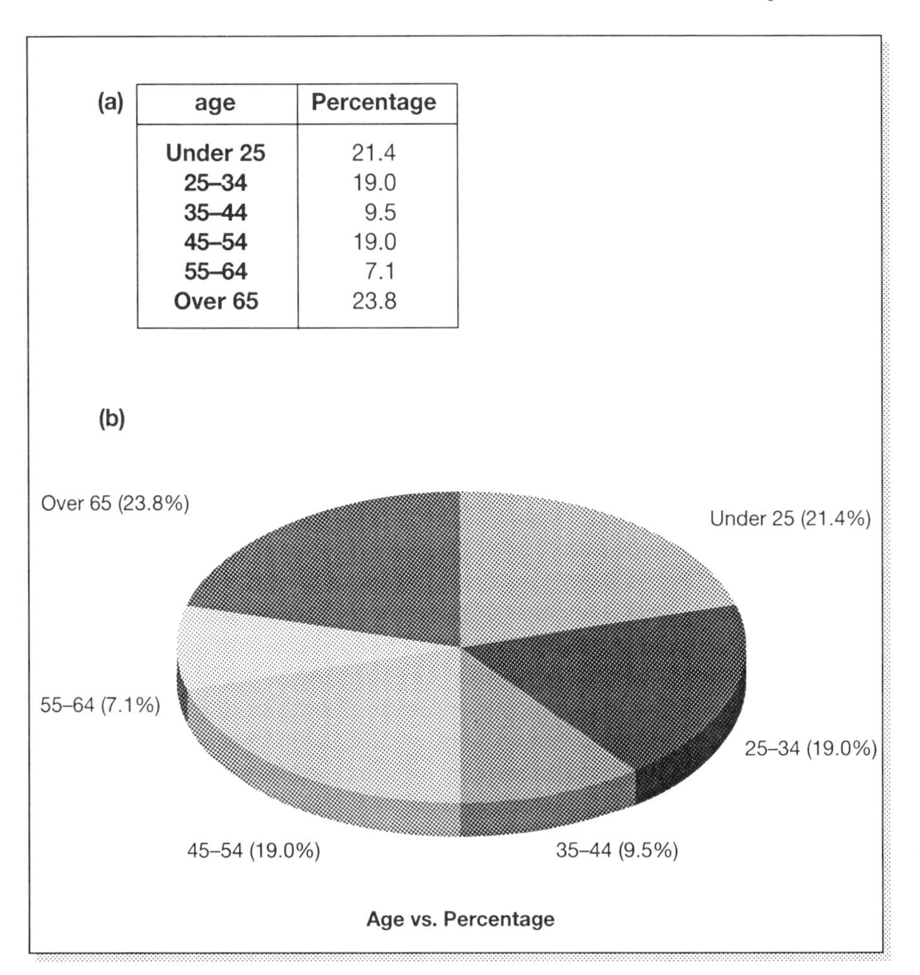
(a)

age	Percentage
Under 25	21.4
25–34	19.0
35–44	9.5
45–54	19.0
55–64	7.1
Over 65	23.8

Fig. 8.1 Two-dimensional representation of tourist information: (a) tabular; (b) pie chart

You will notice that the pie chart is not left as a bald picture of the data but is also complemented by the age range titles and an indication of the percentage of each falling into the separate groups. You may also notice that the percentages do not add up to 100 per cent. The division of this sample into the groups does not make a percentage which can be accommodated in one decimal place. Therefore a certain amount of rounding of decimals may go on. Do not be alarmed if your totals occasionally seem slightly out. This is quite normal and acceptable – within certain limits! If the rounding bothers you, simply extend the number of decimal places being displayed and the problem will disappear, unless you have a series of recurring decimals such as 57.66666 or 42.33333 which, as you will see, will never *quite* add up to 100 per cent!

GRAPHS

Each of the graph types is discussed briefly below with a mention of their uses.

Pie

The pie chart, long the province of the school 'project', is a perfectly acceptable measure of frequency or percentage. Each 'slice' of the pie represents the proportion of that sample identified by a particular characteristic.
Advantages: easy to create and to understand.
Disadvantages: very limited in scope – incapable of displaying more than one series, making comparative analysis of data impossible.

Bar

The simple bar chart represents each proportion of the sample with a single bar, its height representing its level against the scale being used to measure. Typically each *category* has an individual bar, although categories may be grouped so that all the totals from two or more categories are represented by a combined bar.
Advantages: easy to create and understand. Flexible.
Disadvantages: limited in the number of categories that can easily be displayed. This difficulty can be ameliorated to a small extent by reversing the axes and making a horizontal graph.

Pareto chart

This specialised bar chart is used when you are looking to improve processes or rectify faults. It is a useful tool in quality management and quite simply it is a bar chart on which you display the different types of faults in the usual way, grouped together by type. However, the differences between this and a normal bar chart are that the bars are first of all arranged in descending order – the most frequent problem down to the least frequent. This gives an instantly visible indication of which is your greatest problem and therefore, when it is corrected, which will give the greatest return for the time invested.

In addition, some Pareto charts have a percentage line which accumulates above the bars, showing what percentage of the problems are encompassed by the bars to the left of any given point on the line. Therefore, you might see that out of 150 customer complaints around 55 could be rectified simply by fixing one of the causes (Fig. 8.2).

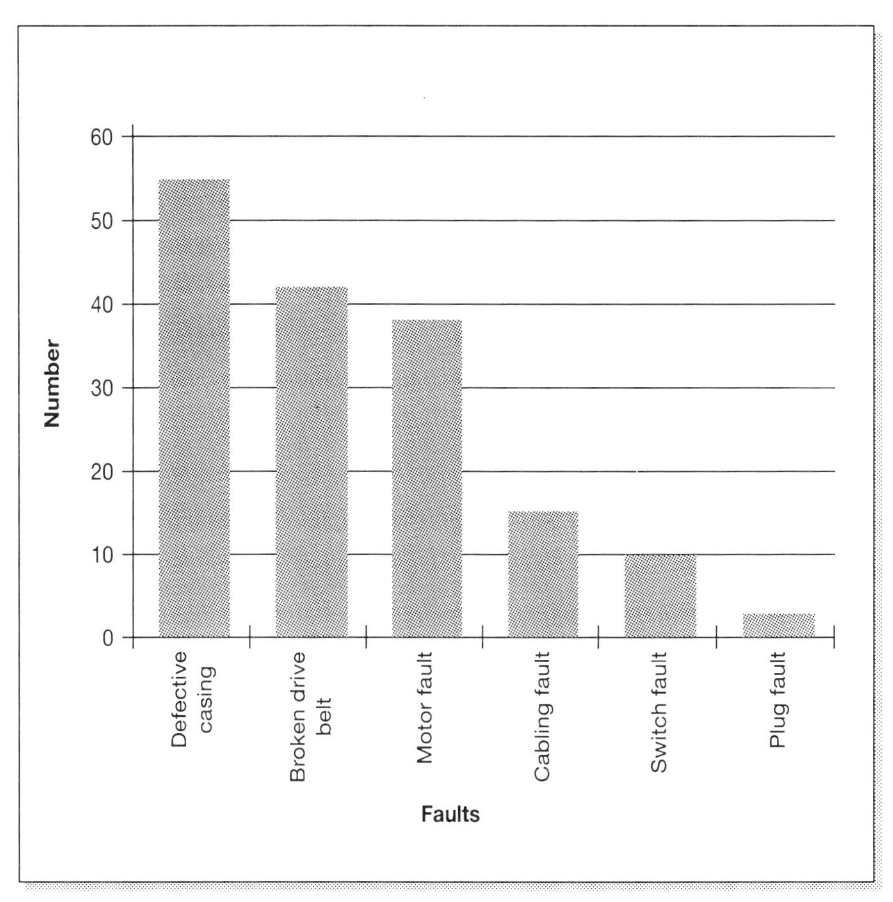

Fig. 8.2 Defects in production

Block

A block graph is similar to a pie chart in that it can deal only with a single series of data but instead of representing each part of the series as a slice of the pie, each one is a layer in the 'layer cake'. The depth of the layer represents the size of that part of the sample (Fig. 8.3).

Advantages: easy to create and understand.

Line

The simple line graph can represent similar data to the bar graph. However, it is better at 'continuous flow' data – information which varies in minute increments along a scale. An example might be a progression of profitability against time. This could be represented as a series of blocks on a bar chart, one per month. However, a line graph which is drawn on a daily basis will give much more idea of the ebb and flow of profitability and the points where trends begin and end because its resolution is finer than that of a bar graph (Fig. 8.4).

Advantage: allows wide variations to be plotted at an acceptable resolution. *Disadvantage:* less effective with groups of data unless class intervals (binning) are used.

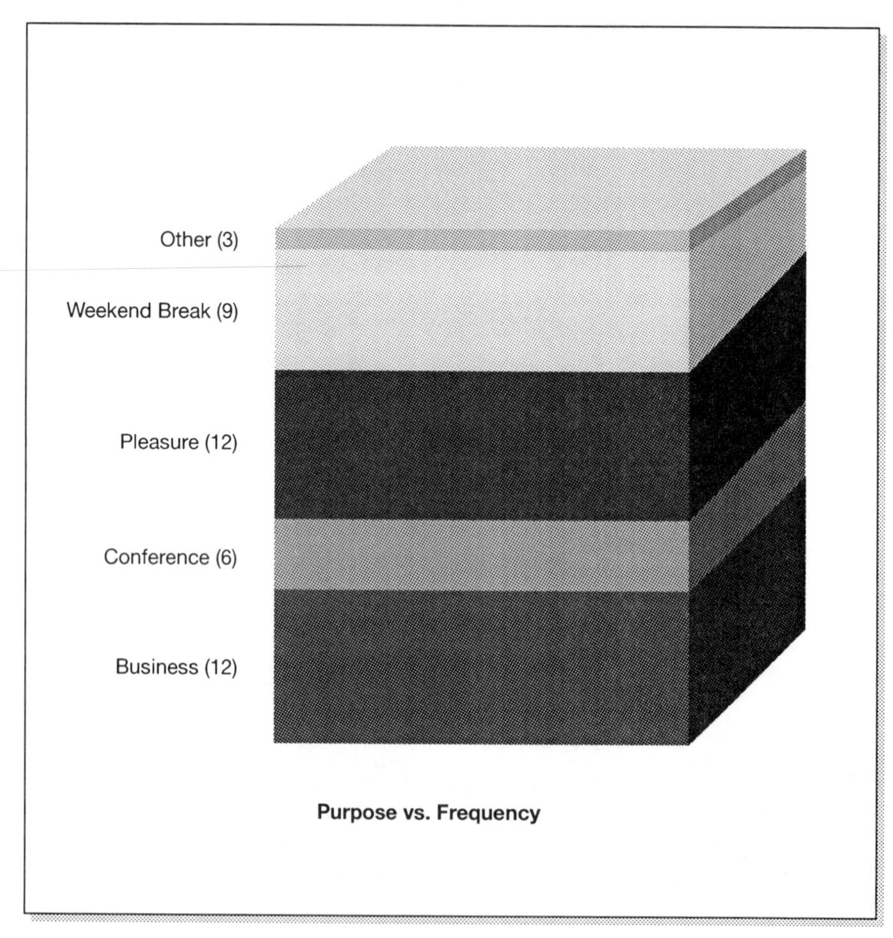

Fig. 8.3 Block graph

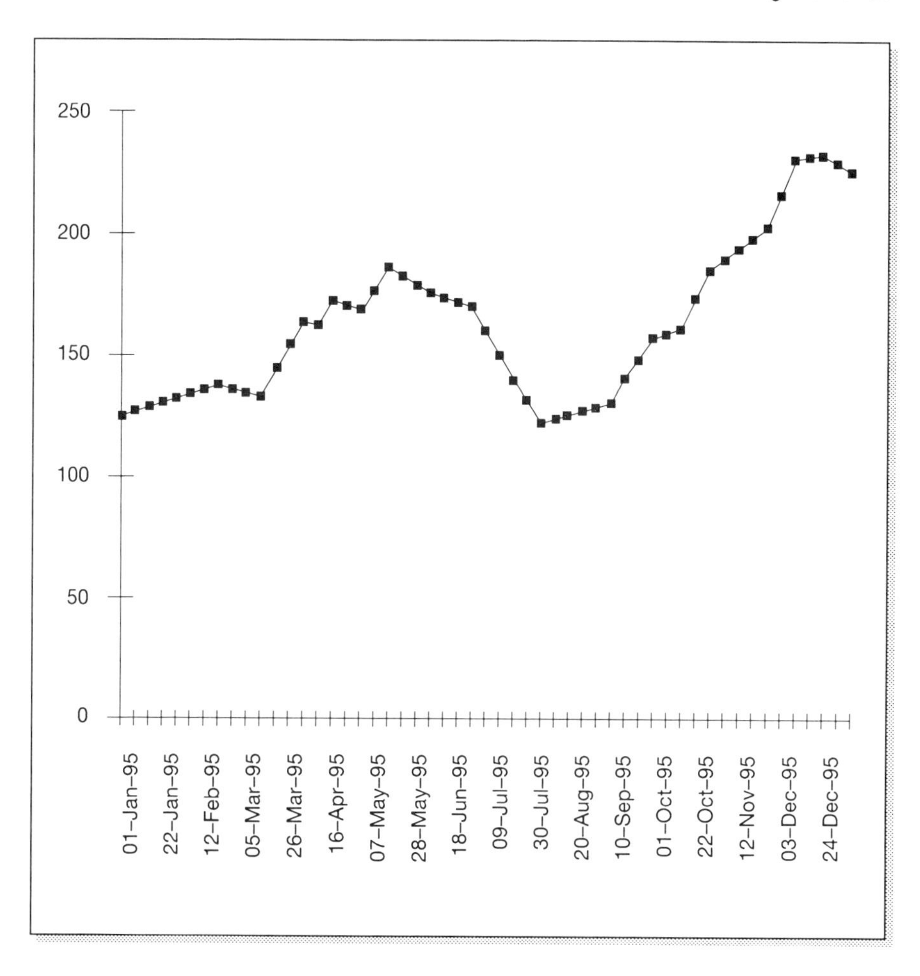

Fig. 8.4 Line chart

Area

An area graph shows, as its name suggests, that the area under the line has a significance. The filled area represents the volume of the variable being measured (Fig. 8.5). Therefore it is possible to gain a pictorial representation of overall percentage by observing the filled and unfilled areas.

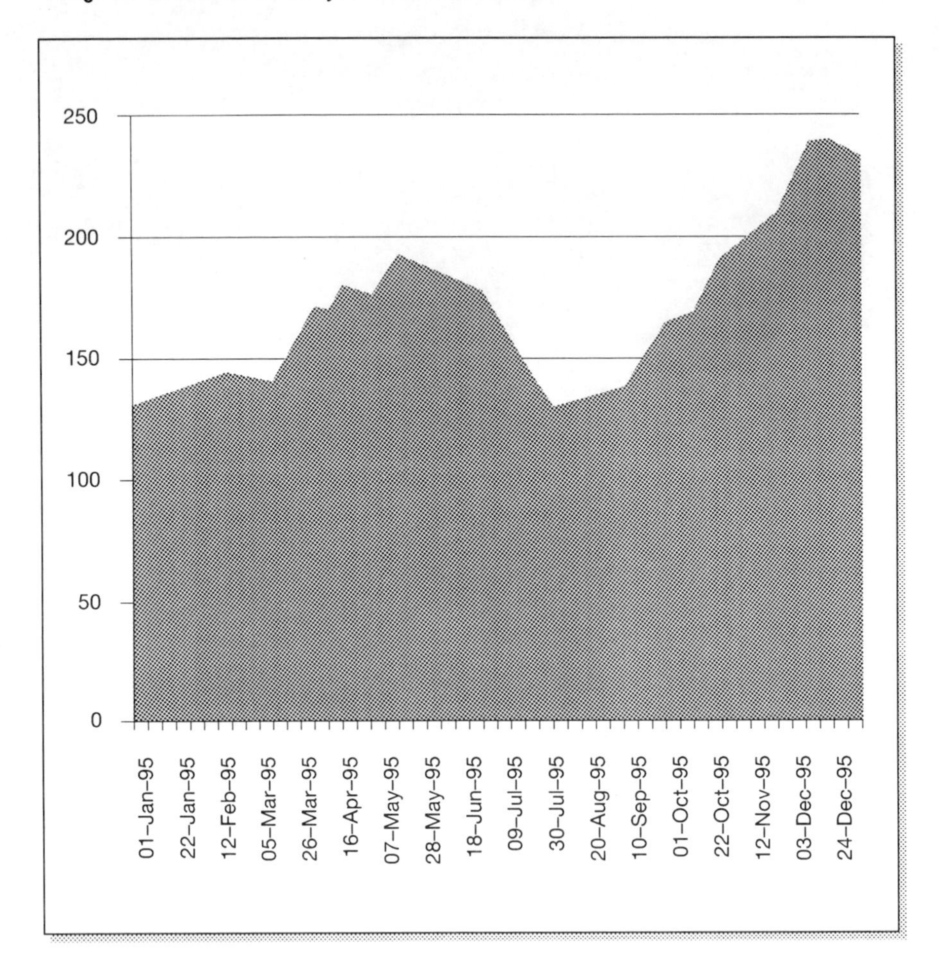

Fig. 8.5 Depicting sales by area graph

Scatter graph

A scattergraph allows you to cross-correlate two separate variables, seeing whether there is a relationship between their distribution. For example, in a survey of children's birthweight, one might reasonably ask the question 'Do big babies grow into big children?' The question can be answered by cross-plotting weight at birth with weight at age 12, for example (Fig. 8.6). If there is any significance to the data it can be shown by drawing a line of best fit.

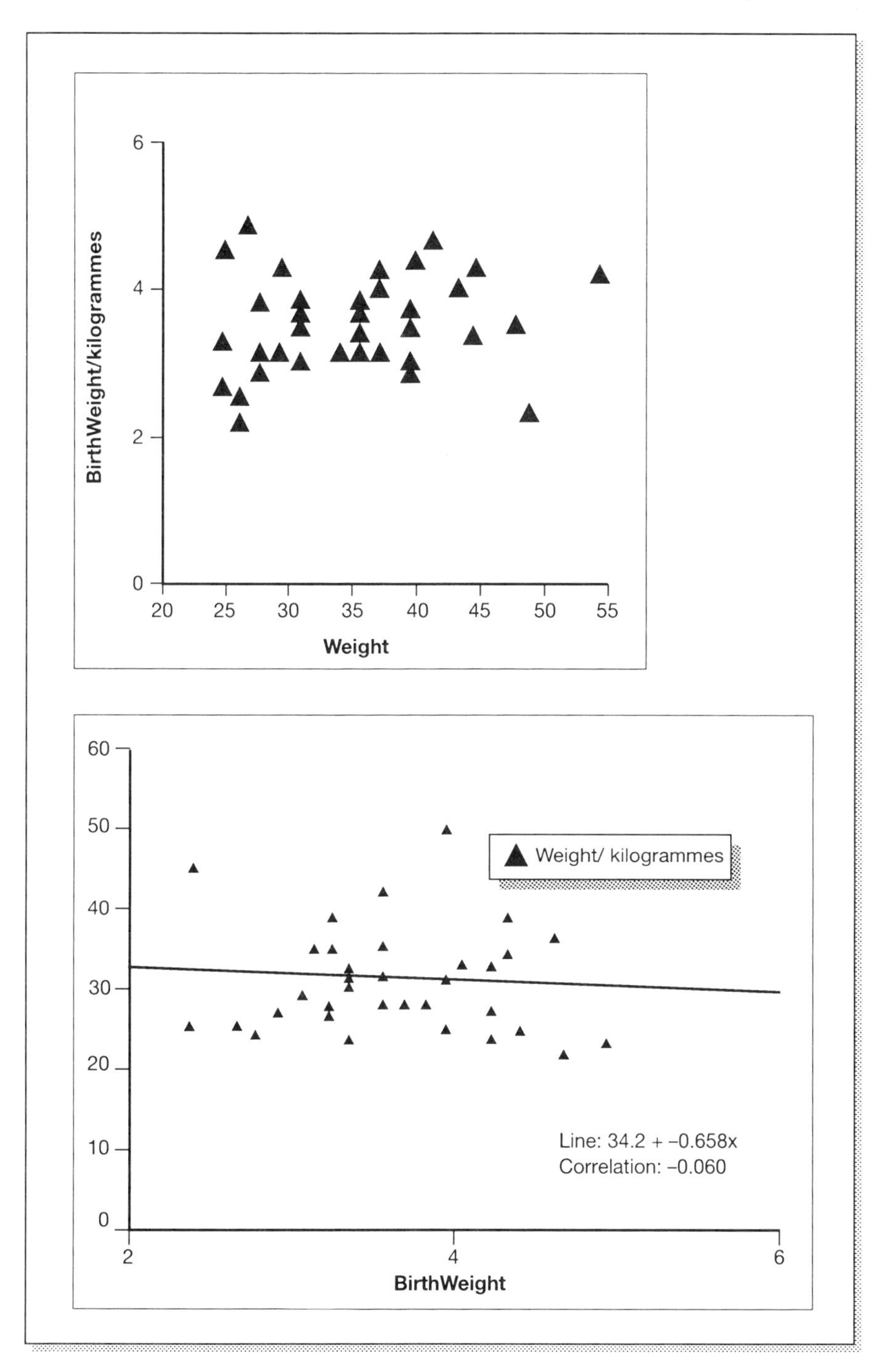

Fig. 8.6 Cross-correlations of birthweight with weight at age 12 years using scattergraphs

Distorting by scale

It is very easy to distort the truth simply by distorting the graph. For example, the humble 3D pie chart can lie profusely simply dependent upon the amount of 'rake' there is in the pie (how far back it is slanted) and which portions are at the front of the image. The nearer portions look proportionately bigger than those at the back because they are! Represent the same graph in 2D and the real truth is told. As you can see in Fig. 8.7, the sector for 'Business' looks significantly smaller than that for 'Pleasure' in the 3D graph, whereas in fact the sectors are identical in size.

Similarly, by stretching the axes on a graph in either direction it is possible to make bars and peaks look larger and smaller than they really are (see Fig. 8.8). Of course that is only because one is looking only at the picture rather than the scale, but the impression remains that perhaps things are not as bad as they seem, a greater proportion of people prefer Sudso or the crime figures really are not growing *that* fast.

A SAMPLE SET OF BAR CHARTS

To illustrate the basics of bar charts, imagine that you need to extract some more information from our hotel customer satisfaction file. You have a need to see the relative proportions of men and women who visit your hotel and then to follow a brief investigative trail to see whether the proportions hold good across the age ranges – you suspect that perhaps they might not!

1. *Identify the whole set of respondents*

You need all the records present for this first pass in your investigation. In your graphing system you need to ask it to show you all the information relating to *sex* which has been stored as a binary choice – yes/no (or in this case male/female) – answer set, and display it as straightforward count. This means that the system will look at every record and tally all those which are *male* and all those which are *female*. The resulting totals, instead of saying 'there are *X* male and *Y* female records', will be displayed as a bar graph which shows the count as in Fig. 8.9.

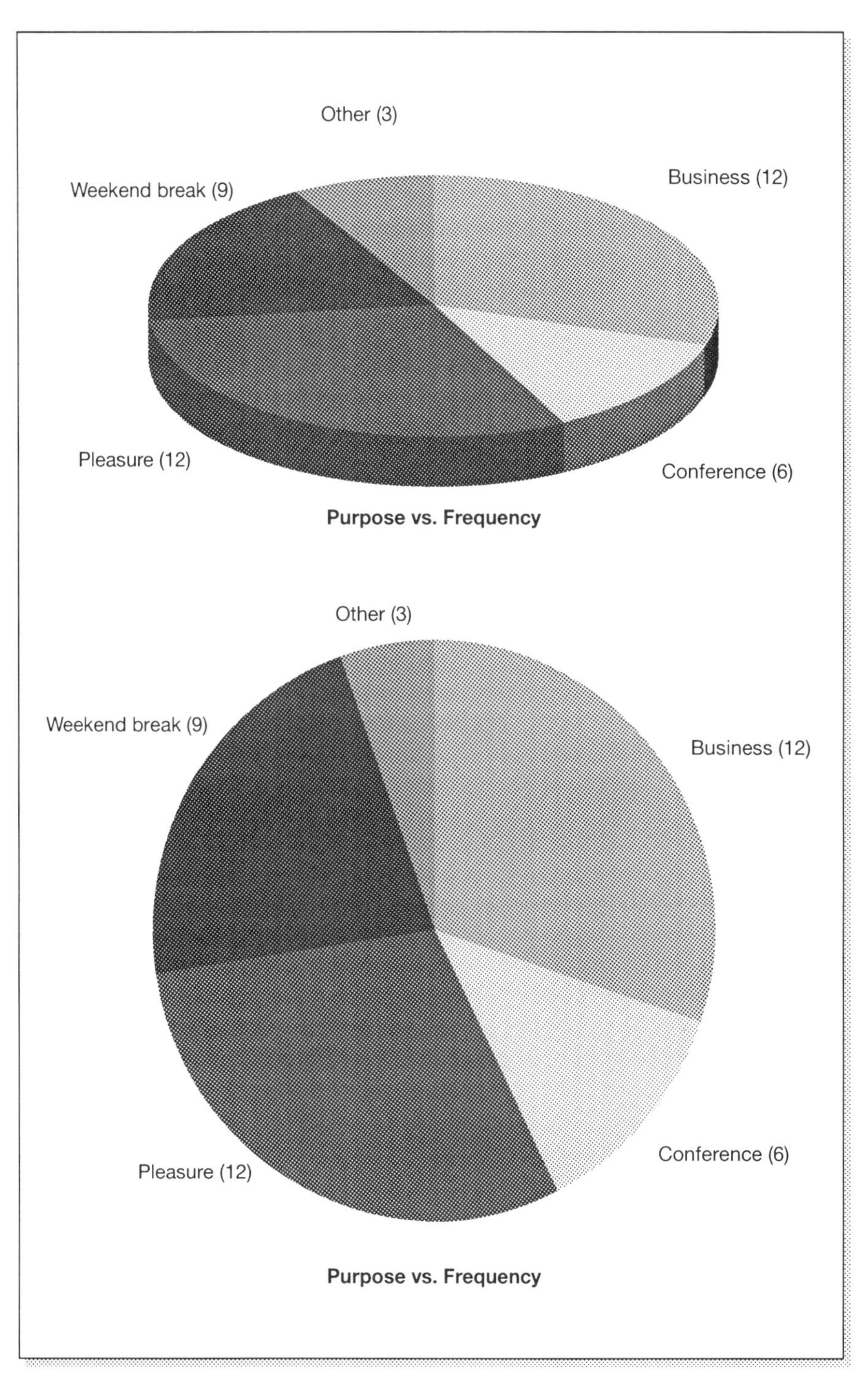

Fig. 8.7 Distorting the scale

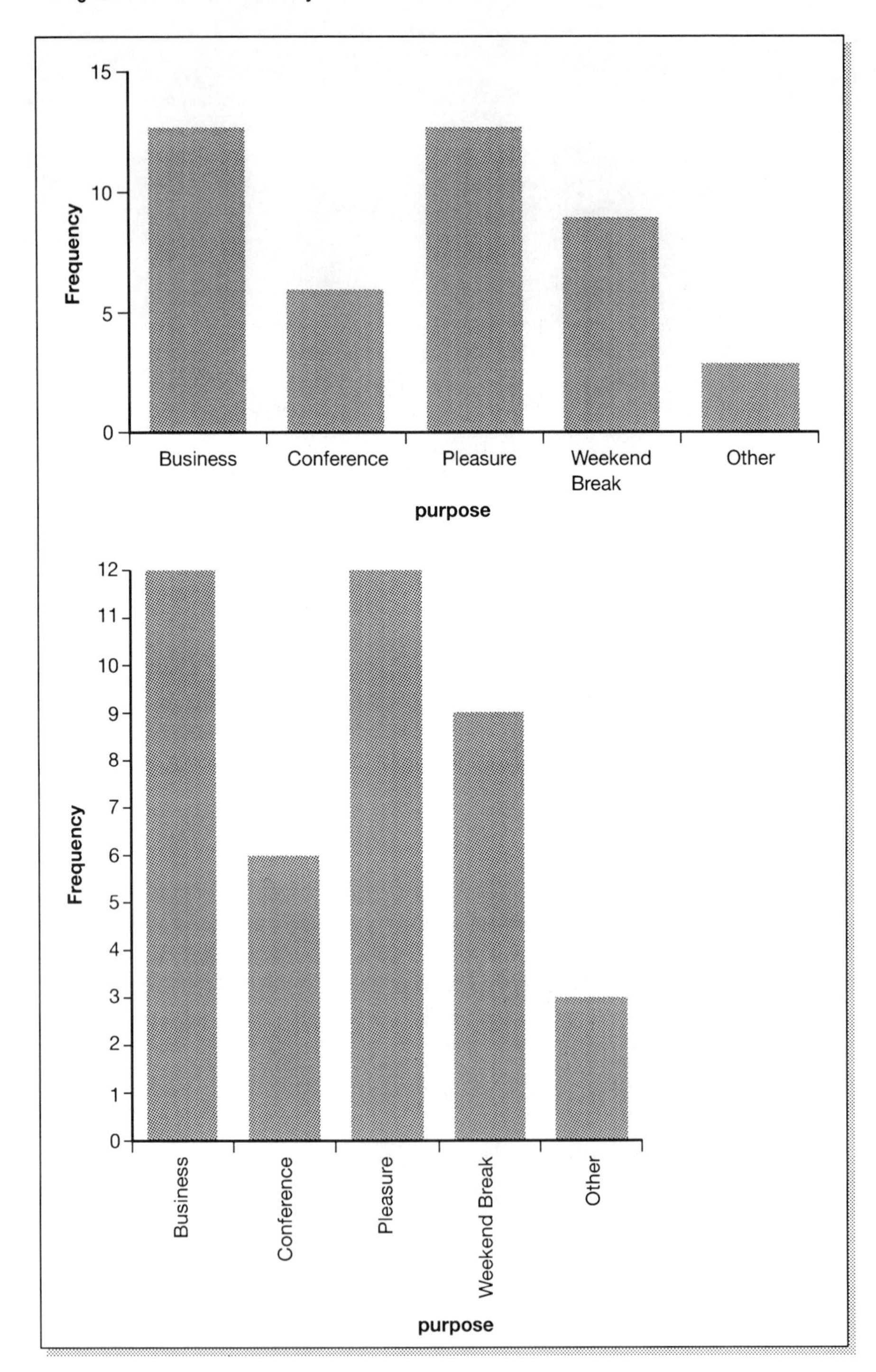

Fig. 8.8 Distorting results on bar charts

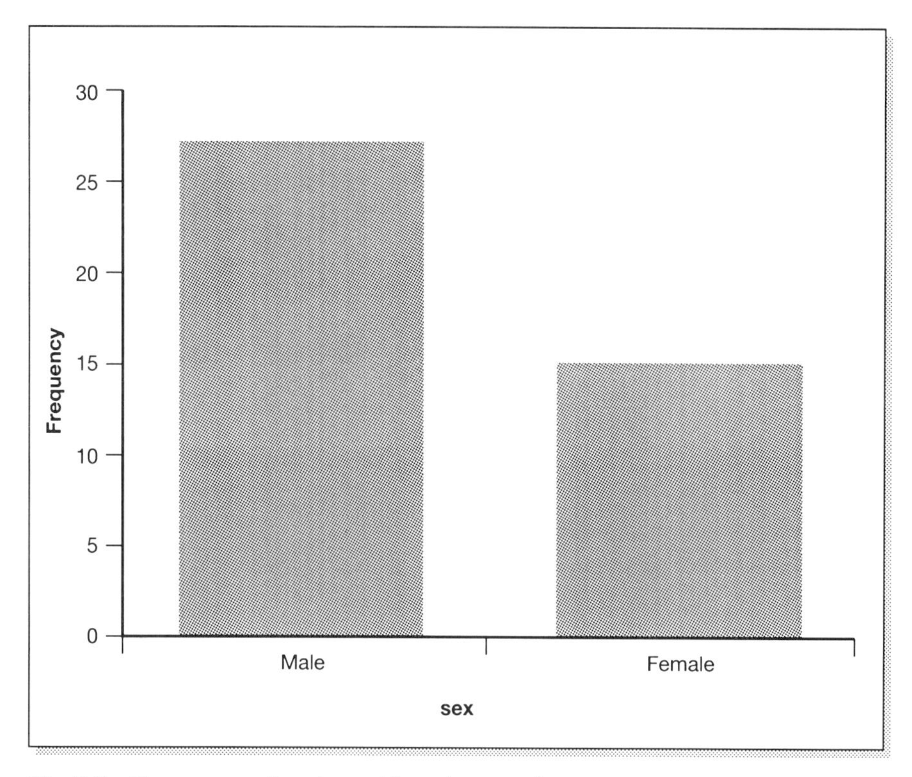

Fig. 8.9 Frequency of male and female records

2. *Use a discriminator to modify the set of data*
In other words, choose a subset, in this case how about choosing all those records in which *age* is between 0 and 34? This means that instead of using the whole set of records we are simply using a subset. Now ask the graphing system to draw another graph relating to *sex*, just like it did before, but this time using the subset information. The result might be a graph like Fig. 8.10.

3. *Use a different discriminator from the same question to identify another portion of the data*
This means, set things back to looking at the full set of data and then choose another different subset. How about all those records where *age* is between 35 and 65? The rest of the set, in other words. Now ask the system to graph that data, again by plotting the *sex* of the people in this new subset, but with one difference: ask the graphing system to plot it on the same axes as the previous graph. This gives a result something like Fig. 8.11.

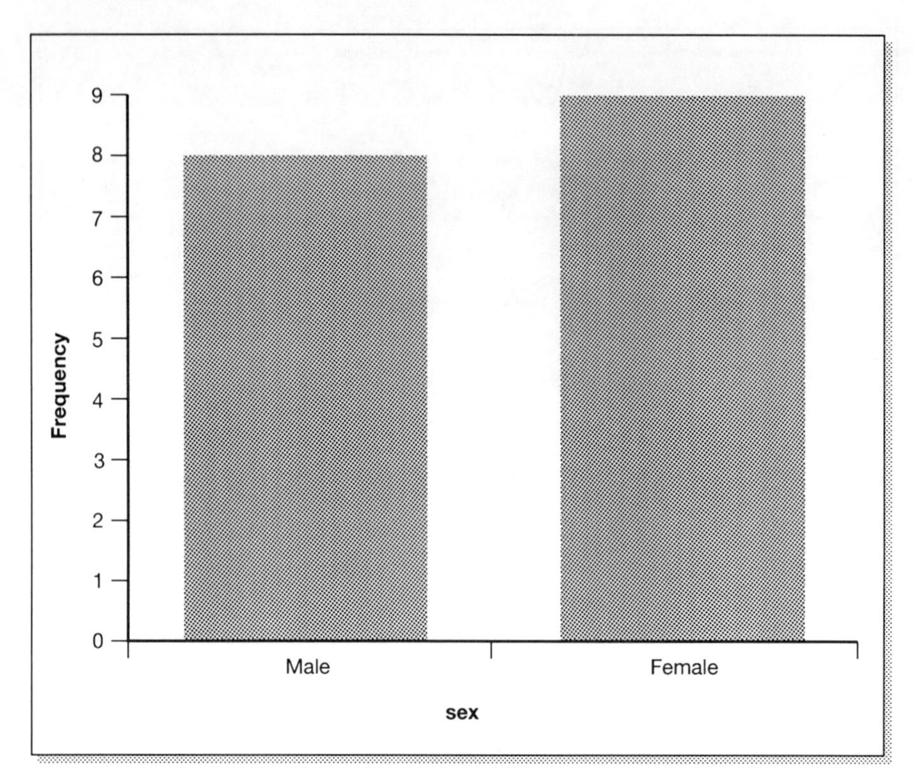

Fig. 8.10 Subset of male/female distribution for age 0–34

As you can see, there is a clear indication that your theory is correct (the proportions of men and women actually change places across the range of ages), a finding which may be significant when you come to examine other aspects of your data.

SOME ISSUES AND TERMS RELATING TO GRAPHS AND CHARTS

Most graphs, with the exception of pie charts are plotted on a grid which is formed around two intersecting lines called *axes*. An *Axis* (singular) is a line along which data are plotted. A standard bar chart or line graph has two axes. These are usually called *X* and *Y*. The *X* axis traditionally is the *category* axis along which the variable against which the data is being drawn, is measured. This might be the different responses or categories found in a question: '*Excellent*', '*Good*', '*Poor*', for example. The *category* axis may also represent a constant flow in one direction – time in a line graph of profits, for example. Axes are sometimes reversed in order to improve the readability of the data. This is particularly useful when the labels relating to the data are long (see Fig. 8.12).

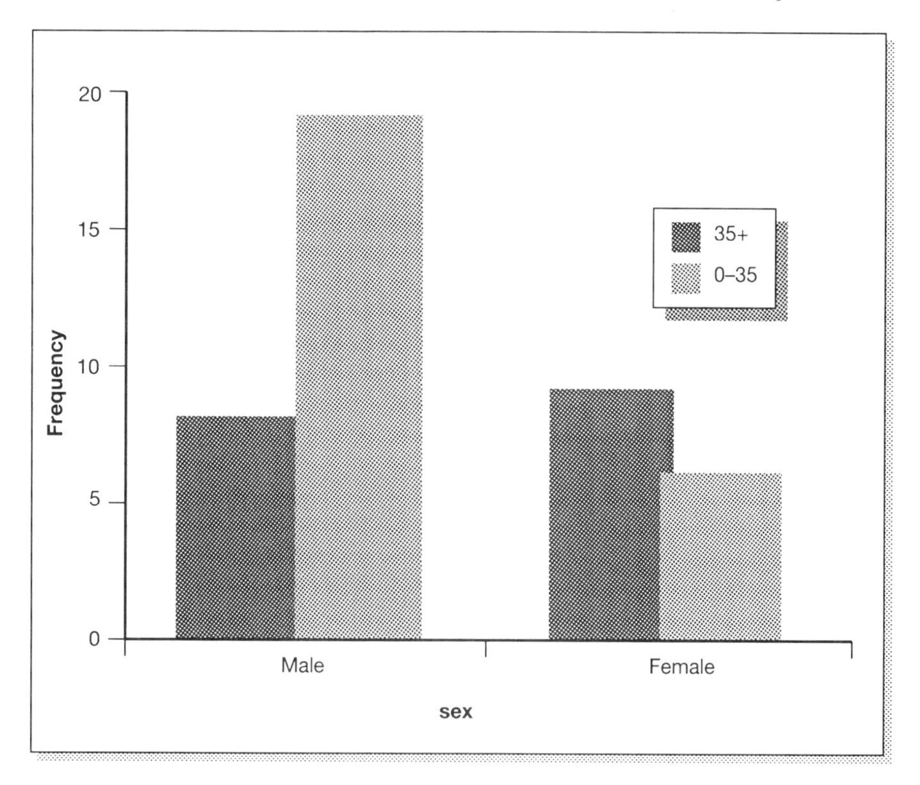

Fig. 8.11 Plotting a different discriminator on the first graph

Each set of data on a graph is called a *Series*. Where more than one series is plotted on the same graph this is called a *multi-series* graph. This type of graph must be plotted with common variables and measures otherwise it will make no sense. It is, however, possible to place two or more graphs of different measures on the same axes, provided that they are displayed separately. This allows the common elements to be observed while not confusing those parts which are different (Fig. 8.13).

Extending the graph

Further information can easily be added to line and bar charts. For example, the mean, median and mode may be represented in different ways on these charts (see Fig. 8.14).

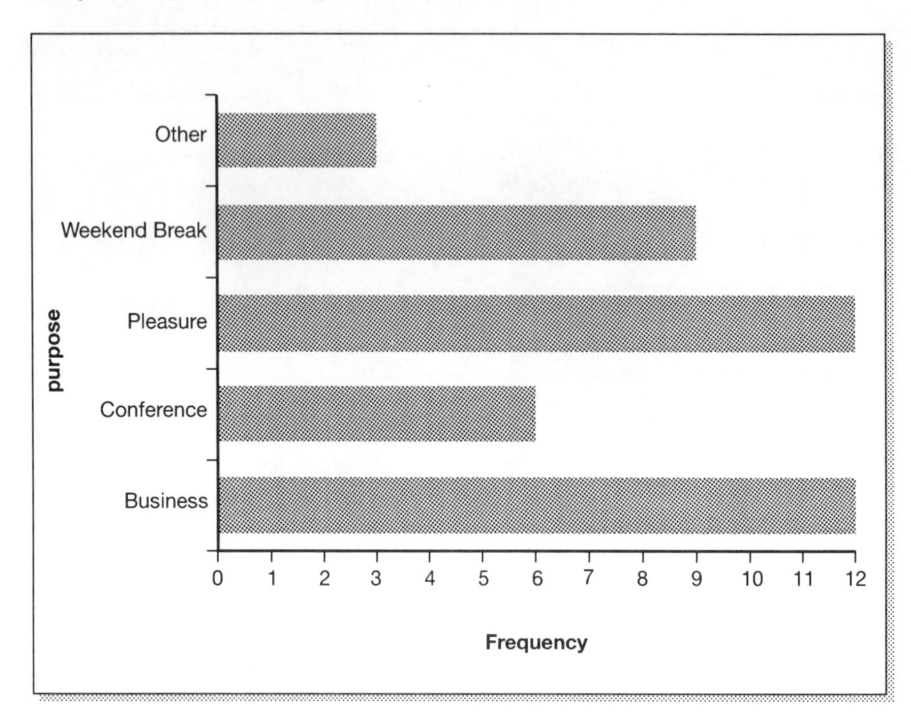

Fig. 8.12 Reversing axes of a bar chart

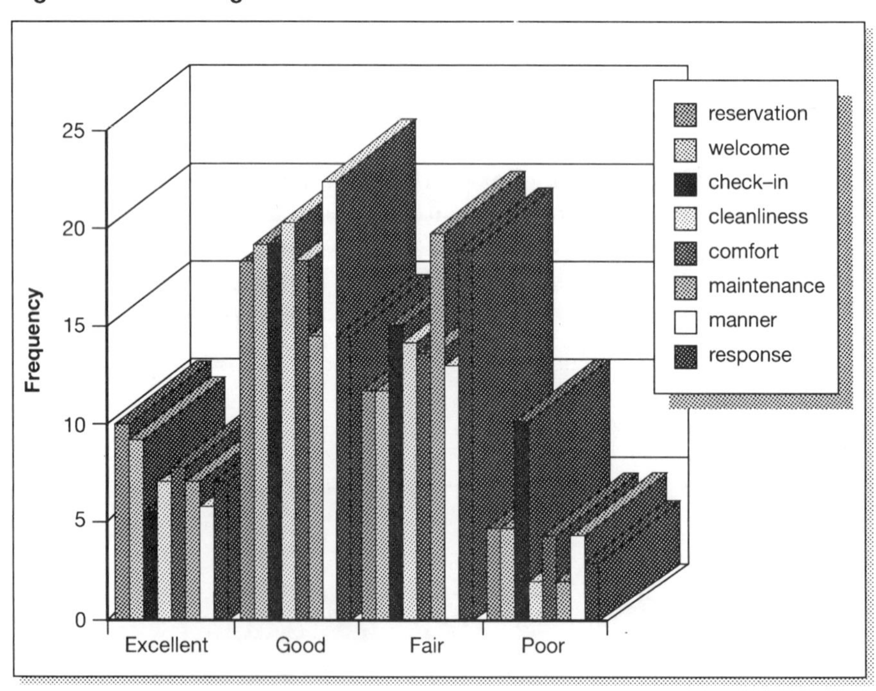

Fig. 8.13 A multi-series graph

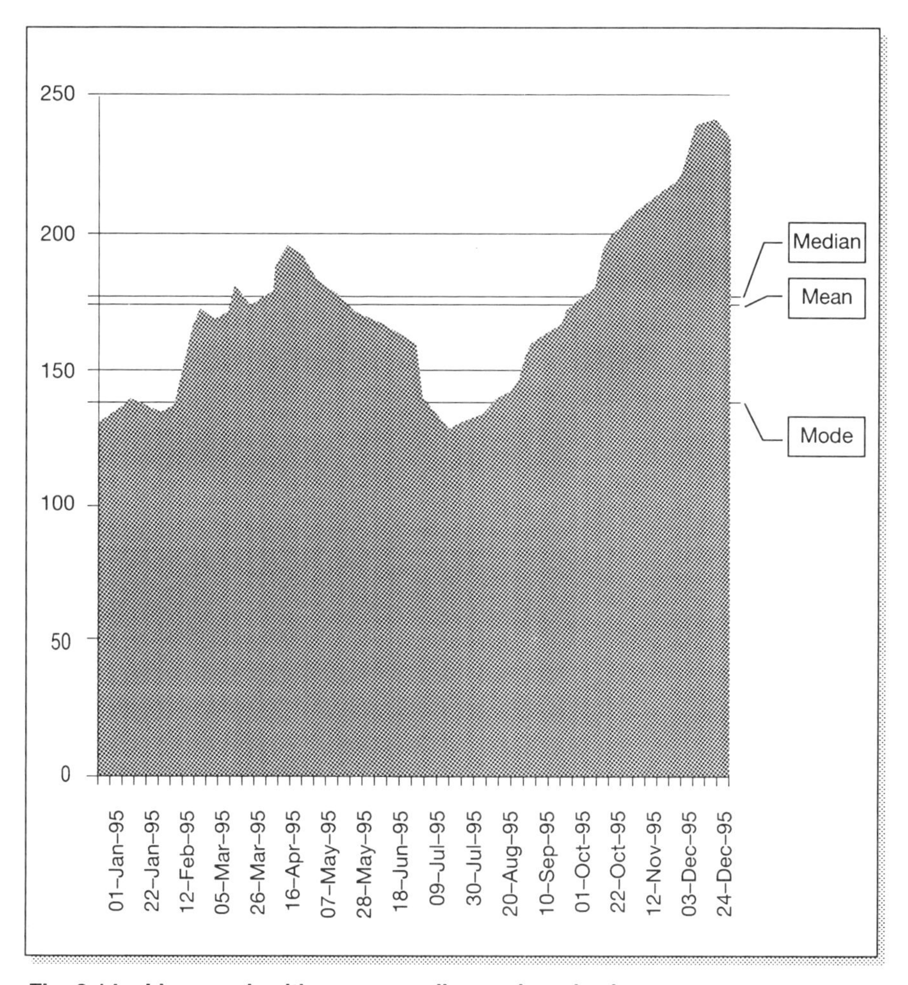

Fig. 8.14 Line graph with mean, median and mode shown

Another way of doing this is to move the 0 point of the *Y* axis so that it represents the mean, for example (see Fig. 8.15). All those bars which represent values below the mean will point one way, whereas those above it will point the other, very graphically demonstrating the relationship of each element.

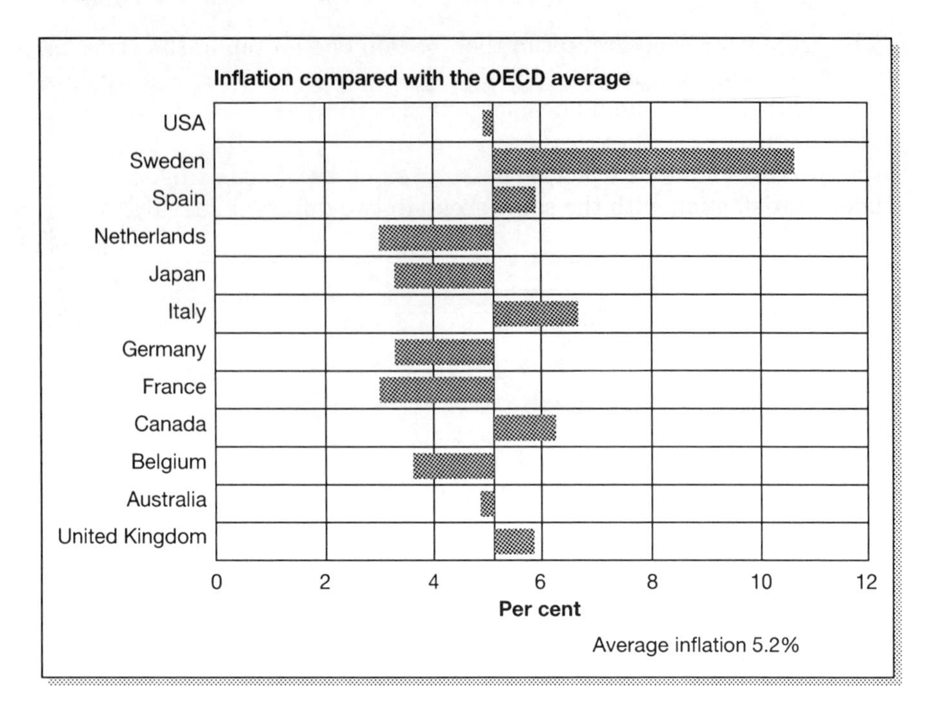

Fig. 8.15 Moving the *Y* axis to represent the mean

Using percentages

Using absolute frequencies (straight counts) on a graph may be acceptable for single series graphs, but for those which are multi-series this process only works when both sets of data have the same number of *cases*. In any other instance where you are comparing two sets of data, use percentages to even out inconsistencies in the population. In the two bar charts of Fig. 8.16 showing the *purpose* in visiting a hotel for each person in the survey, there is a larger number of men than women. In the first graph that difference affects the outcome. What you are really trying to see is what the trend is, not the actual figures. The percentage chart on the right shows the general intention of men and women in this instance.

Multi-series graphs

The multi-series graph allows you to compare two or more sets of data with each other. For example, you may perform a survey on a student population or on your customer base in 1993 to measure their satisfaction with a variety of aspects of your service. As a result of your findings you implement changes to the areas of concern that have been highlighted. In 1994 you run the same survey again, measuring against an identical sample (may even be the same people) in order to see whether your changes have had any impact on their opinions.

The graphs for each group can then be laid one on top of the other in order to see where changes are being shown (Fig. 8.17). If opinion has improved then there should be a lessening in the *average* and *poor* areas and an increase in the *excellent* and *good*. This will be visible immediately if the two sets of data are plotted onto the same axes, as in this survey of student satisfaction with the same group in two different surveys.

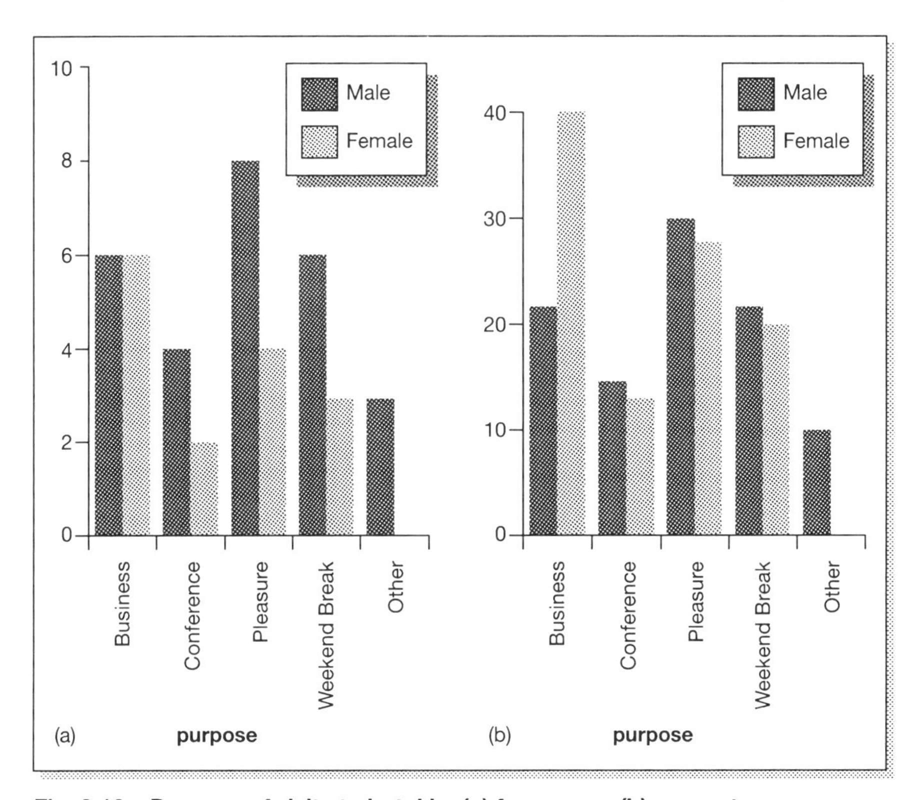

Fig. 8.16 Purpose of visits to hotel by (a) frequency, (b) percentage

In addition, more than one series may be plotted with its elements alongside those same elements of another series, allowing comparisons directly.

3D graphs

A 3D graph is one where multiple series of data are shown on a single graph. This can be done first by adding each series to the graph, and then extending it backwards with a row of blocks for each new series (Fig. 8.18).

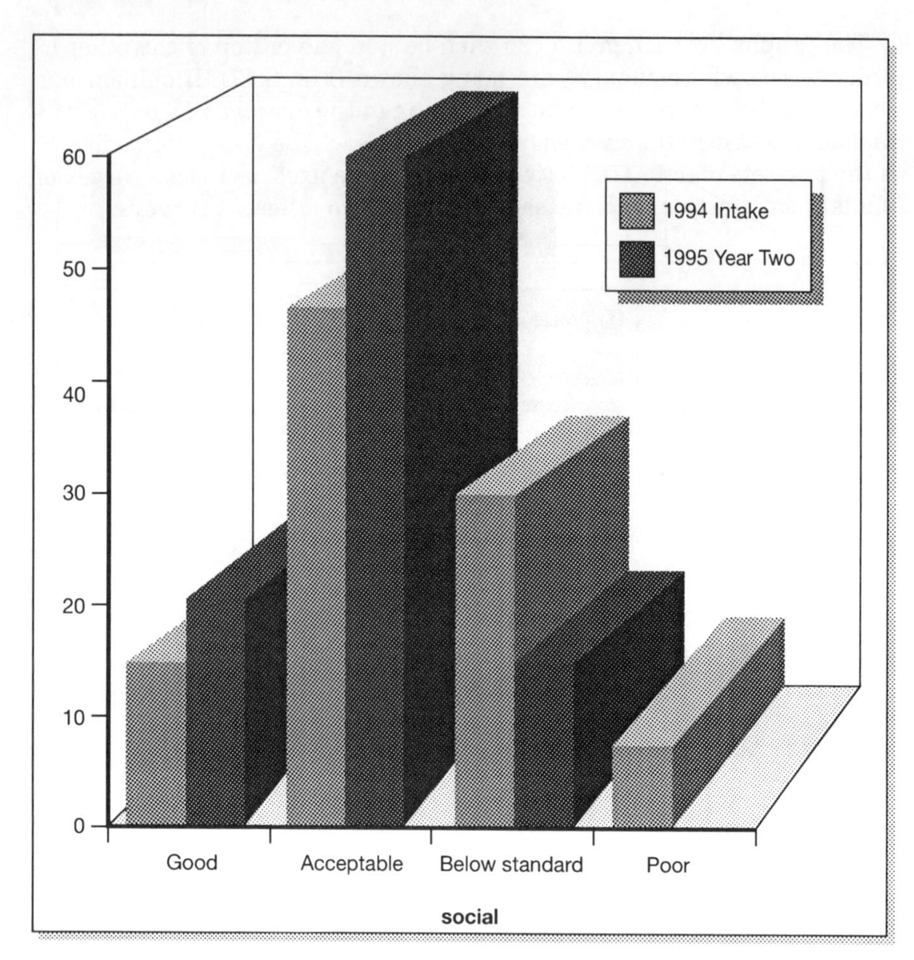

Fig. 8.17 Multi-series graph of student satisfaction

Stacked graphs

The second method is by stacking the graph sectors, using different colours to separate and identify each series (Fig. 8.19). The advantage of stacking is that it enables the total of two or more series to be observed, whereas its disadvantage is that it makes comparing two series more difficult.

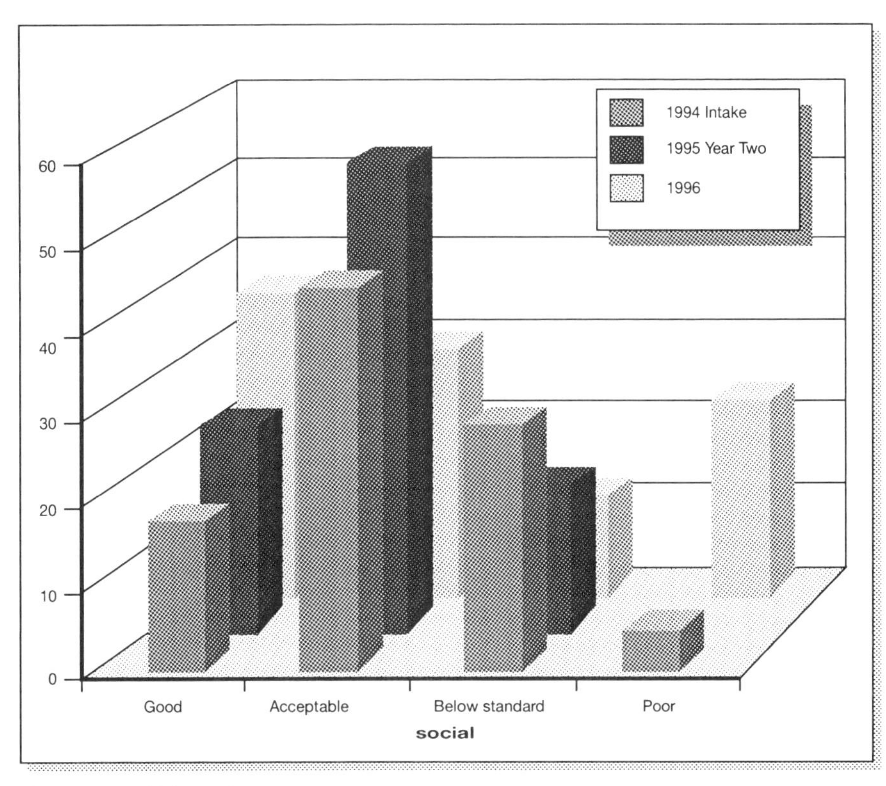

Fig. 8.18 3D bar charts

GRAPHING DIFFERENT TYPES OF DATA

According to the type of data you have available so you will choose particular graph styles.

Numeric (class interval)

Numeric data implies that there will be a range of values which may increment in anything from single units down to many decimal places. Making sense of this type of data depends upon the requirement. For example, if one were to graph the age at death of people from a certain area it would be very much the case that a line graph would be inappropriate – it would simply rise and fall as each case was encountered and give little interpretation. This type of *classification* data needs to use an appropriate graphing style which highlights classified groups. By grouping the data into class interval 'bins', it is possible to see how specific groups have fared. This process means that the data may be represented in, say, 10 bars rather than the possible 100 bars that could be required for a sample of 100 people.

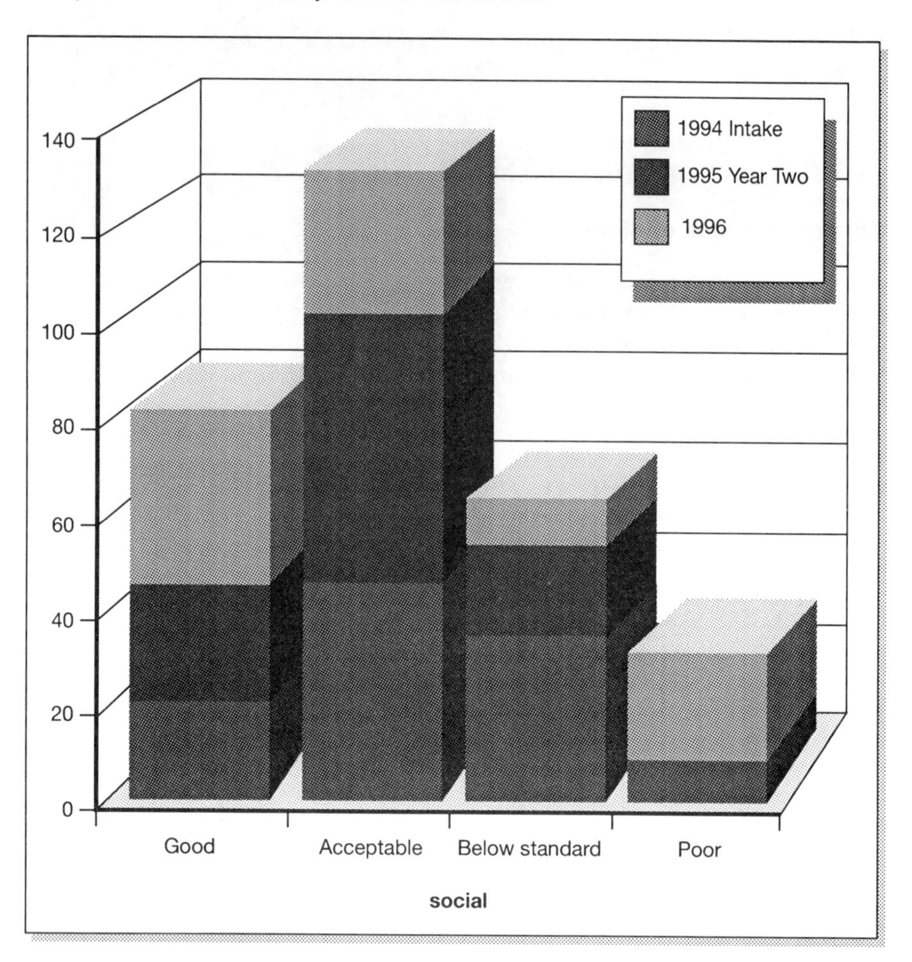

Fig. 8.19 Stacking graphs

This type of numeric does not lend itself to a line graph because it has no direction or 'flow'. A plot of sales figures against time shows a variation which may rise or fall due to factors yet to be discovered. Seasonal variations, for example, can be highlighted by plotting data in this way.

Text

Traditionally it is impossible to 'plot' text responses graphically, yet the frequency of certain words or phrases can be mapped by the classification style of graph. This process is one way of representing customer satisfaction data – count the 'Excellent', 'Good' and 'Poor', and represent them as a bar chart.

Similarly free text may, after being coded (see the section on Coding Questions) be categorised and mapped by bar, pie or block graphs. So in a survey of village life, respondents might be asked to express their views about any further topics which have not been covered in the questionnaire. The frequency of occurrence of particular topics: litter, broken flagstones, speed limit, postal collections, can then be coded and graphed to give an overview of issues that have not been tackled so far.

Ranges (multiple choice)

Multiple choice ranges are once again a classification style of data and therefore lend themselves to bar, pie and block graphing. Since one is counting the number of times which each option has been selected, it is simply a matter of totalling them and displaying the graph.

Popularity (ranking)

Ordered choice or *ranked* questions give a popularity index for any given question. In graphing the results one is counting the scores given to particular components offered in the question. So, for example, in the question:

Please rank these makes of car in order of preference, with 1 being your most preferred car and 5 your least preferred:

☐ Peugeot 405 Diesel
☐ Ford Mondeo GLS Automatic
☐ Reliant Robin
☐ Ferrari Testarossa
☐ Fiat Uno

there are five makes of car, and therefore five scores. For each respondent, the first choice (1) will score the top marks: in this case, because there are five choices it will score 5. The second choice will score 4; the third, 3 and so on. This *inverse scoring* allows the system to profile the popularity of each make simply by adding the scores for each car from every respondent. The end result is a chart which reflects the levels of preference.

Popularity ranking is often used, for example, in employee profiling where attitudes to their work, the management, the environment and so on, are measured and shortcomings may be observed. An example from 'real life' might be the election result where the various political parties are ranked in their overall order of popularity per constituency and then grossed up as a popularity chart (Fig. 8.20). Each bar represents the accumulated popularity score for each party – in this case over a period of elections throughout the twentieth century. Putting this into a workplace example, employees may be asked to evaluate the importance of a number of activities in their role and to place them in order of priority (which in this case is a more appropriate term than 'popularity'). The overall score for an individual will give an impression of their feeling about their value in the total operation, and the accumulated scores from the entire workforce will show where the emphases lie in total or within particular subgroups.

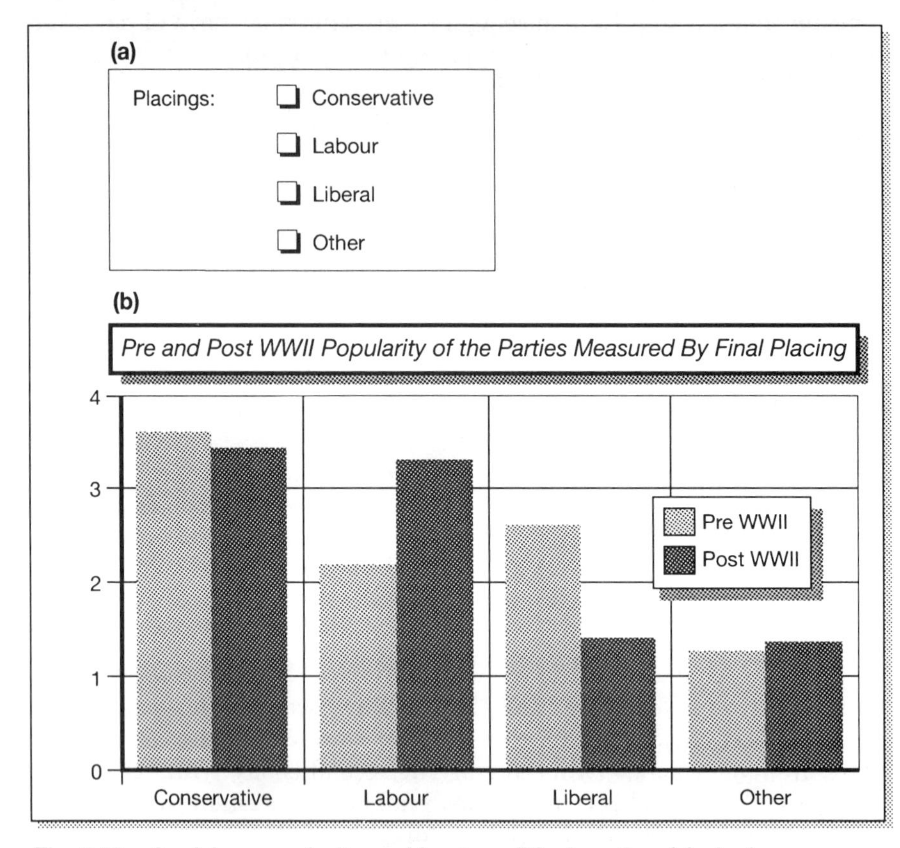

Fig. 8.20 Applying popularity ranking to political parties: (a) placings question; (b) popularity presentation

Frequency (absolute and percentage)

Any graph which simply counts the number of times a particular option is selected is plotting *frequency*. As has been mentioned earlier, frequency plots are fine provided that no comparison is needed with other data sets containing a different number of respondents. In that case, use percentage plots to overcome the difference and highlight the underlying trend.

INTERRELATING CHARTS, GRAPHS AND CROSS-TABULATIONS – A TYPICAL SEQUENCE OF ANALYSES

Single graphs can tell a good deal, but a structured approach to analysing and presenting your data will pay dividends because it will allow you to observe trends that you may have otherwise missed. In the following example we look at the data from the hotel survey which we have encountered already. Here, however, we are starting from scratch.

In the first analysis you need to have an overview of all the data in order to see where anything interesting may lurk. This is no time to be constrained by what you thought you *might* find. A data bureau will provide you with instant cross-tabulations and preliminary analyses which will be undertaken dispassionately. If you are undertaking this work yourself then you need to treat your data with the same detachment. So, first of all, look at the data simply in terms of frequencies. You may find that you can, with suitable software, print out summary data complete with totals for the responses to each question.

Figure 8.21 shows that there is a problem with *check-in* procedures; that although *cleanliness* is generally satisfactory, the perception of the level of *maintenance* is poor; that our hotel, although *friendly* and efficient is slow to *respond* to requests for service. All that information can be gleaned by scanning a single sheet of paper. However, the causes which underlie those facts can be further elaborated and may, in fact, be due completely to outside circumstances. For example, how do we know *who* voted that the maintenance was poor? Is there any correlation between the people who thought that response times were slow and those who found that check-in was unsatisfactory? Were these people drawn from a particular group: male, female, over 65, business visitors?

Nearly all of these questions can be answered very rapidly by performing a simple cross-tabulation. If one cross-tabulates all the maintenance respondents with, for instance, the age groups then one comes out with the grid in Fig. 8.22. As one can see, there are some interesting groupings. Perhaps these areas need examining further. It may be a good idea to see this data in a more graphical format by selecting the 'interesting' columns from the cross-tabulation and rendering them as pie charts (Fig. 8.23).

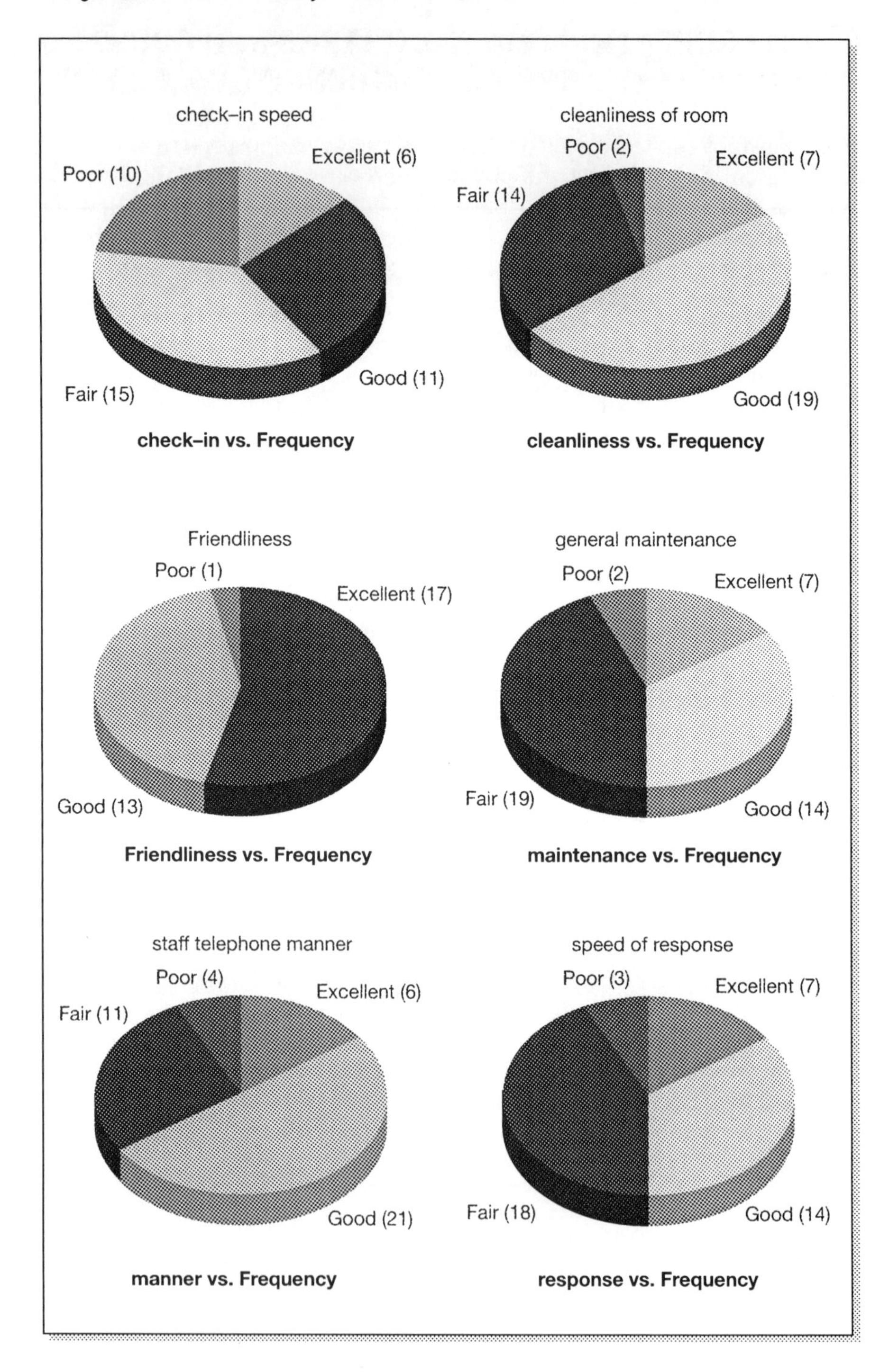

Fig. 8.21 Overview of responses to hotel survey

age counts % columns	maintenance Excellent	 Good	 Fair	 Poor	 Total
Under 25	2 29%	5 36%	2 11%	0 0%	9 9
25–34	2 29%	3 21%	3 16%	0 0%	8 19%
35–44	0 0%	0 0%	4 21%	0 0%	4 10%
45–54	2 29%	0 0%	5 26%	1 50%	8 19%
55–64	0 0%	0 0%	3 16%	0 0%	3 7%
Over 65	1 14%	6 43%	2 11%	1 50%	10 24%
Total	7	14	19	2	42

Fig. 8.22 Cross-tabulating age with maintenance responses

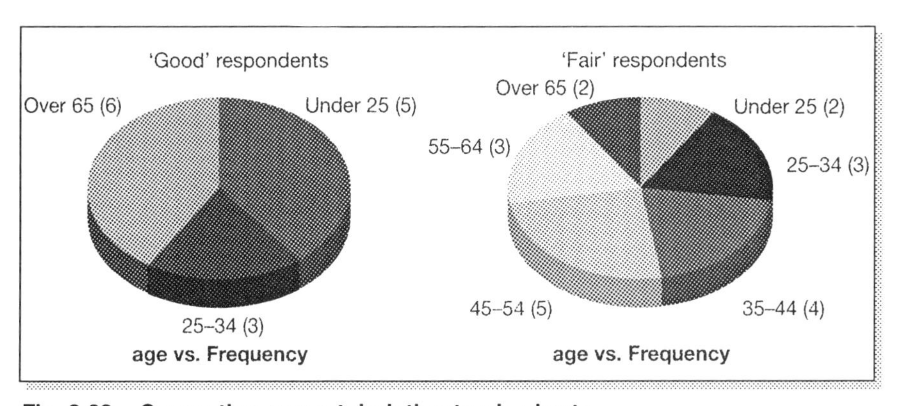

Fig. 8.23 Converting cross-tabulation to pie charts

Now a clearer picture is beginning to emerge. There is a definite bulge in the data which is at the two extremes of the age ranges. It may now be a good idea to move on and cross-correlate these same groups with other areas of satisfaction.

Looking at trends by comparing data from different years/groups/areas

This method of examining the data allows you to identify discriminators – that is, factors which isolate particular types of respondent. In our example above, the discriminator was quite definitely age. Therefore it is not unreasonable to hypothesise that it may also be a discriminator for other factors in the data. It is worth beginning to examine other elements against age. However, do not be drawn into assuming that that is the whole story. There is a chance that a number of discriminators may be at work in your data – the purpose for which people visited, the time of year (related to the efficiency of seasonal staff perhaps), the sex and age of the individuals, and so on. All of these factors may be thrown into relief simply through the intelligent and creative use of cross-tabulation.

However, you have now looked at that data, drawn from it as much as you feel it will render and set it aside to get on with running your hotel. The information is not dead. It lives still because it is the benchmark against which you may measure next year's survey. There are a number of factors which affect the validity of this. First, the survey needs to be conducted in a similar fashion, with a similar group of people at a similar time of year. Remember that you should always compare like with like unless you are trying to establish what characterises the differences between two *unlike* groups.

The next year's analysis may well highlight similar factors to the previous year's. But has anything changed? Have the restructuring and new work practices you brought in as a result of last year's survey had any effect? The way you discover that is by looking for trends. A *trend* is a movement in opinion/sales/growth/satisfaction/output or whatever else you may be measuring, observed by comparing one set of figures with another, more recent, set. Undoubtedly any marked change will be visible simply by looking at the table of totals, but where more subtle changes are taking place the outcome may not be so obvious. For example, how easily, without statistical tools, can you identify the movement in Fig. 8.24.

There is definitely a change, and it is reasonably simple to see in which direction. For the purposes of management it is important to see where the change lies, to what extent it has happened and whether the trend will move across the board. By representing this data graphically we can see that the change is largely in the bottom end, the malcontents – who have become less dissatisfied. However, there is not a significant rise in those who thought that the service was 'Good'.

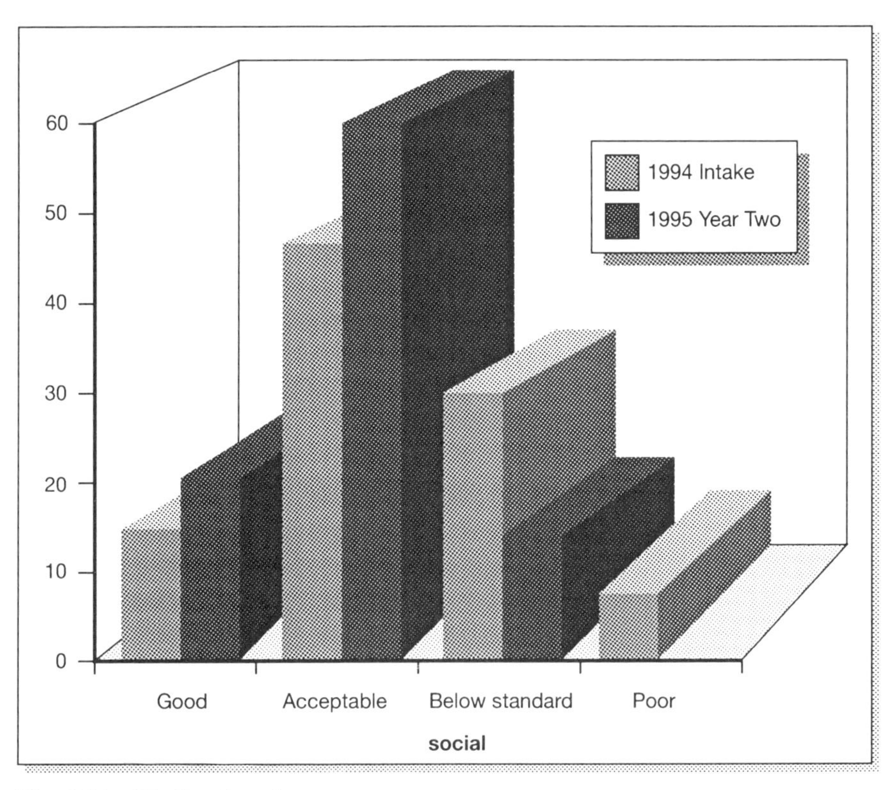

Fig. 8.24 Finding trends

Further changes may allow you to create a three or four layer graph, highlighting the trend. Moreover, you may decide to isolate the results just for the 'Excellent', 'Good', 'Satisfactory' or 'Poor' categories and examine the trend there.

DRAWING CONCLUSIONS

Once the investigations are done and the graphs are drawn, you then need to pull together your conclusions in a final report. There is little point in research if there is no action on the findings. Therefore the final steps must be:

- Analyses
- Conclusions
- Graphs and presentation
- Report
- Consequences.

The report is the vehicle through which your findings are delivered. It is the body of evidence that substantiates the case being brought by:

- presenting the hypotheses
- outlining the research method
- examining the data
- drawing conclusions
- recommending courses of action.

Without those elements the project as a whole is likely to be incomplete. In situations where the process is continuous (quality management, for example) the report is simply a snapshot in time which:

- looks at the state of affairs at one particular point
- elaborates the situation from the data
- compares it with previous data or against planned objectives
- proposes corrective action.

This is a continuous loop which ensures that maximum effectiveness in all aspects of the business is striven for.

What have you learned from your data?

The type of information derived from your data will largely be dependent on what information you have collected and how. Therefore, any shortcomings in the analyses must point back to the initial design of the questionnaire or even the basic remit of the project.

What you have learned from the data must be presented in a way which gets the message over clearly. It must be easy to understand, strong in terms of evidence (comparisons with previous performance or trends), and argued consistently with reference to the original objectives. A report which says that the survey discovered a few interesting facts (all unrelated) is not referring back to its original brief. It is easy to be distracted from that brief by the allure of 'interesting facts'. These may well be important, but your original task was to discover why no-one seems happy with the proposal to bypass Kirkby with a ring-road. The fact that you have discovered exciting trends in people's travel habits may well be the subject of a quite separate investigation.

What are the consequences?

The result, unless you are totally happy with *status quo*, will always be action. If there is no action then there was little point in spending the time and money on undertaking the questionnaire. The action you take will, of course, depend upon your circumstances, but part of it should be to ensure that the data from your survey, the component questionnaires and the identifiers which gave you your population which was surveyed, should all be preserved.

You need to know whether the changes or actions you have taken have worked. You may well be able to see the effect without the need for another survey, but things are rarely that simple. Repeating the survey a year later will give you the opportunity to observe the world as it is now with the world as it was then and mark the changes that have taken place. It may be that you need to evaluate that process with an even finer resolution so that you have a requirement to survey every month, every three months or even every week. This type of work is called a *rolling survey* and, as its name implies, is a continuous process where change is monitored and evaluated. If you work in an area where this type of change is not only your bread and butter but could also be your downfall (financial markets, commodity buying, or simply purchasing high value goods from a range of suppliers on a regular basis), then you need to keep your finger on the pulse. The rolling survey will help you to do that, and will allow you to take action rapidly.

THE CONTENT OF YOUR REPORT

There follows an outline of a research report. Each section heading relates to our original plan for reporting. Ensure that your report is structured clearly so that all aspects may be noted, including when, where and by whom the research was carried out, for instance:

Report for Crown and Castle Hotels on Customer Satisfaction
29th February 1995
Author: N. Evans
© Kirkby Konsultants

The objective (mission statement) of the research

Provide an overview of the task which was set:

- The problem or subject for research.
- The background to the need for research.
- The objectives to be achieved.

A brief overview of the method

- The population being surveyed.
- The sample and how it was derived.
- The questionnaire techniques employed (style of interview, additional research).

A Summary Report

Provide the busy executive with a brief overview of the findings so that they do not need to read the whole report. Thus, you may have:

Summary Findings:
a)
b)
c)
d)

The Findings

This is the part which everyone who has not simply skimmed the *Summary Findings* will read. All of the detail here is important and should be presented as simply and concisely as possible, bearing in mind that the reader is probably neither conversant with the problem, nor with the techniques you used to research it.

A GRAPHICAL OVERVIEW OF THE OUTCOME WITH NARRATIVE

Present all of the points in your findings with illustration wherever possible. This will provide clarity, will make the presentation look less ponderous and will enlighten difficult issues, particularly where sensible narrative is used. Be sure that the narrative expands upon the graphical material and does not simply recite what it says already!

A BRIEF OUTLINE OF ANY SIGNIFICANT STATISTICS RELATING TO THE GRAPHS

Present statistical information in context, explaining how it was derived and what it means wherever that seems necessary. Make no assumptions about people's understanding of statistics and therefore present them only where necessary and with supporting graphs and charts where appropriate.

A SUMMARY OF THE CONCLUSIONS AS CONSEQUENCES FOR THE BUSINESS OR PROJECT

The outcome will highlight a number of consequences. These will be to do with:

- The problem or issue if left alone.
- The problem or issue if particular courses of action are taken.
- The consequences of taking particular actions.
- Argue towards the action points or recommendations.

A SUMMARY OF THE RESULTS AS ACTION POINTS OR RECOMMENDATIONS

Finally, summarise the recommended course of action. This should be written in the light of the objectives defined originally. It may be that no precise course of action is recommended but that a number of alternatives are presented for consideration. The action points may well relate to a number of different departments or individual activities, and should therefore be clearly stated in terms of their responsibilities.

At the close of the questionnaire you may feel that it is appropriate to include a number of appendices:

- The questionnaire.
- A list of respondents.
- Any related literature or materials derived from desk research.

9

Theory into practice!

- **In this section you can examine some contexts and some suggestions for tackling them**
- **The whole process of design and implementation of a survey is discussed here**

IF I WANT TO DEMONSTRATE A FACT OR A HYPOTHESIS TO MY CLIENTS OR EMPLOYERS, HOW SHOULD I DO IT?

First decide:

- Your objectives and the outcomes you propose.
- The make-up of the 'population' which you will survey.
- The degree to which your questions target the issue.
- The style in which the data are collected and, as a consequence . . .
- The manner in which the data may be analysed.

Who are your respondents?

- Who are the people who are your 'population' – the people who can answer on an informed basis?
- What proportion of those will make a valid 'sample'?
- What are the major issues and influences you need to address?
- What language is appropriate? Do you need to avoid or include jargon?
- What are the scales and units by which variables are measured in this situation?
- What sensitivities may people have to the issues you are raising?

Ensure that they are:

- Representative of like-minded people in the *population*.

- Capable of answering the questions.
- Willing to answer the questions.

Remember that:

- the larger the sample, the more likely it is that it will represent the views of the whole group being represented
- a small sample from a small population may miss major contributors to the significance of the data
- the larger the sample, the more expensive it is to administer
- the larger the sample, the more the extremes in behaviour/attitude/opinion will cancel each other out
- practical considerations will limit the size of samples drawn from large populations
- for a sample to be random the population from which it is chosen must be sufficiently large to represent all shades of opinion.

You must ask the right questions in the right way

Ensure that you:

- Keep answer ranges the same to enable comparison of like with like.
- Keep question types the same – don't collect one set of answers as numeric when a similar set in the previous survey were undertaken as a range.
- Survey a similar or the same subset of people to ensure that the style and weighting of answers is maintained.

Keep the questions:

- Short and simple.
- Few in number.
- Jargon-free.
- Easy to understand.

Ask yourself:

- Is the question unambiguous?
- Is the question leading the respondent?
- Will the question elicit the type of responses which are being looked for?

Allow your respondent to know what you want

- By making your intentions clear in your instructions.
- By asking the question clearly and concisely.
- By giving the correct options or opportunities for an appropriate answer.

Collect the data appropriately

Remember that obstacles to reliable data entry are:

- Unclear specification of answer type to enter.
- Poor form layout which has no logical route through it.
- Poor form layout which is difficult to read.
- Poor response quality – lots of written word in bad handwriting.
- Dissimilar form for the data system from the one used in the survey.
- Lack of motivation, especially when the number of forms is large.

Then do suitable and legitimate analyses

Producing:

- Report containing results.
- Statistics.
- Graphs, charts, tables, cross-tabulations.
- Presentation including Narrative.

SOME EXAMPLES

Difficulties experienced by staff in answering the telephone

What exactly is the root cause of the problem? Your customers complain that staff take a long time to respond to the telephone. Be careful of pre-judging the outcome. You need to undertake a small internal survey which will establish the following information:

- Do staff respond to the telephone as soon as they are able?
- Do all appropriate staff respond to the telephone?
- Do staff take too long with telephone calls?
- Is the system for routing calls operating efficiently?

- If not, where is the bottleneck?
- Is there any technological solution which could alleviate the problem?

There is a good deal of potential for antagonising hard-working staff in this issue. Questions should be sensitively thought out. Consider using the technique of 'Buying it for a friend . . .'. Ask questions about what happens with telephone response generally and then home into the specific by asking 'And is that your experience?'

Your analyses of responses will aim to highlight:

- Areas where the telephone is answered infrequently.
- Areas where the length of call is too long.
- Patchiness of cover for telephone reception.

The improvement in satisfaction of our customers since the implementation of new procedures

This is a simple customer satisfaction survey. The prerequisite for seeing the improvement in satisfaction is the use of two or more similar surveys to the same group of customers. The questions, which cover all relevant areas of satisfaction, will yield results which may be compared with previous results month on month, year on year. Use multi-series graphs to demonstrate how the perception of service has moved towards the 'Excellent' end of the scale, with a consequent reduction in 'Poor' responses.

The frequency with which a particular problem in a process is occurring and the value to be gained from fixing it

This quality management problem is the most common in terms of seeking the greatest cost benefit in changing processes, techniques, staffing, etc. It is first of all necessary to discover the range of problems being revealed in your process – be this manufacturing, caring for patients or providing a service. The incidence of the problems needs to be quantified so that you may then represent it as a bar graph.

Taking this one step further, a Pareto analysis will place the problems in order of size and provide a percentage line to show at which points specific percentages of your problems could be eradicated.

Customers' preferences for a particular colour of product

In this situation where preferences are being requested you may decide to offer your customers the direct choice: which colour do you want – red, green or blue? On the other hand, you may feel that it is more appropriate to let them respond by ranking the available options in order of preference. This will give you a finer level of detail about their preferences because, rather than having a single bald choice, they now indicate to you the gradation of choice which, when profiled across the entire group being surveyed, will give you an hierarchy of colour preference.

Assessing employees' attitudes to aspects of their work

The employee attitude survey aims to collect information which will enable management to profile not only the satisfaction of people with their role in the company but, more importantly, their perception of that role. This will involve gathering information about:

- How important they feel the role is in the overall business.
- How important the role is in their division of the business.
- How valued their contribution is.
- How well they believe they perform that contribution.
- How important they see other people's roles to be (particularly those of their managers).
- How well they feel that those roles are being fulfilled.

In many of these questions there is an implicit need for two steps: first, the perception of value of a role and, second, how well that role is actually being fulfilled. In other words: How important is the role and what is the individual's current performance? These two factors will be rated in a scalar fashion using numeric or semantic scales. the results may then be profiled in graphical format so that areas where there is a negative correlation between role perception and role fulfilment may be addressed.

In any survey of this type it is vital to establish the parameters being used to measure before the respondent is asked to do the measuring! This is best seen in the context of the old chestnut: 'How well did the trip meet your expectations?' If you have not bothered to discover what people's expectations are then they cannot say how well they were met.

10

Technology tools

- In this section consideration is given to ways in which computers can aid the process of questionnaire design and implementation
- Some issues related to computer hardware are discussed
- Consideration of the Data Protection Act is encouraged

Without computers, much of what is described in this book would be either difficult or near impossible to undertake. New technology enables us to design questionnaires which look attractive and encourage the respondent to be positive. It enables the capture of data in appropriate forms so that it may then be analysed, cross-correlated so that trends may be identified, questions may be asked and hypotheses may be tested.

TECHNICAL CONSIDERATIONS IN SOFTWARE

As time marches on so too the technological revolution changes techniques and work practices in all areas of business. Keeping up with these changes is demanding and sometimes seems to be pointless. In the area of questionnaire work, however, there have been numerous benefits which have emerged as the technology has improved.

Traditional methods

Traditionally, surveys have been carried out with pencil and paper, using a tally sheet to total up the number of responses to particular questions and then some mathematics to work out the totals, distributions and statistics. These techniques have been the foundation upon which present methods have been built and consequently, in many cases, computer software has been designed simply to replicate and automate those processes. This begs the question – is this the most appropriate approach to exploiting the power of computers in this context? Computers offer us opportunities to do things differently and better. The ways in which computers work are different from the ways in which humans work with pencil and paper. Software which is effective maximises the computer-based facilities and minimises the manual facilities. This is often uncomfortable, particularly for seasoned practitioners in the art or science being rewritten for the computer.

Thus we have a situation where computer software can often appear to fit the bill and yet fails to fulfil the potential which the medium offers.

New methods

Many workplaces are trying to tackle questionnaire work using the tools that they have at their disposal – not unreasonable. The pencil has been replaced by the word processor, the tallysheet by the spreadsheet or database. The process often goes something like this:

- Design a questionnaire using the word processor or desktop publisher.
- Print it and distribute it.
- Collect the completed forms.
- Design a template for data entry on a database or spreadsheet.
- Copy the data from the forms into the database or spreadsheet.
- Perform analyses and produce graphs, charts and statistics, perhaps using a graphing system.
- Copy these graphs, charts and statistics from the database, spreadsheet or graphing system into the word processor or desktop publisher.
- Produce a report.

These stages use anything between two and five different computer applications to perform four essential tasks:

- Design.
- Data entry.
- Data analysis.
- Presentation.

Each of the tools being used is also likely to carry many more facilities than are needed in the relatively simple operations being tackled in the above four stages. This can slow down the process. Moreover, in capturing data from the forms and entering into the data capture system the operator is using two dissimilar media – the form and a database or spreadsheet template which bears little or no resemblance to the form. The possibility for errors here is high. In addition, nearly all such systems including the high powered statistical analysis packages use only numeric data, meaning that all text-based and choice answers must firstly be converted to numeric responses before they can be entered.

Dedicated questionnaire programs

The new generation of software can side-step all of these problems, providing in one package all the tools that are needed for questionnaire work, while retaining the ability to transfer data in and out from the main software tools being used in the workplace if and when required. This book has referred frequently to techniques which can be found in software such as *PinPoint for Windows* (published by Longman Logotron in the UK). This software allows the user to design a form in a simple and easy-to-use environment. Data entry is on an identical screen form to the paper one which the keyboard operator holds. Multiple choice data are entered simply by pointing and 'clicking' at the required response – the response 'Excellent', for instance, is then automatically entered in the data set – no mistyping, no variance in spelling.

In analysis, such responses are counted and tallied, doing away with the need to code every single response that is not already numeric. Statistical functions are applied, and graphs and charts, cross-tabulations and tables are generated at the touch of a button, modified with ease, enabling the user to try out hypotheses, change presentations and, more importantly, to interact directly with the data in an intuitive and flexible fashion.

SCANNING

New technology also offers us 'intelligent' machinery. Scanners which can read forms are becoming more prevalent. The volume of data being collected frequently means that pressures on data input staff are enormous. Forms which are designed appropriately may be 'read' by scanners (see Chapter 6 on Data Entry for more details).

THE DATA PROTECTION ACT

Under the terms of the Data Protection Act it is necessary for any individual or organisation collecting *personal* information which is to be stored and retrieved electronically to be registered with the Data Protection Registrar. This registration also brings with it commitment to a code of practice and the need to give access to the information which is collected both to the individual from whom it was collected and to the officers of the Data Protection Registrar if necessary. If you are in doubt whether your organisation falls under the terms of this Act please contact the Data Protection Registrar.

Contact addresses

■

Market Research Society, 15 Northburgh Street, London EC1V 4AH. Telephone: 0171 490 4911, Fax: 0171 490 0608

Data Protection Registrar, Springfield House, Water Lane, Wilmslow SK9 5AX. Telephone 01625 535711

Longman Logotron, 124 Science Park, Milton Road, Cambridge CB4 4ZS. Telephone 01223 425558, Fax 01223 425349

Corporate Communication Associates, Dell Barn, Stoughton, Chichester PO18 9JL Tel: 01705 631256 Fax: 01705 631724

Index